THE ENGLISH IN AUSTRALIA

Australia is the second most English country in the world, yet, taken as the 'norm', this largest immigrant group has never been analysed in detail. Dr James Jupp provides fascinating new insights into the impact the English have had on Australian life in the first book ever written on the subject. Beginning with familiar stories of convicts, explorers, and early settlers, and then the various waves of immigration over the nineteenth and twentieth centuries, the book concludes with reflections on today's English immigrants, now considered 'foreigners'. Anyone interested in tracing their English ancestry will find this book compelling reading, and helpful in bringing to life senses of the places, conditions, occupations, and so forth that their ancestors lived through.

James Jupp is Director of the Centre for Immigration and Multicultural Studies at the Australian National University. His many publications include, as general editor, *The Australian People: An Encyclopedia of the Nation, its People and Their Origins* (second edition, Cambridge University Press, 2001). He is a member of the Order of Australia for services to multicultural and immigration studies and to recording Australian history.

THE ENGLISH
IN AUSTRALIA

JAMES JUPP

CAMBRIDGE
UNIVERSITY PRESS

PUBLISHED BY THE PRESS SYNDICATE OF THE UNIVERSITY OF CAMBRIDGE
The Pitt Building, Trumpington Street, Cambridge, United Kingdom

CAMBRIDGE UNIVERSITY PRESS
The Edinburgh Building, Cambridge CB2 2RU, UK
40 West 20th Street, New York, NY 10011–4211, USA
477 Williamstown Road, Port Melbourne, VIC 3207, Australia
Ruiz de Alarcón 13, 28014 Madrid, Spain
Dock House, The Waterfront, Cape Town 8001, South Africa

http://www.cambridge.org

© James Jupp 2004

First published 2004

Printed in Australia by BPA Print Group

Typeface Life Roman (*Adobe*) 10/12 pt. *System* QuarkXPress® [BC]

A catalogue record for this book is available from the British Library

National Library of Australia Cataloguing in Publication data

Jupp, James.
The English in Australia.
Bibliography.
Includes index.
ISBN 0 521 54295 2.
1. English – Australia – History. 2. Immigrants –
Australia – History. 3. Australia – Civilization – British
influences. 4. Australia – Emigration and immigration –
History. 5. Australia – Emigration and immigration –
Social aspects. I. Title.
994.00421

ISBN 0 521 54295 2 paperback

CONTENTS

ILLUSTRATIONS

Maps

INTRODUCTION

And there they raised old England's flag, the emblem of the brave.

Australian National Anthem

Australia is the 'second most English country in the world' – a description which might surprise and even annoy many Australians. New Zealand with its large Polynesian population, Canada with French Québec and polyglot Ontario, and the United States with its major Afro- and Hispanic-American component are all less 'English' in their basic composition. All four English-speaking settler societies are also, of course, multicultural, as is England itself. Yet in both the 1986 and 2001 censuses well over one-third of Australians declared their ancestry to be English, while many who ticked the 'Australian' box were also of predominantly English origin. The largest overseas-born 'ethnic group' is now, and has since 1788 always been, English, most of whom would reserve the word 'ethnic' for others. Only in 1996 did New Zealanders replace the English as the largest single immigrating group – and many of them were also of English origin.

Nor is this surprising. Although the Dutch, and arguably the Portuguese, have good claims to have 'discovered' Australia for Europeans, it was the English who first laid effective claim to its territory. William Dampier, from East Coker, Somerset, first explored the west coast in 1688, a century before the convict colony was set up in Sydney and nineteen years before the amalgamation of England and Scotland into the United Kingdom. James Cook, from the Yorkshire North Riding, claimed the east coast in 1770, thus finally pre-empting any rival claims from the Netherlands or France. He was accompanied by the natural scientist, Sir Joseph Banks, from Lincolnshire. Finalising the English stamp on the continent was the

William Dampier (1652–1715)

arrival in January 1788 of the first convict fleet. Its passengers were overwhelmingly English. Its commander, Arthur Phillip, was born in London, lived in Hampshire and is buried near Bath, though of German origin through his father. In voyages between 1798 and 1802, Matthew Flinders from Lincolnshire found that Tasmania was an island, sailed around the continent, and named the new possessions 'Australia'.

What did 'the English' mean then, and still mean today? The massive work of Norman Davies – *The Isles* – reminds us that subjects of the British Crown in 1788 were of very varied origins. While the English tongue was the official language of government and law, it was not spoken or understood by many living in Ireland, Scotland and Wales. They still used the Celtic languages, replaced in England

Matthew Flinders (1774–1814)

by the Anglo-Saxons over one thousand years before, in which the word for the English is 'Saxon' (*saesneg*). Cornish had just died out, but Manx was still the majority tongue of the Isle of Man and Norman French of the Channel Islands. While Anglicanism was the established church throughout England, Wales and Ireland in 1788, this was not true of Scotland, whose church was Presbyterian. Moreover, while Catholicism had no secure legal status in the United Kingdom until 1829, it was the majority religion of Ireland and of parts of the Scottish Highlands. The rise of Methodism in the late eighteenth century strengthened the Nonconformist element, which already included Baptists and Congregationalists from an earlier century.

The English, defined as living in thirty-seven of the counties of England established after the Norman conquest of 1066, adhering to the established church set up by Henry VIII in 1536 and speaking the English language derived from varieties of Anglo-Saxon, were the largest identifiable 'nationality' in the United Kingdom in 1788. They were scarcely as dominant as they later became. The legal system of Scotland was quite different, the administrative system of Ireland (and its parliament until 1800) was distinct; the religious adherence of most Irish, Scots and Cornish was not to the established church, and nor was that of many English living in the North, East Anglia and the Southwest. Moreover, the English language had such a variety of dialects that many of the English could not understand each other. The standardisation of English was not effective until the introduction of universal education as late as 1870, which has still not produced the relative uniformity of English-speakers' accents in Australia.

England did, however, have unifying features, and the English had a strong sense of being different from other British people as well as from their neighbours on the continent and non-European British subjects overseas. Varied evidence for this includes many of Shakespeare's works, and especially his historic plays. Every schoolchild and patriot was reminded during the Second World War of John of Gaunt's dying praise of 'this blessed plot, this earth, this realm, this England' in *Richard II*, written 350 years before.

The rural social system, with its aristocratic and propertied leaders, was reproduced throughout England. The Howards had strong links with royalty, and castles and mansions from Carlisle through Yorkshire to Surrey and Sussex. Unusually, they remained Catholics, and still do. The Dukes of Devonshire owned large parts of central London but had their ancestral mansion in Derbyshire. The Dukes of Bedford also owned London property, but lived in Bedfordshire and owned much of the Fenland agricultural district, which they had drained by Dutch, Belgian and French labour. One part of the framework of England was thus provided by the landed aristocracy and royalty, from the junior ranks of which Australian governors were often drawn. These were not, however, exclusively English; many were Scots, and German inheritance ran through royalty at least until the World War of 1914. Even Jews, Europeans, Americans and, eventually, a tiny number of Indians, were admitted to the upper classes towards the end of the Victorian era.

At the pinnacle of society was the monarchy. But it was unpopular between 1788 and 1837 under George III (who was mad), George IV (who was degenerate) and William IV (a nonentity known

as Silly Billy). Queen Victoria was also unpopular for withdraw-
ing from public life between 1861 and 1874. But from her Golden
Jubilee in 1887 the monarchy became increasingly central to English
national identity. Republicanism was only briefly popular in the early
1870s and has had little credibilty since. Whatever else the English
may not know about their history and culture, they do know from
childhood that they live in a monarchy.

Also binding the English together was a system of law which
operated throughout England and Wales, using the English language
and administered through the rural hierarchies in each county.
English law was assumed to operate in Australia from the first landing in 1788. Consequently there were few lawyers among Scottish
immigrants, as the Scots system was distinct and still is. Country
towns were governed through royal charters granted by the monarchy from London. It was part of the rhetoric of English political
life that these well-developed legal and local government systems
gave the English exceptional freedoms not enjoyed in Europe or
elsewhere. English law was assumed to apply in the English colonies
from their annexation and many English laws and precedents are
still valid in Australia, where English legal dress is still worn in some
jurisdictions. The principle of the common law was that it applied to
everyone, and of the rule of law that it placed the law above the
government of the day.

The English constitutional system did not, however, give democratic rights in the sense of free elections, freedom of religion,
government by representative bodies or freedom of association.
Power was held nominally by the monarchy but actually by the
rural hierarchies. The right of parliament to control budgets and
appointments was still contested by George III in 1788 but was
completely accepted after Victoria came to the throne in 1837.
National political leadership was concentrated in the House of
Lords well into the nineteenth century. The last English peer to be
prime minister was Lord Salisbury between 1900 and 1902. But
later prime ministers such as Winston Churchill, Arthur Balfour
and Harold Macmillan had close aristocratic links, either through
marriage or descent. The last peer to become prime minister was
the Scottish Earl of Home, who renounced his peerage to sit in the
House of Commons in 1963.

The aristocracy in its lower rungs was open to new entrants, who
changed its character over time. It was thus less rigid than in many
European states and able to modify itself rather than being over-

thrown by revolution as in France and, later, Russia. The English ruling classes were more willing to live in the countryside than was common in Europe, consolidating their local support by a combination of patronage, paternalism, political and legal domination, and mild coercion through their control of the local judiciary. The majority of the first convicts transported to New South Wales were sentenced in the assizes of county towns.

The traditional picture of the English was of a rural and small-town population which was ruled by a benevolent local and national upper class, enjoyed relative personal freedom defined by common law, was Protestant, accepted a social hierarchy, and was consciously English within an insular society superior to all known alternatives. This was the 'Old England' praised in song and story throughout the Victorian period, not only in England but also in Australia. It was embellished and expanded as the British Empire grew into the largest political entity in the history of the world, on which 'the sun never set'. The Empire strengthened feelings of pride based on military conquest rather than quiet rural virtues. But the older tradition remained – and still remains in corners of rural England.

The English were bound together by a common Germanic and Nordic ancestry, by a common language, by institutions and by a capital city whose role pre-dated 1066, by feelings of superiority and by relative internal peace and unchanging borders. The last battle fought on English soil was in 1745, in startling contrast to the experience of most European countries, not to mention Ireland. England has not been effectively invaded since 1066, except from Scotland or by rebellious claimants to the throne such as Henry VII. As Shakespeare proudly proclaims in his *King John*: 'This England never did, nor never shall, live at the proud foot of a conqueror'. So it has remained for a millennium, uniquely in European history.

The English were divided by social class, by dialects, by local loyalties, by education and by urbanisation and industrialisation. These divisions, rather than ethnic or religious schisms, remained dominant in English public life until very recently. By 1788 the English were not markedly religious. The Victorian era changed that, at least for the middle and upper classes. But many English immigrants brought religious indifference to Australia with them. Nor were they fiercely political. Until the 1830s political debate was between small coteries of Whigs and Tories to the exclusion of most of the public. The last English revolution was in 1688 and it created a system of parliamentary government which changed but was never shattered or overthrown. All of this was grounds for congratulation, and affected attitudes taken to Australia and other parts of the empire. Peace, order and good government was the formula taken around the world by English administrators and lawyers.

Yet all was not well. Millions of the English emigrated over a period of two hundred years, predominantly for economic and social reasons as there was little overt persecution and no enemy occupation or civil war. Until 1840 in New South Wales, 1853 in Tasmania and 1868 in Western Australia, many of those coming to Australia were convicts, the majority being English. English emigrants travelled the world and many preferred the United States to the Empire. But Australia was periodically the target for mass movement, especially in the 1850s, the 1880s, the 1920s and the 1960s. Each of these waves came from different generations, from different circumstances and for different reasons. Each wave was more English – and less British – than its predecessor.

But it was also from a different England and came to a different Australia. I have taken the common sense position that English immigrants did not arrive out of the blue. They brought with them traditions and attitudes which cannot be understood only within the Australian context. Many passed some of their culture on to their children. All this is as true for the English as for any other large intake of immigrants from anywhere. The difference is that because Australia was colonised and developed after 1788 by more settlers from England than from anywhere else, their distinctive characters and experiences have often been overlooked or taken as the norm to which all others must conform.

While it is often artificial to distinguish between the 'English' and the 'British', this was less apparent in the formative years of Australia. Even today the non-English people of the United Kingdom and many of their relatives and descendants in Australia are conscious of these differences. There are more Scottish clan chieftains in Australia than anywhere outside Scotland, and a wide variety of Burns clubs, Scottish dance groups and even football fan clubs for Glasgow Rangers. Few have denied the distinctiveness of the Catholic Irish, who acquired their independence from the United Kingdom in 1921. Scotland and Wales acquired self-governing institutions much later, in 1998, on a more restricted basis but with the support of majorities in referenda. The Isle of Man and the Channel Islands have never been part of the United Kingdom, only delegating foreign affairs and defence to London.

Perhaps more contested is the distinctiveness of the Cornish and the 'Englishness' of those living in or coming from England but not of historic English ancestry. Cornwall has only a county council, fiercely protected against amalgamation with parts of neighbouring Devon. Yet South Australia hosts the largest Cornish festival and the oldest Cornish Association in the world. Cornish emigration to Australia was at its height between 1840 and 1880 when Cornwall was exceptionally homogeneous and culturally distinct. While Cornish Australians were often imperial patriots (as were many Scots and Protestant Irish) they deserve to be treated as a distinct ethnicity at least within the Australian context.

English immigrants of non-English ancestry have not been so organisationally insistent on their origins. Nineteenth century Jews often referred to themselves as 'Englishmen of the Hebrew persuasion' (which is certainly no longer the case). The late Conservative politician Enoch Powell argued that someone of Caribbean or Indian origin could be 'British' but never 'English'. The very large numbers in England who are of Irish birth or descent are sometimes ambivalent about their origins, especially if they are Catholics. But increasingly it has become recognised that ethnicity in a multicultural society can be a matter of choice. Thus some Australians choose to be regarded as 'English' or of 'English ancestry', which does not prevent them from being equally 'Australians' with those of many varied backgrounds. A small but significant number of the English coming to Australia were born in India or elsewhere in the British Empire within official or military families. Among them were Lord Birdwood, commander of the Australian forces in the First World War, and the ancestors of Gough Whitlam.

Writing about the English

My own interest in this topic is based on the fact that I have spent half my life in England and half in Australia. My origins are 'British', in the fairly common amalgamation of English, Scottish and Irish ancestry which still characterises many Australians. Many object to the term 'Anglo-Celtic', but that is what many of us are. The Jupps have humble but undeniably English origins among the agricultural labourers of East Surrey. Perhaps for that reason I have stressed the rural origins of so many English Australians in the past, while not denying their urban origins in the present.

I have sketched the progress of the English from majority settlers in a predominantly British society to a diminishing minority in a

much more multicultural Australia. In doing so I have been anxious
to emphasise that the English can be found at all levels of Australian society and are much too varied to be stereotyped in the
simplistic terms often used by Australian or English nationalists.
Today Australia is a multicultural country resting on an English
base, part of a global English-speaking society increasingly dominated by the United States, and located in an Asian-Pacific region
from which British imperialism has irrevocably withdrawn. This
suggests a more complicated future than the 'new Britannia' or
'England over the water' created by the English, the Irish and the
Scots more than a century ago.

Writing about such a large and varied population necessarily
involves compression and selection. I have selected individuals
as representative of larger groups or as particularly interesting. In
doing so I have relied heavily upon the definitive *Australian Dictionary of Biography* (*ADB*), which is unsurpassed in its scope
and accuracy. I have confined the term 'English' to those born in
England, while acknowledging that some may have come as adults,
some as children and some as temporary residents. Those of English
descent are a much larger category. But because of the ease of
assimilation it seems reasonable to regard them as unqualified
Australians. After all, they are part of a society which has been more
strongly influenced from England than from anywhere else. They
have 'assimilated' to a variant of themselves.

English influence lessened as Australia moved away from its
colonial origins and developed a distinct character, and as the
cultural influence of the United States has tended to replace it. The
extent to which even English immigrants are still 'English' needs
debating, just as much as whether Australia is still 'English' or
even 'British' in any meaningful sense. There is a degree of sub-
jectivity in my choice of individuals and social groups. Politics has
shaped Australia, and I have dwelt on factors such as religion, sport,
language or culture.

The resources for studying the English in Australia are so vast,
widespread and generally accessible that it is surprising that there
seem to be no books entitled *The English in Australia*. The network of county record offices in England provides invaluable
sources which are often not available elsewhere. Those used most
extensively included East Sussex (Lewes), Staffordshire (Stafford),
Lancashire (Preston), Kent (Maidstone), West Yorkshire (Wakefield), Somerset (Taunton), Oxfordshire (Oxford), Northamptonshire and Metropolitan London. The two great repositories of

nautical studies – the National Maritime Museum (Greenwich) and the Merseyside Maritime Museum (Liverpool) – were invaluable, as was the National Museum of Labour History (Manchester) and local social museums in York, Lincoln, Bury St Edmunds, Beamish (Co. Durham) and elsewhere. The newspaper collection of the British Library at Colindale (North London) is without parallel. Much of this work was done in preparing *The Australian People* (1988, 2001), which includes substantial sections on the English in Australia.

In Australia, the National Library of Australia, the National Archives in Canberra, and the Migration Museums in Adelaide and Melbourne were extremely helpful. It is a matter of some regret that the collections created by the Commonwealth government through the Australian Institute of Multicultural Affairs, the Bureau of Immigration, Multicultural and Population Research and the Department of Immigration and Multicultural and Indigenous Affairs have been split up at various stages by decision of the national government. Extensive collections of newspapers and pictures exist in the State Libraries, and considerable use was made of the Mitchell Library (Sydney), the La Trobe Library (Melbourne) and the State Libraries of South Australia and Queensland. The resources of the Australian National University Library are very extensive for census reports and parliamentary papers.

Genealogical (family history) collections in London, Melbourne, Sydney and on-line should not be overlooked. They include extensive collections of census data, shipping lists and official records of births, deaths and marriages, as well as local and family histories. Convict records are quite extensive and the largest resource is at the New South Wales State Archives in Sydney, while State record offices contain details of birth, deaths and marriages. La Trobe University has a major archive of interviews with migrants arriving in the 1960s, organised by Dr James Hammerton.

All statistics used here are from official sources. They distinguish between the 'English-born' and others from the British Isles wherever possible.

1

WHO WERE THE ENGLISH?

... a British subject, in whatever land he may be, shall feel confident that the watchful eye and the strong arm of England will protect him against injustice and wrong.

Lord Palmerston, 1850

England has been a single political unit for over one thousand years. By the middle of Queen Victoria's reign (1837–1901) the English were the most urbanised people in the world, London among the largest cities, and Lancashire and Yorkshire had the largest industrial concentration. England was proudly proclaimed as 'the workshop of the world' or 'an island of coal surrounded by a sea full of fish'. The British Empire outdid all others in both area and population. However, this was not true of England when the First Fleet sailed into Botany Bay in 1788, nor is it true today. Neither were the English as numerically dominant in the United Kingdom as they are now. Fewer than 60 per cent of its residents were English, compared with 83 per cent today.

England had a uniform legal system by 1788 and a central government located in London, where the landed aristocracy also maintained town houses. But before the growth of the railways in the 1840s it did not have a standardised system of time and its local centres of power were often remote from London. The historic administrative centre of the North, at York, was four days away from London by stage coach, a distance of only 300 kilometres. The functions of the national government were defence, the licensing of corporations and monopolies, diplomacy, postal services, and restrictions and taxes on trade and commerce. There was no income tax until the Napoleonic wars (1796–1815). Most government income was raised through taxes on a variety of commodities and customs duties. The naval budget was the largest single item of public expenditure. Local taxes, which largely went to support the poor, were raised on property, as were the tithes which went to support the Church of England. The electoral system had not been radically changed since the Middle Ages and rested heavily upon small towns and even villages. A few of these had almost no voters at all and most were controlled by the local aristocracy. The state did acquire more power during the Napoleonic wars and had spy systems within the small radical groups then arising. Trade unions were effectively illegal, often being treated as secret societies because they required oaths of secrecy and solidarity. Their activities were limited by *Combination Acts* between 1799 and 1824.[1]

Perhaps the most important state functions influencing transportation and emigration were enclosure of common land, illegalisation of snaring wild game, and maintenance of a Poor Law which dated back more than two centuries. Enforcement of these statutes was entirely in the hands of local agencies such as magistrates and justices of the peace, parish vestries and Poor Law overseers. Yeoman farmers, who employed labour and often owned freehold property, were recruited into local militias. The model of the yeoman farmer was held up as an ideal in Australia for over a century, though few actually emigrated after the first few decades of settlement.

In emergencies, law and order was maintained by local militias or units of the army, in the absence of organised police forces before the 1840s. This sometimes led to armed clashes, of which the most famous and controversial, at St Peter's Fields, Manchester in 1819, was an attack by the yeomanry on a political rally. It was followed by the Six Acts, allowing summary conviction, the suppression of meetings, bans on seditious publications and a heavy tax on newspapers and periodicals.[2]

The rural poor

In 1788 the majority of the English lived in villages and small country towns and worked in agriculture or as artisans and rural craftsmen. There is much evidence that wages and conditions for rural labourers declined in the nineteenth century.[3] In the eighteenth century 'fair wages' were determined by the local magistrates under a system dating back to Elizabeth I. This was being replaced by dependence on the Poor Law to provide for basic needs, which created resentment and a desire to leave the land for the cities and, to a lesser extent, for overseas. Many elderly labourers and widows who remained in the countryside became dependent on charity or went to the workhouse.

The Poor Law system created by Queen Elizabeth in 1601 was reaching a crisis point in southern England by 1830, accompanied by opposition to threshing machines which reduced the need for labour. Unemployment was the usual cause of poverty and the need to apply for Poor Law relief. Village workhouses mainly catered for the elderly, the infirm and orphaned or illegitimate children, until the system was reformed in 1834 and they were moved to urban centres. The principle was then established that able-bodied paupers could only live in the workhouse under conditions worse than for labourers remaining outside. Outdoor relief was prohibited for the able-bodied, which assumed that they would seek work. As work was not always available, the choice was to enter the workhouse with its draconian regime or to seek work by migrating within England or overseas. Some of the new workhouses were attacked and even destroyed in the mid-1830s. The system was modified but not seriously reformed until the welfare provisions of 1909 to 1911, and not abolished altogether until 1948.

Support of the poor rested with the parish of settlement and was paid for from locally raised rates. As rural populations increased, the burden on farmers and landowners also increased. Labourers did not have the income to pay rates and did not own property. Under a system developed at Speenhamland (Berkshire) in 1795, Poor Law support became a device for subsidising wages and controlling the workforce. The local parish vestry, drawn from farmers and employers, could allocate relief funds and attach conditions. This often meant the 'roundsman' system, whereby labourers had to apply for work at all farms in the parish and accept whatever wage a farmer might decide on. Those 'undeserving' of support might be denied it or be lodged in the village workhouse. While not all parishes operated this system, its general effect was to pauperise large sections of the labouring classes, making them 'welfare dependent' in modern terms. Counties using this system, such as Sussex, Kent, Berkshire and Hampshire, were most affected by the 1830 'Captain Swing' rising. This last English rising affected the southern and south Midlands counties. Captain Swing was a mythical figure used to rally support, and rioting, burning of hayricks and threats to farmers were the main tactics used.[4]

One alternative to rising costs was to provide poor relief only for those in obvious need and to stop the system of general subsidy of wages. This allowance system had developed originally at Sevenoaks (Kent) and had come to be looked upon as a right rather than a privilege. Using a measure of support for a healthy male, wife and two children, it bears a strange resemblance to the idea of the basic wage introduced in Australia in 1907. But it was much less generous, was paid by the parish and not the employer, and was criticised as being demoralising.

One reformer, the Reverend Robert Mayne of Limpsfield (Surrey) near Sevenoaks, told the 1832 enquiry into the Poor Law that reducing regular allowances to the poor had made them 'better off, more contented and orderly, and more regular in their attendance at church'. Those fully employed and in good health had not been subsidised for ten years, and expenditure had consequently been greatly reduced. This still meant that Limpsfield, with a population of 1042 in 1831, was spending £568 a year on poor relief or about half the level for Surrey, which was £1 per head of population. Equivalent expenditure in modern terms would be about $A50 000. Many parishes could no longer afford poor relief as they had only a few hundred residents.

A particular problem was the large number of deserted children consigned to the workhouses. The Poor Law enquiry for Sussex, Surrey and Kent in 1833 saw this as a problem requiring emigration: 'Where bastard or deserted children fall entirely on parishes the apprenticing them in the Colonies seems a mode by which the country may be relieved of the charge'. This suggestion does not seem to have been taken up. In 1839 the Dursley Poor Law Union (Gloucestershire) enquired whether the Poor Law commissioners would sanction sending to Australia 'orphan boys from twelve to fifteen years of age in our workhouse'. The commissioners thought not, unless the boy volunteered to go. However, girls from some workhouses were sent out, partly to redress the acute imbalance of the sexes and to meet the demand for domestic servants. Eighty years later, child migration from orphanages was adopted on a large scale with scandalous consequences not fully revealed until quite recently.

Town and country

There were few towns with more than 20 000 people in 1788, and only one really large city. London had almost one million people and was already spreading into Middlesex and Surrey. It had no single administration but was divided into many parishes. Most of it was still within easy walking distance of the old City, which had been rebuilt to the medieval street pattern after the great fire of 1666. The upper classes were relocated in the squares of Marylebone and Westminster, laid out by speculative builders from the early eighteenth century. But many Londoners still lived in crowded slums eastwards along the Thames or within the city limits. Many other large towns were also still medieval in their layout, including Bristol, Norwich and York. A few planned towns were laid out at the turn of the century, and the industrial town of Middlesbrough was one of the first 'green field' developments in the world in the 1830s. But these were exceptional. Most old and new towns were a muddle of alleys and courts. The elegantly planned towns of northern Europe were almost completely absent except for Georgian enclaves, as in London, Bristol or Liverpool, or resort towns such as Bath or Cheltenham.

Sydney followed the English pattern of winding streets, lanes and alleys. Like some English cities it was subject to outbreaks of disease, the most devastating being in 1900 when 101 people died of bubonic plague in the rat-infested Rocks. But other cities, notably

A 'muddle of lanes and alleys': the chimneys of Victorian Waterloo, London

Adelaide, Melbourne and Perth, were laid out by military officers or surveyors along straight lines, a pattern often modified by poorly constructed buildings in back lanes.

The new industrial revolution was already creating larger cities such as Manchester, Birmingham, Liverpool, Leeds, Sheffield and Newcastle. Apart from narrow streets of hastily built cottages and tenements, many industrial workers lived in cellars or in subdivided lodging houses. There was no effective sewerage or fresh water supply, and outbreaks of cholera continued until the 1850s. National laws governing housing standards were not introduced until 1867 and only affected new buildings, which were built in rows as 'bylaw housing' and are still present in the centre of many industrial and mining towns. Most villages had no sewerage or piped water, in some cases until the 1950s. Cabin passengers to Australia in the 1850s were disturbed to find that rural labourers in steerage had never seen a toilet and had no idea what to do with one.[5] As recently as 1945 half the households in England did not have a bathroom.

The population of England grew rapidly after the first national census in 1801, when it was 8.3 million. The largest counties then were Middlesex (containing London), Lancashire, the Yorkshire West Riding, Devon and Kent. The two largest occupations were agricultural labourers and domestic servants. But there were already large numbers of miners, wool and cotton textile workers and metal workers. Industrial, mining and urban influences were already strong in Lancashire, the Yorkshire West Riding, Warwickshire, Stafford-shire and Durham. London's population included many born in neighbouring counties such as Surrey, Essex and Kent. Yet most people lived in the county in which they were born and, probably, within a few miles of the village in which their parents and grand-parents had been born. Even those who did move into the towns usually came from neighbouring counties.

The obligation on parishes to provide Poor Law relief only for their own natives or those with an established residence was a dis-incentive for migration even within England. Once lost, this right was very grudgingly taken up by other places, and many paupers were returned to their native place after moving somewhere else. In some villages, cottages were immediately pulled down when empty to prevent others from moving in. The 'laws of settlement', under the Act of 1662 as amended in 1795, were quite effective in im-mobilising the rural poor. Many did migrate to larger cities and industrial areas. But many more felt bound to their native place until the settlement laws were modified in the 1860s. Moving into the towns usually meant breaking the ties of family and friendship which were a vital source of support, especially as marriages were often between close relatives.

Nearly everyone walked to their place of work, as transport was limited and expensive until the growth of the railways in the 1840s. Of countrywomen in Victorian Surrey, quite close to London, it was said that 'they rarely went ten miles from their home throughout their lives'.[6] Villagers took their spouses from the same or neighbouring parishes, often marrying cousins. Despite an increasing emphasis on moral behaviour there were many unsanctified relationships. Births, marriages and deaths were recorded by the parishes, which also provided information for the censuses between 1801 and 1841. Not until 1837 did the registration of these events become compulsory and centrally recorded.

A strong sense of place and of history bound many to their origins. As Joseph Arch, the agricultural trade union leader of the 1870s, put it, referring to Barford (Warwickshire) where he was born in 1826: 'my country ... is Shakespeare's country, and my home, and what was the home of many of my forefathers as well, lies right in the very heart of old England'. Arch was a skilled hedger and ditcher and owned the freehold of the cottage where three generations of his family had lived, giving him an unusual freedom to challenge farmers and landowners later in life. An advocate of emigration, he still favoured opening up the land to agricultural labourers in their home country. While many labourers were certainly less literate or independent than Arch, they also had a strong sense of place and tradition. This made them reluctant to move even when economic pressures became powerful.

The idea that the rural English were too strongly attached to their native place to be coerced into emigration was used as an argument for changing the protective tariffs of the Corn Laws, which kept the price of bread unduly high in the view of ultimately successful critics. Making this claim, the *Oxford City and County Chronicle* of 6 June 1840 went on to state:

> We do not like to see poor people banished from the land of
> their birth to the furthest point in the world. They are far more
> domiciliated than the rich: their sphere of life is far more
> circumscribed, and they suffer much more from exile than those
> who are rendered more indifferent to the associations of

birthplace by the latitudinarian luxuries of life. The poor
villager has far stronger local affections. The objects of his
locality become as it were the landmark of his sympathies, nor
is there a tree or brook in his native village but has its place in
the fabric of his feelings. We are great sceptics in the Comfort
of the Colonies. Why don't some of those people who are so
loud in lauding emigration, emigrate themselves?

While many country people did emigrate at this time, it was not
always with great enthusiasm. In 1837 a whole shipload of intending emigrants from Norfolk to Australia simply refused to sail.

Rapid growth in the number of the English in the first half of the
nineteenth century is often linked with industrialisation. Certainly,
industry expanded to use the extra labour and to service the extra
market. But much of the expansion was in rural areas. It caused
great concern to Thomas Malthus and to his followers in recom-
mending the Poor Law reform of 1834. Malthus believed that
population would expand greatly beyond the availability of food to
support it. The reduction of smallpox, cholera and infant mortality
caused a population explosion in overwhelmingly rural counties like
Sussex. Its population rose from 159 000 in 1801 to 272 000 in
1831 and 300 000 in 1841, greater than the total white population
of Australia at the time. While some of this increase was absorbed in
the seaside resort of Brighton, much of it was in the villages, and the
rate was high for a rural county. It created a surplus of labour, made
worse by the introduction of threshing machines and other early systems of mechanisation. The same processes were at work in southern
counties and in Kent, where the Captain Swing revolt began.

Reduction of disease and mortality was only part of the problem.
Many rural areas provided employment in traditional crafts such
as handloom weaving, basket making or shoe making, which were
all being undermined by factory production mainly in the North
and the Midlands. Not only were there too many hands to work in
the fields but alternative sources of income were reducing. Crises
developed between the ending of the Napoleonic wars in 1815,
which released many men from the armed forces, and the growth
of the railways in the 1840s, which created a new opening for
labourers to build the lines and tunnels. The number of transported
convicts now reached its peak, and the system of paying for emigrants to travel to Australia was begun.

Religion

England was a Protestant society with an established church. The Reformation of 1536 created a national network through the Church of England with 9000 parishes organising every part of the country, most parishes being already in place. New ones were added later in hilly areas such as Northumberland, North Yorkshire, Westmorland and Cumberland as new land was developed and mining activity expanded. The parish structure was not radically changed to cope with population expansion in the industrial areas. Parishes were not simply an area for religious activity as they later became. They administered the Poor Law and other welfare services, and registered births. Civil parishes, now distinct from the church, are still the lowest level of local government in rural England, using the medieval boundaries. The church, sustained by annual tithes on produce and often by glebe land which produced an income from agriculture, was the largest single landowner in nearly every county in the nineteenth century. Tithes were consistently resented, especially by Nonconformists, who could not benefit from them. Their abolition remained a radical objective until the 1920s.

The local parson was a figure of considerable importance in the villages and was usually a link between farmers, labourers and the squire. Parsons were normally educated at Oxford or Cambridge, as entry to the two English universities was limited to Church of England communicants. This also meant that they were usually drawn from superior social classes to those of most of their parishioners. The Church of England was part of the rural establishment. The secular University College, London was not founded until 1836, and Nonconformist ministers were trained through their own seminaries. But in many industrial towns, employers and local councillors were Methodists or other Nonconformists or 'Dissenters'.

Being established meant that the Church of England was given monopoly powers against alternative denominations. The monarch was head of the church and still is. By law only a Protestant can be enthroned. All Church of England bishops are still nominated by the monarch acting on advice from the government. Catholics were not emancipated from civil disabilities until 1829 and the Catholic hierarchy was not restored until 1851. The Church of England monopoly was originally enforced by law, but toleration set in during the eighteenth century towards Nonconformists or Dissenters. These other denominations – mainly Baptists, Congregationalists

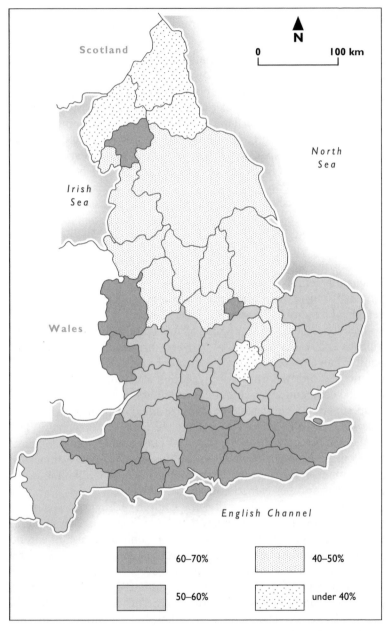

Proportion of Anglicans by county in the religious attendance census of Great Britain, 1851

and Quakers – had developed out of the religious enthusiasms of the Civil War (1642–51). 'Enthusiasm' in religion was frequently condemned as unseemly by the established church.

By the time Australia was being colonised the Church of England was being challenged by another form of Nonconformism: Methodism. By 1851, when the only religious census in England was taken, Methodism had often replaced Anglicanism as the most important denomination in the northern half of England. It also recruited support in isolated areas such as Cornwall, Ulster and the Shetlands. Methodism grew out of the reforming movement of John Wesley within the Church of England and became a distinct denomination after his death in 1791. In 1851 Methodist attendances outstripped Anglican in Cumberland, Cheshire, Durham, Yorkshire and Lincolnshire. In the industrial towns Methodism was stronger than Anglicanism in Leeds, Bradford and Rochdale. Baptists were particularly strong in southern farming counties such as Cambridgeshire, Huntingdon, Bedfordshire and Suffolk.

The strength of Methodism and Baptism often reflected resentment at the indifference of the Church of England towards industrial workers and rural labourers and its basis in the rural hierarchy. The radical journalist, William Cobbett, noted this in 1822 while travelling through an area of Kent from which many assisted immigrants went to Australia a few years later:

> that the labouring classes have, in great part, ceased to go to church; that their way of thinking and feeling with regard to both church and clergy are totally changed; and that there is now very little moral hold which the latter possess.[7]

The Church of England has often been described as the 'Tory Party at prayer'. The Conservative Party, which grew out of the Tories after 1838, was regarded as hostile to the interests of Nonconformists, who tended to ally with the Liberals and later with the Labour Party. Until reform began in the 1830s the Church of England was noted for its patronage and sinecures. Bishops could expect a large and comfortable palace and stipend of £3000 at a time when the annual income of a labourer's family was estimated by the Poor Law enquiry as £30.

Much of the work of parishes was done by curates eking out a miserable living. The *Barchester Chronicles* of Anthony Trollope (who did not approve of evangelical church reformers) graphically describes these problems. Those evangelicals who did not defect to the Methodists were an important element in establishing the Church of England in Australia. Their traditions still influence Sydney, the largest Anglican diocese.

The Church of England in Australia lacked the rural structures so important in England. Convicts were obliged to attend church services but free emigrants were not. In a few instances English landowners tried to recreate the English village, with church attendance obligatory for their workers. But this could not be sustained and was swept away by the huge influxes during the gold rushes of the 1850s. By then, at least half the population were Irish Catholics, Scottish Presbyterians or Cornish Methodists. An influential minority in South Australia were German Lutherans.

Messianic sects swept through England in the 1830s, when numbers coming to Australia were rising. The most important (detailed by Edward Thompson in his *The Making of the English Working Class*) followed Joanna Southcott, but they do not seem to have influenced Australia. Other nineteenth-century creeds like the Mormons, Jehovah's Witnesses, Christian Scientists and Seventh Day Adventists all have an Australian presence but are mainly inspired from the United States. The specifically English Salvation Army established a strong presence in 1880, only a few years after it was launched in London. Its leadership was taken over by Major James Baker, who was sent out from England. It had an important role in assisting immigration to Australia in the 1920s, chartering its own ship, the *Vedic*, from Liverpool.

Most of the early English settlers came from areas dominated by the Church of England. The London convicts were notoriously irreligious, and London was criticised by the 1851 Census for its paucity of attendance and provision of places and Sunday schools. By then, the Church of England was becoming what it remains, a largely middle-class, southern English and rural organisation. Nevertheless, it was assumed to be the established church in Australia until the New South Wales *Church Act* of 1836. The strongest remaining Anglican districts are still in the earliest areas of settlement in and around Sydney and in Tasmania. As in England, there was a great expansion of church building in the second half of the nineteenth century, with designs influenced by such English architects as Gilbert Scott and Augustus Pugin. Most Australian settlements thus acquired an Anglican church. Until 1996 Anglicans still made up the largest single Australian denomination, as they had done since 1788. They then lost this position to Catholics, whose level of church-going is also higher. Of those Australians born in England, about one-half still claim to be Anglicans and about one-quarter to have no religion.

Methodism came to Australia from Cornwall and Wales and from English villages and mining districts. The first chapel was established in Sydney in 1817. Immigration from Northern England was less important than from London and the South before the 1850s, and Methodism did not reach its peak until the end of the century. It remained divided into several sects until then, most numerously the Wesleyans, the Primitive Methodists and the Bible Christians (mainly from Cornwall and Devon). Methodists were not finally united until 1904, by which time they made up 13 per cent of the population.

Primitive Methodists were especially strong among Australian miners, as in England. They had their origin in Staffordshire and became particularly strong in Durham. These two counties contributed the most miners to the Victorian goldfields in the 1850s and to the New South Wales coalfields in the 1880s. Consequently central Victoria and the Newcastle and Hunter regions became Methodist strongholds. Methodist support in South Australia and Broken Hill was mainly Cornish. Methodists were strong in other mining areas such as Lithgow, Ballarat and Bendigo and in a few scattered towns like Geelong, Kempsey and Camden.

Despite the evangelical influence on the Church of England, the importance of Methodism and substantial support for Baptism and the Salvation Army, Australia did not develop the strong religious commitment which is so influential in the United States, with mainly Baptist origins. Periodic revivalist campaigns temporarily raised the profile of Christianity but left only a limited imprint. One effect of evangelical Christianity was a strict observance of the Sabbath, especially in Victoria and South Australia, and the efforts of those the *Bulletin* called 'wowsers' to limit access to alcohol, gambling and other sources of amusement for the less religious. Most of this survived until the 1960s but has now almost disappeared. It was an aspect of Australia which many English immigrants in the post-war years found oppressive.

Churchgoing levels are now higher than in England, but that is not saying much. This is largely due to Catholic attendance, which has also declined, and to Pentecostalism, which caters for all ethnic backgrounds. Methodists disappeared into the Uniting Church in 1977, along with Congregationalists and many Presbyterians. Between 80 and 95 per cent of Anglicans, Uniting and Baptists are Australian-born, with about one-in-eight Anglicans coming from England. These churches represent the descendants of previous generations from Britain, together with a minority whose ancestors were converted in various parts of the British Empire. The main churches derived from England are in relative decline, and the limitations placed on Sunday observance, trading, alcohol and gambling by Nonconformist and evangelical Christians are declining even more rapidly.

Measuring the emigrants

The English have often been confused in official figures with others from the United Kingdom. Even the Irish with their independent state were lumped in with the United Kingdom in Department of Immigration statistics as recently as 1999. The Australian Bureau of Statistics in its annual publication on migration continues to put England, Scotland and Wales together under 'United Kingdom'. It was common in the Victorian period to include the Welsh with the English and to classify Monmouthshire (now in Wales) as an English county. The Cornish have, of course, always been included with the English, which most seriously affects statistics from South Australia. There were more Cornish than Welsh immigrants in the nineteenth century, and far more from Ireland and Scotland than recently. However, Australia does have excellent immigration and population statistics from the early years of settlement and it is often possible to determine not only how many English were arriving but even from which counties they were coming.

The major sources for measuring the English population of Australia include convict records, local musters in the new colonies, assisted passage records, census data and shipping lists. A limitation on census data is that for the past century census records have been destroyed, making it impossible to trace ancestors or to measure immigrant settlement from particular districts. This practice was not amended until 2001, when census respondents were able to notify that their details could be stored and released a century later, as in the United Kingdom. Otherwise the census has become the main source, measuring birthplace, language, religion, parentage and, in 1986 and 2001, ancestry. Because the English have been the dominant ethnicity since 1788 and have intermarried with others, mainly from the British Isles and Australia, their 'boundaries' are often blurred. It might be assumed that Anglicans are of English origin, and that was largely true before the 1950s. It was always assumed that Catholics were Irish, though some, like Mother Mary McKillop, were Scottish. This assumption is now quite misleading except in some rural areas unaffected by recent immigration. Religious adherence was a useful indicator of English settlement in the past but has become much less convincing as Australia becomes more secular and multicultural.

The limitation on convict records (apart from some losses due to destruction and wastage) is that they normally show place of trial rather than of residence or origin. The work of professors Robson and Shaw suggests that many convicts were tried away from their place of origin, especially the large number in London and Lancashire. In the convict period everyone was assumed to have a place of origin or residence for Poor Law purposes, but these are recorded only at the place of trial and not at the point of transportation or of arrival in Australia. One very thorough survey has been done for Gloucestershire, listing every village or town of those sentenced to transportation between 1783 and 1842. This shows that 81 per cent were from Gloucestershire and 11 per cent from adjoining counties. The samples taken by Robson and Shaw differ, and are strongly influenced by the domination of London and Lancashire in the totals and the numbers of Irish-born tried in England and Scotland. Another debate, raised by Nicholas and Shergold, concerns the proposition that most convicts were from the 'criminal classes'. Their sampling, which includes Western Australia, suggests that convicts were a cross-section of the working classes, including many rural labourers and urban artisans.

Nineteenth-century records normally distinguish the various British nationalities. It was the policy of the agency which controlled assisted passages, the Colonial Land and Emigration Commission, to reproduce in Australia the English, Scottish and Irish, and the Protestant and Catholic, proportions found in the United Kingdom, and all their reports detail figures accordingly. Records exist for Poor Law assisted emigrants from the 1830s to the 1850s which detail the parish from which they have come. The British Census of 1841 also listed emigrants by county, though not specifically those going to Australia. The largest numbers left from Lancashire, West Yorkshire, Sussex, Devon, Kent and Somerset, and the last four rural counties were a major source for Australia.

The various colonies periodically enumerated assisted arrivals by their county of origin. Queensland continued to do this as late as 1879. As assisted passages were available only for defined skills, relevant occupational statistics were also produced, as were figures for literacy. It was often alleged that many applicants claimed to be agricultural labourers to secure a passage. This may have been true, but then many recently urbanised people retained close links with their villages of origin. The rural component of English emigration to Australia, while less than from Ireland, remained very significant for more than a century after first settlement. Nor was the English level of literacy particularly high; the Scottish level was almost always higher.

Consciousness of local, national and religious differences was less apparent in the figures when the Commonwealth assumed its census power in 1911 and its immigration power in 1920. Shipping lists then become more important. They always were for unassisted immigrants, who often made up half the English arriving, especially during the gold rushes. Many of the lists of assisted passengers were held in England and destroyed by the Board of Trade in 1900, but Australian lists were kept from 1924. Lists of passengers arriving by air since 1934 are sometimes available, but assisted passages were ended in 1983. Sampling done both in Australia and in Britain shows the occupational and regional backgrounds of English migrants in the post-war period. Recent records are much more concerned with educational and skill levels than with the kind of fine detail available for the English in the past. Both in the census and in immigration statistics the English have become 'invisible' by being buried within the broader United Kingdom category. But as over 80 per cent of modern UK immigrants have been English, this is less of a problem than in the past.

Where did they come from?

England was not as varied as the United Kingdom or many European powers such as the Austrian, Russian or Ottoman empires. It was much smaller, and of course very much smaller than Australia. But limited transport, illiteracy and poverty immobilised much of the rural population within narrow regional and local societies. With no national school system, there was no agency to develop and enforce standard English. The élite public schools were not reformed until the 1840s, town grammar schools were very localised and the

Church of England did little to standardise its village schools until mid-century. Mass popular newspapers did not develop until the 1890s. So until the public schools adopted 'received pronunciation' or 'Queen's English' in the mid-nineteenth century, there was considerable variety in dialects and pronunciation. When this change came, it created an 'upper class' English which marked out class boundaries.

Consequently, the English were culturally varied by region, class and degree of urbanisation. Most importantly, they were varied by the extent to which modern industry was developing in some areas but not in others. In Manchester and Leeds huge mills were turning out cotton and wool textiles, while less than 50 miles away in the valleys of the North Yorkshire moors there was a general belief in witchcraft. Wages varied considerably, depending on the availability of industrial employment, being lowest in the South despite its generally better land and climate. Agricultural wages kept dropping during the nineteenth century in some areas, whereas factory workers and miners in the Midlands and the North were living in brick cottages which, by the end of the century, some were even buying. Skilled industrial workers in many parts of England were not poor by the 1880s. Agricultural labourers and city slum dwellers were.

These variations led to two quite different influences on migration to Australia and elsewhere. One was the poverty of southern rural life; the other the disruption of old ways and traditions in the new industrial cities. The first led eventually towards assisted emigration for paupers and agricultural labourers, the second to conviction and transportation. The main English counties from which assisted immigrants came between 1830 and 1855 were Middlesex, Sussex, Somerset, Kent, Devon, Norfolk, Buckinghamshire, Bedfordshire, Wiltshire and Cambridgeshire. Those from which convicts came between 1788 and 1852 were, in order of numbers, Middlesex, Lancashire, Yorkshire, Warwickshire, Surrey, Gloucestershire, Kent, Somerset and Staffordshire. In Western Australia from 1850 to 1868 they were Middlesex, Lancashire, Yorkshire, Staffordshire, Warwickshire, Kent and Surrey. While there is some overlap, the basic difference is that all the 'convict' counties included large cities or industrial areas – London, Manchester, Liverpool, Leeds, Sheffield, Bristol and Stoke-on-Trent. The 'assisted migration' counties were much more rural, some overwhelmingly so.

Why did they come?

The English came to Australia for a variety of reasons. The first large input – the convicts – came because they were forced to and the alternative was often the death penalty. Between 1788 and 1868 the transported English numbered over 156 000. Of these, 80 000 came to New South Wales, 66 000 to Van Diemen's Land (Tasmania) and 9600 to Western Australia. Some were located in what became Victoria and Queensland. A few came to South Australia once freed, though the colonial authorities did their best to discourage this. Of those transported to eastern Australia about 71 per cent of the males and 57 per cent of the females were tried in England. Some were of Irish birth. Western Australia requested that no Irish should be sent, and transportation there was exclusively male. However, some tried in Liverpool and other parts of the North were born in Ireland. This Irish component reflected the large numbers who had fled from the famines and civil disorder to London and the industrial cities from the 1830s. The peak period for convict transportation was between 1825 and 1840, years of considerable social tension in England, but also of the growth of effective police forces.

The second and much larger input – assisted emigrants – came because they were paid to do so in various ways, ranging from loans to outright free passages. Assisted migrants need to be divided into historic periods to understand their variety. Between the 1830s and the 1860s they were predominantly rural labourers, many paid for by the sale of land in Australia, organised from England and given some further support from their parish or Poor Law Union. They were encouraged to come in family units. In the 1880s another large intake came with passages paid for and organised by the colonial governments, and especially by Queensland. They were more urbanised, including miners and railway workers, and more likely to come from the Northern and Midland industrial counties, but still included a large number of agricultural labourers. In contrast to their predecessors, they often had the vote (if male) and were enrolled in trade unions. Before and immediately after the First World War assisted immigrants came from urban, industrial and coalfield locations, including many from London. By the last and greatest influx, following the Second World War, they were reasonably representative of wage-earning English society.

The largest assisted intake of all was between 1947 and 1983. Immigrants were selected from all over England and with only limited regard to their occupations or qualifications. As previously, families were encouraged, in this case by giving free passages to children. About 85 per cent received assistance from public funds. They were overwhelmingly urban with a large component from London and the Home Counties and from Manchester and Merseyside. They could be nominated by relatives, churches, employers or the Commonwealth. State governments also gave incentives such as low-rental housing, most notably South Australia. There was mostly full employment before 1973, and the huge assisted intake of the 1960s were beneficiaries of a system which originated in the quite different circumstances of 130 years before. Immigration offices were maintained by the Commonwealth in London, Manchester, Leeds, Birmingham and Bristol during the 1960s.

Smaller numbers assisted by private organisations, charities or by loans were mostly not eligible for government assistance. The assisting institutions ranged from Caroline Chisholm's Family Colonization Loan Society in the 1850s, to the Salvation Army and Barnardo's from the 1920s. A large part of this charitable emigration was for children, which was at its peak in the 1920s and 1950s. Trade unionists were sometimes assisted by their organisations, but the numbers were not great.

This left a large residue who paid for themselves or were paid for by employers. They also were very varied. Many came for the gold rushes of the 1850s through to the 1890s, and others were pioneering agricultural settlers who brought their workers, animals and tools with them before assisted passages were developed. Many skilled artisans and coal miners had enough resources to get to Australia even when not eligible for public assistance. Repayable loans were often available for them.

Probably the largest unassisted group after the gold miners were white collar and professional people, ranging from lawyers and doctors to teachers and merchants. These non-manual classes were not encouraged in the nineteenth century but today dominate the English intake. Thus the intake moved from the labouring classes, through skilled artisans, building workers and miners and, eventually, towards highly skilled élites. Consistent decline in numbers after 1975 has not invalidated the generalisation that English immigration to Australia has involved a transfer from one working class to its equivalent. Today it is more likely to be from one professional class to another.

The primary reason for coming to Australia before 1945 was economic. Obviously the gold miners hoped to achieve wealth in a quite new way. Many agricultural labourers simply wanted higher wages. The desire to own a farm was also important, being almost impossible for a labourer in England as so many farms were tied up in landed property or traditional families. Miners and engineers went around the world seeking better wages, and Australia was only one of the countries in which they settled. As the coal industry went into terminal depression in the 1920s miners were attracted from counties such as Northumberland, Durham, Lancashire and South Yorkshire which had been officially designated 'depressed areas'. Lancashire cotton workers had similarly moved to Australia sixty years earlier during the cotton famine caused by the American Civil War.

These migrations, then, were quite materialistic. They were not necessarily inspired by the imperialist rhetoric used from the 1880s. Nevertheless, the English, unlike the Irish, did prefer Australia and New Zealand as destinations from the 1850s. There are still more English-born in Australia than in Canada or the United States, despite their larger populations. Material reasons seem predominant, and letters home are full of prices, wages and the availability of food. But the English also seemed most comfortable within the Empire when at its height.

The reasons for coming after 1945 were, perhaps, more complex. England had finally achieved full employment and was developing the 'welfare state' under a Labour government pledged never to return to the pre-war depression. Post-war rationing, shortages,

The Euripides *carried many coal miners to Australia after the general* *strike of 1926*

fuel crises, hard winters and the winding up of the Empire all contributed to an air of depression. The largest selling newspaper, the *Daily Express*, put a knight in armour held by chains on its front page every day for years. He would only be released when Britain was unchained from government restrictions. The newly elected Conservative government of Winston Churchill in 1951 promised a 'bonfire of controls' in the same spirit. This did not stop the flow towards Australia which escalated into the 1960s. Nor did it save the *Daily Express*, which declined nearly as rapidly as the empire it so strongly supported.

A docile and insular people?

In the eighteenth century the English were often described as 'ungovernable'. England had a long history of rioting, most seriously in London in 1780 against Catholics. Similar riots against the Irish broke out in Lancashire in the 1860s. More than a century later they were still rioting against 'foreigners' – now Pakistanis, and not foreigners at all but British-born youths. English football hooligans are the bane of Europe. All this suggests a degree of repressed frustration in an otherwise rather obedient and docile people. In 1847 a witness to the UK Select Committee on Colonisation from Ireland stated that 'possibly the Englishman is the most obedient and the least troublesome'.[8] But he was also insular and reluctant to leave home as compared with the Scots or the Irish.

There is clearly a contradiction here between the fear of civil disorder current until the late 1830s and again in the early 1920s and the reality that for the past century most major conflicts in England have been on the coalfields or around race and have rarely had a political motivation. The general strike of 1926 was the last serious confrontation between the state and the unions until the miners' strike of 1984. In both cases the miners were defeated, and in both cases there were breakaways from the miners union in the Midlands coalfields favouring conciliation. In all instances of social conflict – from the Chartists in the 1840s, through the union-isation of agricultural workers, miners and waterside workers in the 1870s and 1880s, to the industrial strife before and after the First World War – the English have sought a parliamentary solution to their grievances. Communism was negligible throughout the United Kingdom, and its most significant following in the 1920s and 1930s was in Scotland and Wales. The Irish were the only truly revolutionary people in the British Isles, and some of them are still fighting each other into the present.

During the first sixty years of Australian colonisation, the disturbed and violent state of England was transformed to a fairly conservative and reformist society. Conservative prime minister Benjamin Disraeli foresaw, when he granted them the franchise in 1867, that urban householders would not be very radical. He and his Conservative successors mobilised urban support around the expansion of the British Empire, a tactic of considerable relevance in Australia. Hesitation about enfranchising rural men was due to the landed aristocracy in the House of Lords being fearful of losing its political hold over them, as was obstruction over secret balloting until 1872, fifteen years after it was introduced in Australia. Many rural areas did support the Liberal Party after that, but very few transferred their loyalties to the Labour Party in the twentieth century. Many urban and industrial areas remained Conservative at least until 1945, including Liverpool, Birmingham and some textile towns of Lancashire and Yorkshire. The most severely depressed area of England in the 1930s, the Northeast coast, turned away from Labour in 1931 and did not come back until 1945.

All of this gave the English a reputation in Australia for conservatism, deference and lack of class militancy. But Australia, too, was under conservative domination between 1920 and 1941 and again between 1949 and 1972. Part of the contrast between the two societies rests on the perennial shortage of labour in Australia when compared with England. The English touched their caps to the squire because they would not get a job otherwise. The Australian 'called no biped lord or "sir", And touch their hat to no man', as Henry Lawson put it. He could always move on to somewhere else. But Banjo Paterson noted in *A Bushman's Song* that farmers in the Illawarra 'haven't the cheek to dare to speak without they touch their hat'. Paterson and Lawson notwithstanding, there were many tenant farmers of English origin in early Australia.

In both countries radicalism and trade unionism declined when unemployment loomed. The importance of labour shortages was never lost on employers. As James Unett cynically wrote to his father in Birmingham in 1836, 'suppose all, no we will say the greater part of the working men of this Country, were to save their money, in lieu of drinking it all away as quick as they get it, what would the consequences be? Labour would be impossible to be had unless at ruinous terms, for these very men would in a short time become Masters'.[9] A similar fear was expressed by the landowner Edward

Macarthur in 1847, linking labour shortage to demands for better wages and conditions, which was 'a political evil, because such a state of things tends to promote Democracy'.[10]

The insularity of the English was more of attitude than of concrete reality. They left home in their millions either as emigrants or as soldiers and sailors or as colonial administrators and traders. But they often took notions of superiority with them, based on the technical advances and imperial expansion of the Victorian era. Their prejudices were engrained and outspoken, especially against the Irish, Catholics, French, Indians, Africans and Americans. Australian racism had local dimensions based on conflict with Aborigines and Chinese immigrants. But English racism was well established, often based on feelings of superiority towards those conquered in India or Africa or fleeing from starving Ireland. Some retained prejudices against 'colonials' which shocked and annoyed middle-class Australians returning 'home' as late as the 1960s. It is not surprising that the movement for a White Australia reached its height during the mass English immigration of the 1880s, nor that many of its leaders were English. But these very same leaders were among the founders of the Australian Labor Party.

The myth of 'Old England'

Nostalgia for rural England continued strongly until the final years of the nineteenth century, by which time the English were coming largely from urban, industrial or mining areas. A popular mid-Victorian song, *The Miner's Dream of Home*, sums this up:

> I saw the old homestead and faces I love,
> I saw England's valleys and dells,
> And I listened with joy,
> As I did when a boy,
> To the sound of the old village bells.

The myth that the 'real England' was in the countryside was appropriated by middle-class and conservative romantics, who were correspondingly derogatory about immigrants from the cities. British Conservative prime minister Stanley Baldwin told the Royal League of St George in 1924 that 'to me England is the country, and the country is England'. This meshed with Australian notions that migrants ought to go to the bush as their forefathers had done, an idea not yet dead. The bush was not, of course, the orderly English

How they saw things 140 years ago

countryside with villages and towns established since the Middle Ages and churches and pubs every mile or so. Nor did most of those doing the urging actually live there. These illusions had their most damaging influence on migrant settlement policy in the 1920s.

The thoroughly urbanised English coming in the twentieth century could not conform to these expectations. Italian and Greek migrants did come largely from villages and small towns, and in the 1920s many went to the bush. But this was no longer the case for most in the 1950s. As for the English, most wanted a better life within an urban setting. They missed many aspects of English urban life, but not 'the old village bells'.

2

CONVICTS, LABOURERS AND SERVANTS

The Emigrants must belong to the class of Mechanics and
Handicraftsmen, Agricultural Labourers or Domestic Servants.

Instructions from the London Government Emigration
Office *c.*1840

The largest numbers of men in England during the formative years of Australia were labourers with limited skills and education. The largest number of women were either unpaid wives and daughters or domestic servants, who were even less likely to be literate than the men. Those coming to Australia before 1850 fully reflected this pattern. Labourers and agricultural workers made up about 40 per cent of the male convicts. The English were more likely to be industrial workers than the Irish, especially those sent to Western Australia between 1850 and 1868. Women were harder to classify, but of those who had employment a large proportion were servants. Labourers and servants were even more strongly represented among assisted emigrants after 1831. Public policy deliberately encouraged the immigration of a manual working class for at least a century after settlement. This distinguished the Australian colonies from the West Indies – which depended on slaves – or from Africa or India, which relied on the local population.

Social conditions in the large cities and the new industrial towns created massive social problems, which were tackled by deterrence and severe sanctions but with limited efficiency. Unlike Europe, England did not have organised police forces until the 1830s, following the creation of the London Metropolitan Police in 1829. Watchmen and constables were appointed by the parishes, but there was no co-ordination or discipline. The *Rural Police Act* of 1839 encouraged the creation of county forces but most were not in place until the 1840s. One consequence of reform was an increase in arrests leading to transportation. Prisons were often ancient and insanitary and used to house debtors until they could repay their creditors.

Crime increased greatly after the Napoleonic wars, when large numbers of soldiers and sailors were discharged into unemployment. Three alternative punishment systems tried to deal with these problems: hanging, transportation or convict hulks. A fourth possibility, imprisonment in a 'model' penitentiary, became increasingly important after the first was built at Pentonville (London). Others soon followed, so that by the end of transportation it was possible to incarcerate convicted criminals in specially built prisons, many of which are still in use. These replaced the older London prisons such as Coldbath Fields, Marshallsea, Fleet and Clink, although Newgate remained in use until 1902. Prisons on similar lines were built in Australia, the most famous being at Port Arthur (Tasmania).

Prisoners from Pentonville prison were sent to Australia as 'exiles' in the 1840s in an attempt to circumvent local opposition to transportation. The first 21 arrived in Melbourne on the *Royal George* in November 1844, and 1727 had arrived by June 1848. But the 'Pentonvillains' were unacceptable and their transportation soon ended, frustrated by large hostile demonstrations. Hulks of disused battleships remained in use until the 1850s, but the prison crisis was being overcome by the new model penitentiaries. Eastern Australia no longer wanted convicts and England did not have the same need to send them. However, there was great difficulty in attracting immigrants to Western Australia until the gold rushes of the 1890s, and transportation provided a temporary solution between 1850 and 1868. Even before this, 51 boys from Parkhurst juvenile prison on the Isle of Wight were sent to the West on the *Orient* in 1848 to work as farm boys, following 36 who had been sent in 1842 and 1844.

London as a sink of iniquity

London had become the largest city in western Europe by 1788, and retained that position until after the Second World War. Not surprisingly, Londoners have been a major source of emigrants to Australia from the convict intake onwards. The city itself grew from English, Irish and European immigration and is still attracting newcomers from throughout the world. In its most rapid period of growth – the nineteenth century – it drew in people from surrounding rural areas, with those from Surrey and Kent tending to settle in

South London and those from East Anglia in East London. Apart from the small City of London, the business and banking district, London was variously defined until the creation of the London County Council in 1888. Before that, Middlesex extended as far as Bow Creek in the East, taking in Westminster, the City and the East End. Surrey extended to the south bank of the Thames, including Southwark, Lambeth and Bermondsey. A small part of Kent embraced Deptford, Greenwich and Woolwich along the Thames. Figures for convict or assisted immigration from these three counties often conceal the extent to which emigrants came from built-up areas of London, especially as these expanded rapidly.

The Irish coming to England were generally poorer and less skilled than those going to Australia or America. They could travel on the deck of passenger ships to Liverpool for a few pennies, arriving 'starving and half naked' as the Liverpool Poor Law guardians complained in 1849. Those in London settled in the poorest districts, becoming unskilled labourers especially in building, transport and the rapidly expanding docks. Among them were what the Victorian social commentator Henry Mayhew, writing in the 1850s, called the 'cockney Irish', who were Londoners of Irish origin but local birth. He believed this group to be especially liable to juvenile crime.[1]

Jews, Huguenots, Italians, Germans and small numbers from throughout the British Empire also settled, especially in central districts such as Soho, Clerkenwell or Whitechapel. Following the pogroms in Russia and the assassination of Tsar Alexander II in 1881, thousands of Jews from the Russian Empire flowed into Whitechapel and Stepney, which had Jewish communities dating from the seventeenth century. Most of these newcomers were Ashkenazic and Yiddish-speaking, whereas the well-established and increasingly rich Jewish élite were Sephardic, like the families of Benjamin Disraeli or the Sassoons, or from Germany like the Rothschilds. Opposition to this large influx eventually led to the *Aliens Act* of 1905, the first serious attempt to restrict immigration to the United Kingdom. Jewish organisations in London sent some of the new immigrants to Australia, but most either remained in London or moved onwards to the United States. Of the London Jews in the convict period, a magistrate commented that 'the bulk of the Jewish population had no knowledge of skilled trade and were inevitably implicated in the wave of crime which spread over the third quarter of the eighteenth century'.

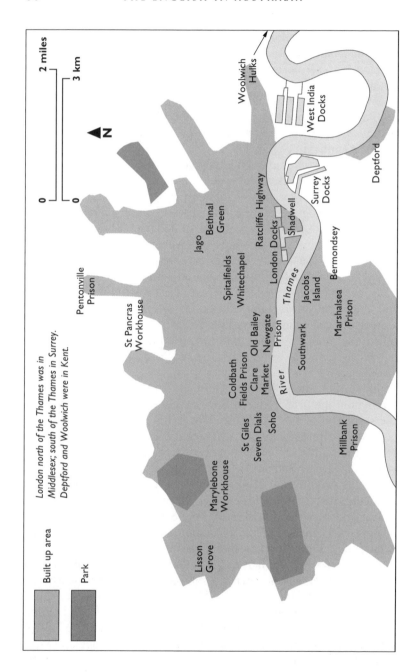

Criminal London, c.1840

London was cosmopolitan, rapidly expanding, but also a sink of squalor, crime and disease. The Victorian dilemma was that as England became richer it left behind a residue of those who were either very poor, such as agricultural labourers, or had turned to crime, such as many London slum dwellers. A long history of literary and investigative studies of the London poor and criminal classes extends back as far as John Gay's *The Beggar's Opera* (1728), through Charles Dickens's *Oliver Twist* (1837), to Henry Mayhew's *London Labour and the London Poor* (1851 and 1862), Arthur Morrison's *A Child of the Jago*, the Congregational Union's *Bitter Cry of Outcast London* (1883) and the massive social survey of Charles Booth, *Life and Labour of the People in London* (1889–97). While the general condition of Londoners improved over this 150 years, criminal-infested slums remained. They were the main recruiting area for the 43 000 convicts sent to Australia from London and the Home Counties before 1868.

The largest slum area was in what is now the London borough of Tower Hamlets, including Spitalfields, Stepney, Limehouse and Bethnal Green. Criminal concentrations were notorious around Spitalfields, Whitechapel and Ratcliffe Highway. Smaller but equally bad areas included Shoreditch, Seven Dials and St Giles, Clare Market and Lisson Grove (Marylebone) north of the river, and Southwark, Lambeth and Bermondsey to the south. In the latter was the 'rookery' Jacob's Island, immortalised by Charles Dickens as the hiding place of Fagin. While these areas gradually reduced in size, they remained at the core of London criminality for two centuries.

London-born convicts had a varied experience. The Jewish group, which included John Harris, Israel Chapman, Isaac Solomon and Emanuel Solomon, became respectively an innkeeper, a policeman, a failed settler in Van Diemen's Land, and a merchant and South Australian politician. Esther Abrahams, transported on the First Fleet for shoplifting, eventually married the lieutenant-governor of New South Wales and is often regarded as the 'mother' of the Australian Jewish community. Of non-Jewish convicts, Andrew Bent became a newspaper publisher in Hobart, but David Bracewell escaped from custody and lived with Aborigines for some time. George Bruce from Shadwell in the London docks became a sailor but made little more progress, while Robert Cooper of Ratcliffe Highway remained in the liquor trade and was a moderately successful distiller. James Underwood from Bermondsey and Thomas Dowse from Hackney both became successful merchants, and George Gatehouse became a brewer in Hobart.

Middle-class London convicts did well. James Blackburn was a forger who succeeded in Australia as an engineer and architect. Another forger, George Crossley, became a lawyer in Sydney. William Bland, a doctor transported for killing a man in a duel, established a flourishing medical practice and became a Legislative Council member in New South Wales in 1843. This was a fairly distinguished selection from such a large number. Those who had been well placed in London usually did well in Australia. Most others probably did not. On the evidence of Mayhew, many returned convicts took up their former criminal life in London again. In 1850 he interviewed a returned convict from Tasmania. His tale of repeated floggings helps to explain why he was ready to turn his back on the London lodging houses which he claimed to be full of criminals hiding from the police.[2]

It is unlikely that many voluntarily emigrated to Australia from the slum core of London after the convict period. But there were regular complaints from receiving colonies about the quality of assisted emigrants sent from London. In 1850 the Colonial Land and Emigration Commission in London responded to complaints about the behaviour of girls sent out from the Marylebone workhouse: 'it is not safe, as a general rule, to accept as emigrants young women from a workhouse in a large town'. Mayhew, in that year, drew attention to the especially bad reputation of the very same workhouse. Nevertheless, 60 paupers from Marylebone were sent to South Australia in 1853.

Police, health and character checks would have kept out many paupers or criminals from London, apart from the normal requirement that families had preference, as did agricultural labourers, artisans and domestic servants. The main agencies for sending emigrants from the poorest parts of London were not the publicly funded schemes but private charities. A particular concern was the thousands of abandoned children on the streets. By mid-century about one-third of the inmates of many workhouses were children, most of whom eventually became professional criminals or prostitutes. Neither fate was acceptable to Christian charities. Child offenders could be transported after the age of seven, and many organisations like the Waifs and Strays Society, the Ragged School, the Children's Friend Society and Barnardo's saw emigration as a solution. A Metropolitan police magistrate commented in 1826: 'London has become too full of children. There has been a great increase of juvenile offences, which I attribute to want of employment for people between the ages of twelve and twenty. I therefore suggest emigration as a remedy'.[3]

Many areas were cleared away as London became more prosperous – notably Clare Market, which was replaced by Aldwych and its grand buildings, including Australia House. Wartime bombing was severe along the Thames and the population declined drastically between 1940 and 1945. Slum clearance produced exceptionally high levels of public housing. In 1991 Tower Hamlets led England with 58 per cent council houses, followed by Southwark with 51 per cent, the only English municipalities with an absolute majority in public housing. The Jews had left Tower Hamlets by 1960, to be replaced by the largest Bangladeshi community in the country.

Criminal traditions had not entirely disappeared. Bethnal Green and Hoxton was the home base of the Kray twins and their gangsters until their arrest in 1968. They were regarded as local heroes by at least some of their neighbours. It is arguable that the Australian tradition of admiring criminals – epitomised by the Ned Kelly legend – is not entirely Irish, but may have some origins in the slums of London. Tilly Devine, the famous brothel-keeper of 1920s Sydney, was born and brought up in south London. She is remembered in the thoroughly respectable feminist restaurant and bar in Canberra named in her honour. Another hero for some, Londoner Ronnie Biggs the 'great train robber', lived in comfort in Melbourne for some years while escaping justice. He was not a local 'hero', as he had to hide his identity.

The industrial areas

The industrial areas were not as cosmopolitan as London, nor did they have such a large class of professional and hereditary criminals. During the convict period they were still rough and raw. Many workers came from elsewhere, especially Ireland, while workhouse children were important recruits in the factory labour force. Women worked in large numbers in the cotton industry of Lancashire, improving the family income but leading to child neglect. They were also employed in even less attractive occupations such as sifting coal at the pit head or making chains and nails by hand. Female mine work below ground was made illegal in 1842. Industrial injuries and ill-health were prevalent and trade cycles made life even more insecure. The protection of various Factory Acts between 1819 and 1850 was available to women and children but only alleviated intolerable conditions and excessive working hours. Men were assumed to be able to look after themselves, and increasingly did so by forming trade unions. Pauper children, who were sent in large numbers to Northern factories from Southern workhouses, were given some nominal protection by the *Health and Morals of Apprentices Act*, 1802.

Between 1788 and 1852, 27 000 convicts were transported from the Northern and Midland industrial counties of Lancashire, Yorkshire, Warwickshire, Cheshire, Worcestershire and Staffordshire. These included the main cotton and wool textile towns, the iron and steel industries, the potteries, and most of the English coalfields other than in the Northeast. Their major cities were Liverpool, Manchester, Sheffield, Leeds, Birmingham, Wolverhampton, Bradford, Stoke-on-Trent, Oldham, Bolton and a range of middle-sized industrial towns and mining villages. The coalfields and shipbuilding districts of the Northeast in the counties of Durham and Northumberland sent relatively few convicts or assisted immigrants before the 1850s. Altogether, 50 per cent of English convicts sent to Western Australia were tried in the Midlands and the North, compared with only 26 per cent of those sent to New South Wales and Van Diemen's Land. The Western Australia totals were, of course, much smaller and over a shorter period (1850–68).

Convicts from industrial areas, like those from London, were unlikely to be rural labourers. In contrast to London, some were transported for political activity, mainly in the Luddite and Chartist

The home of an impoverished Lancashire cotton worker in the 1830s

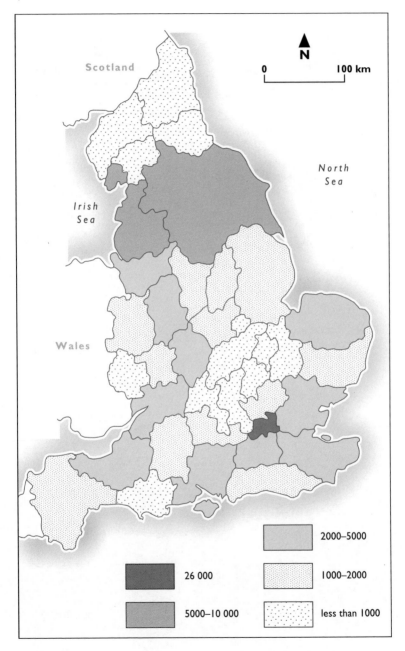

County of trial of convicts transported to Eastern Australia, 1788–1853
Source: Robson (1977), The Convict Settlers of Australia, *tables 4d, n*

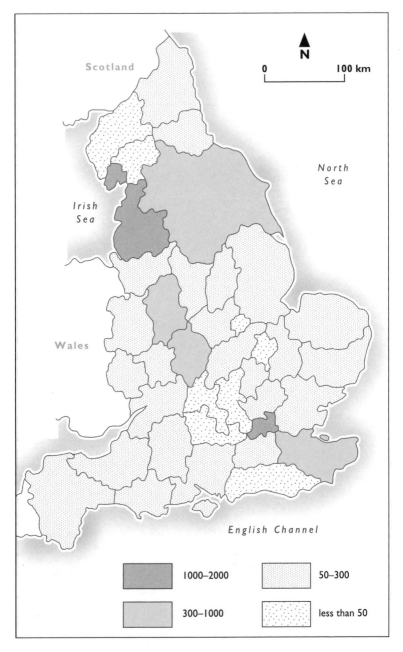

County of trial of convicts transported to Western Australia
Source: Nicholas and Shergold in Jupp (1988), p. 28

movements. The Luddites, named for the mythical Ned Ludd, broke machines which threatened hand-frame knitters in the Nottingham area. Seven were transported in 1812. The Chartists were a much larger, highly organised and directly political movement between 1838 and 1848. Their objectives were to democratise the parliamentary system. Many of their activists were also socialists wanting a different social system. The claim of the social historians, the Hammonds, that 'the village Hampdens ... sleep by the shores of Botany Bay'[4] was even more relevant to those from the industrial areas. However, as with the rural revolts, few major political leaders were transported for political offences. This fate was reserved for the Irish, Scots, Welsh and Canadians. The thousand or so English Luddites, Chartists and followers of Captain Swing who were transported were from the humble ranks of the discontented.

Fifty-one miners and potters from around Stoke-on-Trent in north Staffordshire were transported to Van Diemen's Land on the *John Renwick* in 1843, the last English group who can be described as political prisoners. Most were tried at a special commission of assize at Stafford on 1 October 1842 for crimes arising from large-scale rioting in Stoke and adjacent towns starting on 15 August. But very few were transported for specifically political offences. William Ellis, aged thirty-two, was charged with having 'with divers other persons ... traitorously compassed, imagined, and devised, and intended to levy war against her Majesty, our Sovereign Lady the Queen, in order to force or compel her said Majesty to change her measures and counsels'. He was transported for twenty-one years, not for this offence but for 'feloniously demolishing a house'. Another leader, Thomas Cooper, was charged with 'inciting and persuading a great number of people to assemble and gather together, and riotously and tumultuously, creating a great noise and disturbance'.[5] He was sentenced to only two years' local imprisonment, and wrote about his activities in his autobiography thirty years later.

Virtually all others transported were indicted for destroying houses, stealing valuables from them, rioting and arson. These charges obscure the extent to which the crimes were committed as part of a political and industrial dispute. They illuminate the very uneven nature of punishments, which were most severe for crimes against property. They also mark the declining extent to which violence was associated with political protest in England, being replaced by trade unionism and the extension of the franchise over the next twenty years.

Convicts from the North and the Midlands often did well in Australia. John Boothman of Bolton, an embezzler, became a Tasmanian public servant. Daniel Cooper, also of Bolton, became a merchant and investor in New South Wales. Mary Reibey, an orphan from Bury, Lancashire was convicted of stealing a horse at the age of thirteen and transported in 1792.[6] She became a very successful business woman, taking over her husband's commercial and shipping activities. She was accepted as an emancipist in polite society, returned temporarily in triumph to Lancashire and died a pillar of the Church of England in Sydney in 1855. Simeon Lord of Todmorden, West Yorkshire was transported in 1791 for theft and became a highly successful trader, property owner, whaler and sealer. He was a founder of the Bank of New South Wales in 1816. Samuel Terry of Manchester, a labourer transported in 1801, also became a major property owner, Freemason and leader of the emancipists. Careers like those of Mary Reibey, Simeon Lord and Samuel Terry underline the opportunities open to convicts who arrived early in New South Wales.

Others from the North led a more desperate existence. Matthew Brady of Manchester became a bushranger in Van Diemen's Land and was hanged in 1826. Michael Howe of Pontefract, a highway robber, took the same path and was killed in 1818. The best known escaped convict from the North was William Buckley from Macclesfield, who spent many years among the Aborigines of Port Phillip. He became an object of curiosity when he finally returned to white society in 1835. John Wilson, convicted at Wigan in 1785, sailed on the First Fleet and spent long periods living with Aborigines, one of whom eventually killed him in 1800. William Gould of Liverpool was a minor artist in Van Diemen's Land, and regularly in trouble with the law.

The provinces

From the industrial Midlands, Thomas Bock, an engraver of Birmingham, established himself in his profession in Hobart in 1824. Joseph Lycett of Staffordshire, also an engraver, was convicted of forgery in 1811 and continued to forge bank notes in Sydney, being eventually pardoned and returning to England where, incorrigibly, he appears to have forged more bank notes. Frances Greenway of Bristol, an embezzler, became the leading Georgian architect in Sydney, and the best-known of his many buildings is

the convict barracks in Macquarie Street. Forgery and embezzle-
ment might today be called 'white collar crimes', and those transported were often able to find a niche in colonial society denied to
less skilled convicts. Transported at thirteen from Plymouth in 1846,
William Henry Groom in 1901 was the only convict ever to be
elected to the Commonwealth parliament. He had previously
held Toowoomba in the Queensland parliament for nearly forty
years. The Federal electorate centred on Toowomba is named in
honour of his son, who succeeded him in the seat then called
Darling Downs.

Few convicts from rural areas distinguished themselves, in contrast to the free and assisted settlers and urban convicts. James
Austin of Baltonsborough, Somerset established a rural dynasty
in Tasmania with his relatives, who came free. John Grant, public
school educated and from Buckinghamshire, became a poet in New
South Wales. John Knatchbull of Kent, transported in 1824, was
also among the few English convicts with a public school education
– at Winchester. He was convicted of forgery in New South Wales,
was then involved in a mutiny and was eventually hanged for
murder in 1834 – evidence that family background is not everything. Robert Murray of Shropshire, educated at Westminster, was
transported for bigamy, established the Hobart press and retired to
his ancestral home in England. In contrast Henry Kable, an illiterate
Norfolk labourer, did quite well in business after arriving on the First
Fleet, and has descendants in New South Wales. Molly Morgan,
daughter of a ratcatcher from rural Shropshire, was transported in
1790, escaped to England, was transported again in 1804, became a
land developer around Maitland, but died relatively poor.

The English convicts were mostly urban and rural labourers. But
they were quite diverse and had various careers. A few were very
well educated, including at least one Oxford University graduate,
Michael Robinson. Most were sentenced to seven years and many
were able to take up land or business if they were unwilling or
unable to return to England. The socially acceptable forgers and
embezzlers sometimes had good relations with the ruling élite, as
skills were in short supply, as was business ability. The 'first families'
in New South Wales were not quite as distinguished as those in
Virginia or as the Pilgrim Fathers. Indeed the founders of Australia
in the first forty years were predominantly English convicts –
farmers, bankers, artists, traders and speculators as well as manual
workers and sturdy pioneers.

Rural unrest and transportation

For most of the convict period England was still a rural country. But the English convicts, as contrasted with the Irish, were more likely than the average to have an urban residence or birthplace. Discounting the large numbers from London and the North and the Midlands, rural England produced transported convicts for three major reasons: simple theft (including animal theft), the game laws and rural unrest. The hierarchical and closely knit village systems, the discipline of the Poor Law and the workhouse, limited horizons and religious practice all combined to control rural criminality. Many convicts originally from rural villages had moved to the cities or joined the armed services.

Within rural counties, convicts were more likely to come from large and growing towns or textile and mining districts than from the villages. These included new resort towns such as Brighton and Cheltenham, which both sent about one hundred convicts, mainly servants and building workers. Bristol was divided between the otherwise rural counties of Gloucestershire and Somerset; Portsmouth, Chatham, Southampton, Plymouth, Hull and Middlesbrough were all ports relatively isolated in rural surroundings and drawing their populations from a wide area. Seafaring towns had fairly high crime rates and many men detached from family and parish. Sailors and soldiers were quite common among convicts, especially after the Napoleonic wars when many were discharged away from home and without employment.

In general the rural counties away from the coast and the larger towns sent few convicts. This was particularly true for South Midlands counties like Northamptonshire. Gloucestershire was a fairly typical county. Bordering on the seaport of Bristol, with a textile and coal mining industry, over half its people in 1831 lived in rural villages, if Bristol is excluded.[7] Eighty per cent of convicts transported by the courts in Gloucester and Tewkesbury between 1788 and 1841 lived in the county, with only a small number from London, Ireland or overseas.

The largest number from Gloucestershire came from the Cotswold wool industry district centred on Stroud. This antiquated industry was being decimated by competition from Yorkshire. The census of 1841 attributed population decline to 'the falling off of the woollen cloth manufacture ... four extensive manufactories in the parish of Uley have been discontinued since 1831'.[8] The shoemaking industry was similarly affected by factory competition from Northamptonshire. About 5 per cent of those transported were weavers or other textile workers, nearly twice their proportion in the workforce. Others included shoemakers, miners, soldiers and sailors, butchers and servants and a wide range of specialised occupations, most of which have long ago disappeared. By far the largest number were simply described as labourers, including nearly all those from the smaller villages. Among the very few women, only Mary Sheppard of Bitton was described as a prostitute. This was quite a different cross-section of society than would have been found in London or Lancashire.

Sussex was even more rural than Gloucestershire. It included only one large town, Brighton, and no mines or factory towns. Connected to London by railway in 1841, Brighton grew to become London by the Sea, the largest seaside resort in England. The population of Sussex rose by 26 per cent between 1811 and 1831. The Poor Law enquiry commented that 'the excess in some districts of labourers beyond the actual demand must be taken to be established beyond dispute'. As in Cheltenham, Brighton attracted a range of casual labourers, building craftsmen, servants and washerwomen, from whom many convicts were drawn. The rest of East Sussex was rural, with small towns such as Lewes, Uckfield, Hastings and Rye. This was rural England at its purest and poorest. The Poor Law enquiry in 1832 picked out East Sussex as among the worst areas for pauperising the population through subsidising low agricultural wages. East Sussex in the 1830s became a centre for the Captain Swing revolt, and in the 1840s a major source of assisted emigration to Australia. Today it is very prosperous, with pockets of disadvantage only in the seaside resorts which line its coast.

Almost 300 Sussex men and 25 women were transported between 1810 and 1840 by the East Sussex Quarter Sessions sitting at Lewes.[9] A small number of them were from elsewhere but, as in Gloucestershire, the great majority gave their place of settlement as in East Sussex. One-third were from Brighton and its adjoining parishes of Hove and Preston, 19 from Lewes and 7 from Uckfield. The rest were scattered through most rural parishes, with the highest numbers from East Grinstead (6), Maresfield (7), Framfield (7), Salehurst (5), Ringmer (4) and Rye (4) – all but East Grinstead and Rye being villages rather than towns. As in Gloucestershire nearly all parishes in East Sussex sent at least one convict to Australia by 1840.

Those transported from Sussex were mostly labourers and their crime larceny (theft). Only 17 were transported for their part in the Captain Swing rising, all going to Van Diemen's Land. Only one was middle class – George Camp, an attorney from Brighton, convicted for fraud. Other occupations included servant, cordwainer, butcher, baker, bricklayer, sweep, plumber, carpenter, farmer, fisherman and fellmaker. There was one case of wounding and one highway robber but not a single murderer. Most were transported for seven years. Nearly all those from East Sussex were unskilled men caught stealing the property of others.

Crime in rural areas indicates poverty and social discontent, and general discontent amongst labourers and redundant craftsmen was evident between 1788 and 1850. As in the industrial districts, though more rarely, this sometimes manifested in violent outbursts which brought punishment and transportation. A small rising in Pentrich (Derbyshire) marched on Nottingham in 1817 but was easily dispersed, and 14 were transported. This kind of leaderless and undirected rural rising, known as a *jacquerie* after its French equivalent, is still common in under-developed peasant societies. The most important in recent English history began at Lower Hardres near Canterbury (Kent) in August 1830 and spread rapidly through the southern counties.

The Captain Swing rising was the last purely agrarian revolt in England.[10] Its significance for Australia was threefold: it brought 500 transported convicts with rural labouring skills to colonies with less than 70 000 settlers; it dominated review of the Poor Law in 1832 and 1833; and, through that enquiry, it inspired the assisted passage schemes which helped to build the Australian population for the next 150 years.

Alleviating rural discontent and over-population by emigration from the affected Southern counties was an official priority for the next twenty years. This shifted colonisation policy away from the convicts of London and Lancashire and towards the villages of the South and Southwest. The second wave of founding fathers were thus law-abiding Church of England adherents from structured and conservative rural society, rather than from the chaos of the London slums and the new industrial cities. The contradiction in Australia between hostility to authority and a genteel suburbanism might have its roots in these two quite different intakes.

Captain Swing and other rural dissidents engaged mostly in burning hayricks, threatening farmers by word or letter, smashing

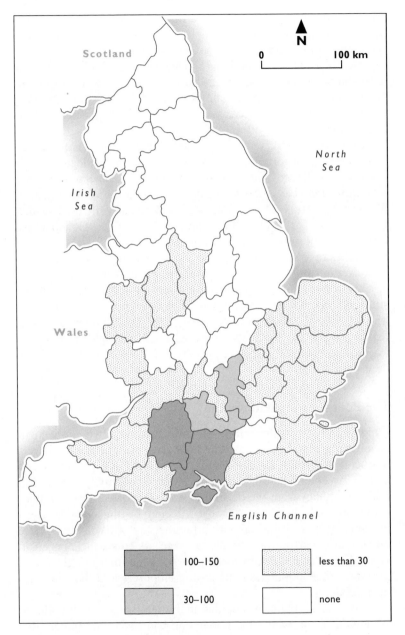

County of trial of Captain Swing convicts transported to Eastern Australia, 1831
Source: Hobsbawm and Rudé (1973) Appendix II

threshing machines and resisting arrest or dispersal. Another misdeed, forming a trade union, was less common but attracted more sympathy from liberal reformers. Once the *Combination Acts* were repealed in 1824 it was no longer illegal to form a union. But their legal status remained doubtful at least until the *Trade Union Act* of 1871. Unionists could be penalised for conspiracy or for breaching the *Master and Servant Acts*, the first of which was passed in New South Wales in 1828 on the English model.

Six farm labourers in Tolpuddle (Dorset) were sentenced to seven years' transportation in 1834 for administering illegal oaths.[11] They were released and returned to England between 1837 and 1839 after massive protests, becoming a symbol of trade unionism for over a century. Most remigrated to Canada with their leader, George Loveless, a ploughman and Methodist lay preacher. No further transportation for trade unionism took place unless strikes and rallies involved violence, as in some manufacturing towns but no longer in rural districts. Most of the Captain Swing convicts were also pardoned, but the majority remained in Australia. A detailed study of their fate (*The Convicts of the* Eleanor) concludes that 'the lives of the Wessex protesters were not fundamentally different from what might have awaited them in England, with one major difference – the spectre of hunger did not consistently haunt their door'.[12]

The Poor Law and emigration

Emigration to Australia before 1851 was driven by two public institutions – the penal system and the Poor Law – and private initiatives frequently depended on land grants and patronage appointments by British or colonial authorities. Thus state activity characterised migration policy from the beginning, and still does. The urban poor and industrial classes were most affected by the convict transportation system. Rural labouring families and artisans were more directly affected by the assisted passage systems which began in 1831. The solution seen by many parishes in southern England was to reduce their populations by paying labourers and their families to emigrate.

This was particularly popular in East Sussex and the adjoining area of Kent, where the population had risen rapidly. The Rye Poor Law Union was the most active in England in sending assisted emigrants to Australia and Canada between 1836 and 1847 under the *Poor Law Amendment Act* of 1834. This area lacked size-able towns but had reasonable access to the emigration port of Gravesend on the Thames downstream from London. Central Kent around Maidstone was even closer. Between 1836 and 1847 Sussex sent 3914 Poor Law assisted emigrants to Australia, and Kent sent 1213.

The heaviest emigration in East Sussex was from Salehurst, Beckley, Northiam, Brede, Icklesham and Burwash, each of which sent more than 50 emigrants to Australia with the support of the Land and Emigration Commissioners and the local parishes.[13] Parishes would equip the emigrants and pay for their transport to the ports. The commission would use money from Australian land sales to pay for the passage out. This entitled it to lay down regu-lations and to supervise chartered shipping. Villages on the Kent side of the River Rother sending similar numbers were Rolvenden, Sandhurst, Benenden, Woodchurch, Goudhurst and Hawkhurst. All were purely rural villages of about 1000 inhabitants. The only towns to send a few assisted emigrants were Hastings, Rye and Eastbourne. So massive was the exodus that the New South Wales Legislative Council was told in 1846 that one-eighth of the pop-ulation of the Rye Union had emigrated.[14] The same was no doubt true for the Tenterden Union in neighbouring Kent.

Other areas of Sussex which sent many Poor Law emigrants included Framfield near Uckfield and Pevensey near Eastbourne; Kent parishes included Yalding, Nettlestead and Pluckley near Maidstone. The largest sailing from Gravesend from these two counties was in 1839 on the *Cornwall*, the *Neptune*, the *Florist* and the *James Pattison*. Altogether, 34 East Sussex parishes and 46 Kent parishes used the new Poor Law to unload surplus people between 1836 and 1847. Nearly all were agricultural labourers and their families. Somerset sent 3000 between 1844 and 1867, mainly from villages around Yeovil and Shepton Mallet.

In other parts of England the enthusiasm for emigration was less apparent. Many witnesses told the Poor Law enquiry that there was no surplus of labour in their areas while others, mainly from the North and the Midlands, denounced pressures to emigrate as inhuman. The reputation of Australia for convict colonies discouraged many, who otherwise left for the United States. Pay-ment of assisted passages influenced this to a limited extent; they were not available for the United States, though many went to Canada and later moved south.

The Colonial Land and Emigration Commission maintained a network of selection agents, which indicates their focus on rural recruitment. In 1852 all but four were south of a line between the Mersey and the Humber. They were in the Southwest (Bristol, Ilminster, Bath, Trowbridge, Gloucester, Salisbury, Pewsey and the main embarkation port of Plymouth); the Southeast (Brighton, Dorking, Canterbury, Staplehurst, Oxford, St Albans, Aston Clinton, Royston and Chelmsford); Eastern England (Ipswich, Cowlinge, St Neots, Norwich, Kings Lynn, Holt, Long Sutton, Grantham and Lincoln); and the Midlands (Worcester, Northampton, Coventry, Shrewsbury, Leicester and Burslem). Most were in agricultural districts and some in large villages. Applicants were sent for approval to the commission's London office, in conjunction with the Poor Law Commissioners.

Not all parishes wanted to lose their people or had funds to assist. One solution was to amalgamate parishes into Poor Law Unions, to fund administration and a larger and more efficient workhouse. These took over the costs of the Poor Law from the parishes in 1865. The Unions became an important local government unit for the rest of the century, forming the basis for elected Rural District Councils which lasted from 1894 until 1974. They were subject to scrutiny by the Poor Law Commissioners (later Board) in London and developed uniform systems of recording and accounting.

All this was useful reform. But it was vitiated by the role of workhouses built by Unions in central locations to replace the smaller and often dilapidated village workhouses.[15] These large and prison-like 'Bastilles' were hated and feared. The separation of elderly married couples was especially resented. The basic principle of the 1834 reforms, 'lesser eligibility', required that conditions in the workhouse should be worse than for the lowest paid labourer outside. Public exposure of abuses, such as at Andover (Hampshire) in 1846, led to better administration. Eventually they mainly accommodated the elderly and infirm and provided 'casual' accommodation for tramps.

As a general rule, workhouse inmates were not eligible for assisted passages to Australia after the first few years of the system, following complaints from Australian employers and politicians. Recruiting material often used the absence of pauperism as an incentive to emigrate. Despite the intentions of the reformers, most pauper assistance was still distributed outside the workhouse system for the century of its existence. Control over public assistance was transferred to local authorities in 1929 and finally taken away from elected committees in 1934, not because they were oppressive but because in Labour Party controlled mining areas they were seen as too generous. Dependence of the unemployed on public assistance was onerous, but the threat of the workhouse mainly applied to the elderly, to unwanted children and to the mentally disabled.

The search for farm labourers

This search dominated assisted passage schemes throughout the nineteenth century and was still influential into the 1920s. Queensland made a heart-rending appeal to the labourers of Suffolk through its Bury St Edmunds agent in the 1880s.[16] Free passages were offered to single women going as domestic servants, to single men labourers, and to married labourers and their families provided not more than two children were under twelve. Queensland, it was claimed 'was no foreign land but only England over the water'. It had elbow-room, wages were better and prices cheaper, there was no pauperism, the climate and the prospect for children were better, the utmost political freedom existed, education was perfectly free and paying ninepence an acre for five years would secure a freehold homestead of 80 acres. This generous offer was extended:

Lincolnshire field workers in the 1880s when Queensland was actively recruiting rural labourers

[to those] who find little chance of saving, whose energies have
not sufficient scope, who would make provision for old age,
who wish to take their labour to a better market, who are heart
sick of care and anxiety, who desire relief for overburdened
wives, who wish to deliver their children from future distress,
and who would escape a pauper's life and a pauper's death.

Queensland attracted more immigrants in the 1880s than in any
other decade before or since, largely through this contrast between
the problems of England and the promise of a new life. The appeal
was entirely economic and pragmatic and did not use imperialist
rhetoric. Queensland was not, of course, just England over the
water, but it certainly had a more attractive future than East Anglia
during an agricultural depression.

Recruitment of agricultural labourers was difficult. Until the
1870s almost half were illiterate. Newspaper and handbill advertising was widely used, and personal canvassing was assisted by
some parsons and Poor Law guardians before the 1870s and agricultural labourers' union officials afterwards. Josias Johnson of
Barley, Hertfordshire and the Royston Poor Law Union were responsible for persuading 1000 to emigrate from southern Cambridgeshire in the early 1850s. Altogether, 1846 left Cambridgeshire for
New South Wales between 1851 and 1859 and a similar number
went to Victoria. In Bedfordshire the Bedford Poor Law Union
supported most of its parishes in sending more than 150 agricultural labourers and their families to Australia between 1834 and
1844, mainly from Stevington, Riseley, Sharnbrook, Wilstead, Great
Barford, Bolnhurst and Colmworth. Unfortunately, many from these
last three villages were drowned in the *Cataraqui* off King Island in
1845, the worst disaster in Australian maritime history. The same
fate befell labourers sent from Tackley (Oxfordshire) and from
Guilden Morden (Cambridgeshire). Tackley lost 42 emigrants in
eight families, of whom 30 were children or adolescents.[17]

Benevolent squires and parsons sometimes took the lead. The
Rev. Scott Surtees of Banham (Norfolk), publishing letters from
former parishioners in gold rush Victoria in 1852, argued that 'there
is more labour in this parish than there is profitable employment
for'. Fares were now so low that almost anyone could afford them
if they abstained from spending money at the beer-house: 'You can
hardly credit, that many who worked as labourers alongside of you
a few years since, now have well-stocked farms of their own, and
write to you about the rate of wages they give their labourers'.[18]

In Northamptonshire, the vicar of Pytchley, Rev. A. W. Brown, organised the emigration of the Dainty and Flavel families to South Australia on the *Prince George* in 1838. Another six Flavels left for Adelaide in 1850. Three large families were sent to Melbourne on the *Felix* in 1844 and twenty-nine others with the Flavels in 1850. The *Northampton Herald* reported on those who had left:

> the large funds necessary were provided over the parish, of which the landowners paid three-fourths of the expense and occupiers the other fourth. The lands belong almost entirely to Lord Overstone and to Mr. Hensman of Pytchley. Both his lordship and Mr Hensman entered warmly into the measure.[19]

Samuel Simpson wrote to the Rev. Brown from Plymouth to thank him: 'I shall not want to come back to Pytchley again for I am thankful I have been on board for another country for I was tired of England'. This mirrored the recorded attitudes of many leaving England for Australia a century later.

Private charities assisted emigration. Kelsall's Emigration Charity of Mayfield (Sussex) assisted 3027 to Australia between 1865 and 1874. These small emigrations from rural England were not like the mass migration to Australia from East Sussex, Kent, Somerset or Devon, or to North America from East Anglia. But they helped spread the idea of escape from rural poverty, even if it meant crossing the globe. This idea resurfaced in the 1870s when a long agricultural depression set in, mainly caused by growing imports of food from North America and Australasia. Objections from colonial authorities had ended Poor Law assisted emigration, and the agents were now officials of the new agricultural labourers' unions. The National Agricultural Labourers' Union was formed under the leadership of Joseph Arch in 1872 and had nearly 60 000 members three years later, In 1874 and 1875 the union spent one-third of its income on assisting emigration, sending 2500 men to Australia.[20]

Immigration authorities in Queensland and South Australia saw in the successful union an instrument for reaching rural workers who had been so hard to recruit. Control had passed from London to the colonial capitals by 1872, and British authorities retained almost no interest in assisting emigration. The Kent and Sussex Labourers Union sent 332 to Queensland and South Australia in 1872 and 1873. From Buckinghamshire 355 were sent to Queensland on the *Ramsey* in 1873 and the *Indus* in 1874. They were organised by an official, Edward Richardson, and arrived wearing the union ribbon. Although the union organised mainly in southern and eastern England, its officials also sent 800 to South Australia from Northumberland in 1879.

Servants

Popular Australian concepts of pioneering and equality overlook the role of domestic servants.[21] Most modern homes have replaced servants with electric equipment, and employing anyone more than a temporary cleaner or child minder is regarded as the preserve of the very rich. Yet from the earliest use of convicts, through the training and employment of Aborigines, to misguided attempts to recruit Greek girls in the 1950s, there is a long history of domestic service, to which English immigrants made an important contribution. Domestic service was widespread in Victorian England, where even bank clerks and teachers would employ at least one live-in maid. Most farms would employ 'farm servants' to cook, clean house and manage the dairy. As for the mansions of the rich, these were awash with servants, sometimes running into hundreds in the stately homes and palaces which were the major employers of labour in many villages.

Not all servants were women, but it was assumed that most female assisted immigrants to Australia would engage in some form of service prior to marriage. From the start there was much concern with the moral problems associated with single girls. Colonial Office instructions of 1833 offered not more than £12 towards 'the Passage of Un-married Females of good character' aged at least eighteen.[22] This covered the entire cost and was payable to the ship's master on arrival. Various conditions had to be met: 'the accommodation of all such Female Passengers in his Vessel as are not accompanied by their Parents or Relatives, shall be effectually separated from the accommodation of the other Passengers'. Two respectable 'householders' known to the applicant had to certify that 'we believe her to be of good Health and good Character, and to be capable of earning her livelihood by Industry'. The certificate had also to be signed by the minister of the parish or a Dissenting minister.

Domestic service provided a home and food as well as a wage. The daughters of rural labourers were taken off their parents' hands until married, and lifetime servants, such as nannies or housekeepers, might remain with a family for more than one generation. But these advantages were often outweighed by the deference and

At left: An emigration recruiting poster, c.1912

Below: A Commonwealth government recruiting poster, 1929

obedience required and the sometimes erratic course of their master's personality and livelihood. Many Australian employers were newly and uncertainly rich, and life could be unpredictable. There was a shortage of women, which bringing out domestics was designed to alleviate but which also led to hasty marriages. Later immigrant domestics frequently preferred factory work as it allowed greater freedom and more ready cash. These factors combined to maintain the demand for domestic immigrants, especially as the middle classes became more prosperous into the 1880s.

Even during the First World War the British Women's Emigration Society continued to organise. In February 1916 it sent 100 to Australia and was arranging for two more parties: 'These young women are destined for domestic service only; they must be between the ages of 18 and 25, and if they have up to the time of leaving this country received no training it will be provided for them in the Colonies'. It was assumed that returning men would reclaim the many jobs being done by women. The Australian government assisted,[23] and was still actively advertising for 'the British domestic girl' in the 1920s under the slogan 'Men for the Land, Women for the Home'.

Young women emigrating in the 1920s

From place of exile to land of promise

Australia ('Botany Bay') was known during its first fifty years as a convict colony. Its reputation was consequently unattractive. The radical journalist William Cobbett painted a dismal picture in 1819, just as free emigration was in its early stages:

> the distance in the first place, makes the voyage a terrible undertaking. When arrived you depend on the public authorities for a grant of land. If you have money to purchase pieces of ground already cleared and cultivated, your servants are convicts, and you are at the joint mercy of them and the murdering natives. Even for the service of the convicts, your sole dependence is on the pleasure of the public authorities ... If you find yourself miserable, and wish to return, preferring the wretched state that you have left to that which you find, your means of return are gone, and you have to undergo another voyage of seven or eight months, and to return to England a dejected and broken-hearted beggar.[24]

Most towns and rural parishes in England had seen at least one transported convict removed during the half-century, so this poor reputation was widespread even among the semi-literate rural majority. Advocacy of pauper emigration during that period did not improve Australia's reputation, and many rural people saw Poor Law assisted emigration as little better than transportation. The failure of the Swan River settlement did little to improve things. The creation of South Australia as a free colony was an improvement, but it too was almost bankrupt by the early 1840s.

The Australian economy could not prosper without extra labour, which was increasingly drawn to the British cities or to North America. The problem was largely resolved by the gold rushes, which completely changed the reputation of Australia and especially the new colony of Victoria. Victoria added 140 000 English to its population between 1851 and 1861, but New South Wales only 33 000. Indeed Victoria could afford to dispense with assisted migration altogether, while New South Wales saw many of the immigrants it had paid for moving south. Overall, eastern Australia had become a land of promise, as it remained until the depression of 1891. It did not need transportation or the Poor Law any more.

3

FARMERS, MINERS, ARTISANS AND UNIONISTS

Oh what a difference there is between this country and home for poor folks. I know I would not go back again – I know what England is. Old England is a fine place for the rich, but the Lord help the poor.

A woman from London to Caroline Chisholm, 1846, quoted in M. Kiddle, *Caroline Chisholm*, Melbourne University Press, 1990 (1950), p. 195

The convict system was replaced by two methods of recruiting labour – free emigration and assisted passages. Free settlers were often able to finance themselves and their workers and dependants. They could secure land grants through the patronage system which was the basis of English politics. Frequently, land was acquired without any payment, especially in Western Australia. While settlement in New South Wales was initially confined, many moved outside the boundaries to become squatters, eventually consolidating their originally illegal hold on the land. The squatters were the equivalent of an upper class in colonial Australia but became the subject of criticism and land tenure reforms from the 1860s.

This method of settlement was not, of course, open to the average English immigrant. Many early families came with landowning farmers who saw better opportunities in the colonies. All land was held by the Crown and allocated to these pioneers either by sale or without cost. Land not taken up was treated as 'waste land' and remained with the Crown, much being later allocated on leases to pastoralists. Prior occupation by Aborigines was recognised but not as the basis for ownership under the principle of *terra nullius* or belonging to nobody. The colonial government held that ownership, as in England, implied settlement on a defined territory and the application of productive labour. Land was surveyed and given, sold or leased as though there had never been a prior claim on it. Many of the original agricultural pioneers benefited from this system, including time-expired convicts and retired military officers. *Terra nullius* also assumed that there was no government with which treaties or land allocations might be organised, as they were in many other colonies.

Free settlers

The early free settlers, other than soldiers, guards and government employees, were prosperous farming families with their labourers and servants, the much praised yeoman farmers who were regarded as the backbone of 'Old England'. Among the best chronicled were the Hentys, from West Tarring near the Sussex coast.[1] The early development of Western Australia, proclaimed a colony in 1829, depended on labourers brought out by their employers to work their land, which in this case was freely allocated. Thomas Henty secured a free land grant in Swan River after selling his West Tarring property in 1828. His son James and a party of 36 labourers sailed on the *Caroline* in 1829. This was nearly 6 per cent of West Tarring's population, which declined between 1821 and 1831 as a result. Of those enumerated in the 1829 muster at Swan River, which excluded soldiers and recent arrivals, 92 per cent were English, mainly from London and the Southeast. Six members of the Christmas family from Sussex came in 1829 but, like the Hentys and many others, soon moved to eastern Australia. The Swan River settlement was a failure for many years. It was initially developed by Thomas Peel from Lancashire, who was related to a cotton manufacturing family and the future prime minister, Sir Robert Peel, and was in a strong position to secure land. He spent his life in Western Australia but he did not prosper, unlike the Hentys who left for the east.[2]

Henry Dendy, a farmer's son from Abinger in Surrey, took advantage of the sale of land in the new Port Phillip district (Victoria) in 1840 at the considerable cost of £5120 (about $385000 in modern values) and sailed for Melbourne, forming a partnership with Jonathan Were (from Somerset) and using the bounty system to bring out emigrants to work the land he had paid for.[3] Under this system purchasers were entitled to free passages for nominated immigrants 'of the labouring classes' at a rate of one adult for each £20 paid for the land. These emigrants left England on the *Earl of Durham* and the *Platina* in 1842. Apart from women with children, the great majority were labourers and domestic servants, mainly from Surrey and Sussex but including some from Ireland. Those on the *Platina* included two large families from Warnham in Sussex, the Charmans and the Patchings. Most of the English passengers

*Henry Dendy (1800–81), a Surrey farmer who developed
land in the southern suburbs of Melbourne*

came from districts in which Dendy had farms or other interests.
With Dendy they developed properties around Melbourne, to one of
which he gave the name Brighton, after the rapidly growing Sussex
seaside resort. For all his enterprise and investment Dendy did not
profit. His colleague J. B. Were established the still existing stock-
broking firm, while many of Dendy's nominees settled in what are
now the southern suburbs of Melbourne.

Another major shipload of immigrants were recruited by the
Macarthur family at Camden (NSW). The bounty system allowed
potential employers to nominate emigrants from England, usually
using agents located in rural areas or at seaports. Many also came
from Kent and Sussex in the large intake of Poor Law assisted
immigrants in the 1830s. Others came from the almost wholly
rural county of Dorset, from which the Macarthurs recruited over
100 between 1836 and 1842, including many from the villages of
Chettle and Woodyates. John Macarthur and his wife Elizabeth,

though of Scottish and Cornish ancestry respectively, both came from Devon. Their descendants are still an important element in New South Wales society.

Potter Macqueen, born in Norfolk, was a substantial property owner of Segenhoe near Woburn (Bedfordshire). He was granted land in the Hunter Valley to which he sent two shiploads of emigrants on the *Hugh Crawford* and the *Nimrod* in 1825. The estate, named Segenhoe, also employed convicts, and Macqueen arranged for some of their families to join them from England. This was the first organised use of emigrants to colonise New South Wales, predating the assisted passage schemes introduced in 1831. Macqueen moved to New South Wales in 1834 but did not remain, despite being an advocate of emigration. Like Dendy he did not flourish in later life. It was said that he brought sixty families from Bedfordshire, all of whom left him within six months.

Most early free settlers came from the farming areas of southern England such as Sussex, Devon, Bedfordshire, Dorset, Kent, Hampshire and Surrey. One exception was the Methodist group from Yorkshire and Lincolnshire which arrived in Western Australia on the *Tranby* in 1830. Like the preceding Hentys, they were unable to benefit from assisted passages as Western Australia did not yet have an established government. They were, however, offered a generous free grant of land. Their leaders, Joseph and John Hardey of Barton-on-Humber, chartered their own ship, taking 40 passengers: 'A respectable local preacher in the Wesleyan connexion goes with them with the laudable intention of preaching the Gospel to the degraded and long-neglected natives of the country'.[4] In 1834 Joseph Hardey founded the first Methodist chapel in Perth, before moving further up country to an area named after two Yorkshire towns, York and Beverley.

Another unassisted northern family were the brothers Thomas and Peter Manifold from Bromborough, Cheshire. Like many early pioneers they came from a farming family, had an introduction to the authorities and were given a grant of land. After several years in Tasmania, where they employed convict labour, they took up land in the Western District of the new Port Phillip colony in 1838, where many others had come from Scotland. The Hentys had already moved there from Western Australia. These early settlers had the benefit of early arrival and generous land grants. Many of their descendants are still socially prominent at the core of the 'old money' made from the rural economy.

Rural labour – convict and free

Unlike New South Wales and Tasmania, Western and South Australia were not founded as penal colonies. The Swan River colony at Perth and Fremantle was established largely by private initiatives. It was not very successful. South Australia was more deliberately planned by evangelical Christians as a free society which would never accept convicts – and never did. Both were settled predominantly by English immigrants. South Australia had much more success by using assisted passages from the beginning, whereas Western Australia was founded before that system was invented and had eventually to recruit convicts to maintain a viable society.

The early practice of bringing out labourers to work for particular masters led to concentrations from some English rural counties. In Western Australia, which did not have a convict past, a census taken in 1832 (though inaccurate) showed 113 from Kent, 81 from Sussex, 56 from Hampshire, 48 from Somerset, 38 from Surrey, 30 from Devon, 27 from Suffolk, and 26 each from Dorset and Gloucestershire. These southern rural counties contributed 445 to a recorded total of 880 born in England. But there were also 185 from London, and 24 from Middlesex who were mostly not engaged in agriculture, as well as 47 from Lancashire and 32 from Yorkshire and Lincolnshire, including those from the *Tranby*. Altogether, 1229 had birthplaces recorded, the minority mainly from Scotland and Ireland. This combination of farm workers from southern England, Londoners and Scots and Irish was fairly typical of early settlement, with most northern, Midland and eastern English counties sending very few. As was also common, many from London and Middlesex were families and servants of the colonial and military administrators. In the early absence of convicts in Western Australia, Londoners came from the respectable rather than the criminal classes. Among those from the Home Counties whose descendants are still prominent were the Drake-Brockmans, who originated in Cheriton, Kent and arrived in 1830.

Because it was so expensive to reach Australia – and because the convict settlements had a dubious reputation – most settlers in the first fifty years came with their employers or were former convicts and soldiers granted land. Working the land was seen as the basis of colonial wealth until the gold discoveries of the 1850s. In Australia, as in England, this demanded a substantial labour force, particularly in the early stages of clearing land, building roads and fences and minding sheep and cattle meanwhile. The dilemma was that convict labour, phased out in New South Wales by 1840, was never introduced to South Australia and was absent from Western Australia for the first twenty years. Only in Van Diemen's Land were convicts the basis of rural labour, and very few free English settlers went there. One exception was Joseph Archer from a Hertfordshire family, who chartered the *Emerald* in 1820 and established a dynasty at Longford near Launceston which sent nine members into the Tasmanian parliament.

Assisted passages

As no agricultural or general labourers could afford to come to Australia, employers had to pay their passages by chartering ships. Few parishes had the wealth to pay for paupers to emigrate, and those who did go before the mid-1830s went to the United States and Canada. As the Colonial Land and Emigration Commission reported in 1849, 'labouring men with families, of whom the great mass of the emigration ought to consist, can usually pay little or nothing', while parishes and Poor Law Unions could only defray preliminary expenses such as travel within England. The situation before 1834 was even worse as the legal basis for parish support of emigration was very doubtful. The Poor Law commissioners eventually recommended that 'the Vestry of each Parish be empowered to order the payment out of the rates raised for the relief of the poor, of the expenses of the emigration of any persons having settlement within such Parish, who may be willing to emigrate'.[5]

Many whom parishes sought to send away were unsuitable. As Governor Arthur of Van Diemen's Land warned in a despatch of 9 July 1831, 'the parishes would probably send habitual paupers and the worst characters they could select'. This echoed a view widely held by the parishes themselves. A reporter from Essex told the Poor Law enquiry that 'most parishes would be glad to be taxed to rid themselves of their idle and dissolute characters'. But the contrary view was also put, from Heveningham in neighbouring Suffolk: 'it is the good labourer that emigrates, not the idle and profligate'. One concern of parishes was that returning emigrants might claim support from their previous place of settlement. Australia was too far away for that to be a problem.

Assisted passages, whether paid directly to 'government emigrants' or as a 'bounty' on arrival, were primarily designed to attract rural labourers. The first annual report of the Colonization Commissioners for South Australia in 1836 laid down that free passages were for 'poor persons' under thirty, of the 'labouring class only'. The British government fully endorsed this view in response to the theories of Malthus and the findings of the Poor Law enquiry that the agricultural counties were faced with an over-population crisis. As Governor Bourke wrote to Lord Glenelg in October 1835, the parishes should 'remove those who were out of employment to the colonies' to relieve 'the distress prevailing among the agricultural labourers in the south of England'. The origins of assisted passages were in the Poor Law reforms of 1834, and were supervised by the Poor Law Board in London. But increasingly, assistance came from the resources of the colonies and the sale of land, which was supervised from London by the Colonial Land and Emigration Commission set up in 1840. Under the system developed by Londoner Edward Gibbon Wakefield, landowners could bring out labourers by purchasing land at a price the labourers could not afford – thus maintaining the English rural class system by using public funds derived from land sales.

Schemes ranged through absolutely free passages, nomination by colonies and British authorities, the bounty system operated essentially by colonial employers and British agents between 1835 and 1841, loan systems, land grants, remittances on behalf of relatives and a variety of targeted recruitments aimed at filling labour market gaps. British involvement from 1831 until 1872 was resumed between 1922 and 1930, and briefly in 1938. Taken up again in 1947, it was modestly sustained until 1972. The main significance of the British connection was to restrict assistance to United Kingdom subjects. With rare exceptions, this was supported from the Australian end. Victorian immigration regulations of 1861 required that 'the Persons to be brought to this Colony shall be British subjects of sound mind, in good health and of good character'.

One consideration, which became irrelevant by 1900, was the large number of Irish getting assisted passages. British policy that 'national' and religious groups be selected in the same proportions as existed in the United Kingdom meant that the Irish, who were almost invariably assisted, could command almost one-third of the places. South Australia complained to the Colonial Land and Emigration Commission in 1850 and 1862 about the large numbers of Irish, who in 1862 outnumbered the English. Official figures were mathematically precise: in 1850, 59 per cent were English, 10 per cent Scottish and 31 per cent Irish. Of more than 15 000 assisted immigrants between 1857 and 1864, 56 per cent were English, 13 per cent Scottish and 31 per cent Irish.[6]

In a debate in the Victorian parliament in April 1862 the Scottish liberal James Service argued that the balance must be maintained, otherwise the Irish would 'in the first half of the year, absorb the entire vote for immigration purposes'.[7] A consistent opponent of high Irish assisted immigration was Sir Henry Parkes. New South Wales did in fact have exceptionally high Irish levels in the 1860s, although Parkes went further than most in wanting assistance to the Irish terminated altogether.

The various forms of assisted passage were absolutely crucial in the peopling of Australia between 1831 and 1982. Even during the gold rush era of 1851 to 1861, 40 per cent of immigrants were assisted. Between 1861 and 1900 this rose to over half, and between 1919 and 1929 to over two-thirds. Altogether, 3 186 723 were assisted over 150 years. Of these, the majority were English. Australian governments deliberately and consistently created a society in which the majority were English or of English descent, and they moved away from that principle less than a generation ago.

Private charities

A major object of assisted passage schemes was to rectify the gross imbalance between men and women inherent in the convict system. The New South Wales Legislative Council reported in March 1832, 'as the proportion between the sexes in this country is already alarmingly great, it ought not to be increased by encouraging an influx of unmarried men, but that it will be advisable to direct attention to married couples'. This view was endorsed from London by the Earl of Aberdeen, who wrote to Governor Bourke in February 1835 that disparity of the sexes 'render[s] the accession of females of virtuous and industrious habits in the highest degree essential'.[8]

For the first few years passages were given to single women, starting with 4000 Irish workhouse girls. Before 1837 assistance was limited to single women between fifteen and thirty. This created new problems, for women and children were vulnerable to exploitation and abuse in such a male dominated society. The New South Wales Legislative Council committee on immigration of 1835 recommended that single women should always be related to accompanying emigrants, for moral reasons. They complained that

41 prostitutes had arrived on the *David Scott* in October 1834. Policy priority shifted towards established families by 1837, and continued for many years. Criticism of single women remained. In 1855 the New South Wales Agent for Immigration commented in his annual report on the 'uselessness of the majority of the single females'. However, single women were still encouraged, both as domestic servants and potential brides.

Many women and children needed immediate assistance on arrival. Caroline Chisholm, born in Northampton but coming to Australia from India with her husband, set up the Female Immigrants' Home in Sydney in 1841.[9] Until her health broke down, she dedicated herself to assisting emigration from the United Kingdom and settlement in Australia. Many loans were not repaid and she died in relative poverty in 1877, being buried in her native Northampton.

Because Caroline Chisholm was a Catholic it was sometimes argued that she favoured Irish immigrants. The first residents in the Female Immigrants' Home were predominantly Irish Catholics, but this does not seem to be the case for emigrants given loans in the 1850s. The *Slains Castle*, sailing from Gravesend to Melbourne in 1851, was the first ship commissioned by Chisholm's Family Colonization Loan Society. Of its 104 passengers only 10 were Irish and 91 were English, mainly from London, the Southeast and the Southwest. Passengers brought by her to New South Wales in 1855, to Victoria from 1852 to 1854 and to South Australia in 1851 included farmers, agricultural labourers and servants, but also a wide range of occupations which would not have attracted official assisted passages, such as 33 printers, 139 clothing workers, 115 building tradesmen and 50 in food trades. Some middle-class included 43 clerks, 3 nurses, 4 governesses, 3 school mistresses, a pawnbroker and a gentleman.[10] Wives left behind by their husbands often applied to Caroline Chisholm for assistance. This was not always granted, as John Pickering of Cannock complained from Salisbury (South Australia) in 1853 after four years of separation: 'she cannot afford to come and was disappointed by Mrs Chisholm's Society'.[11] Without such assistance many families remained apart for years or eventually dissolved altogether.

Several other charitable loan societies sent out artisans, clerks and middle-class women, none of them eligible for the passages reserved mainly for agricultural labourers and their families. The most important was the Female Middle Class Emigration Sociey

*Caroline Chisholm (1808–77) provided for immigrant
women and families in early Sydney*

founded by a Londoner, Maria Rye, in 1862. These helped to modify
the social character of emigration, which would otherwise have been
confined to the assisted poor and the well-off. Private charitable
loans helped skilled artisans and the lower middle classes. Towards
the end of the nineteenth century charities also assisted the urban
poor, orphans and illegitimate children, but not in large numbers.

Early miners

Coal mining developed in Northeast England in the late Middle
Ages, mainly to supply the London market by ship from Newcastle
and the Tyne. Cook's *Endeavour*, in which he explored the Australian
coast, was a Whitby collier previously engaged in this trade. It was
from the Tyneside counties of Durham and Northumberland that
most coal miners emigrated to Australia, and from the Midlands
county of Staffordshire. Coal was first mined by convicts at Newcastle (NSW) and on the Tasman peninsula near Port Arthur. Some

Longbenton, a Northumberland village typical of many from which miners emigrated

had been coal miners already, but relatively few. Robson's sample of convicts sent to eastern Australia before 1852 found only 1 per cent had been miners or quarrymen. Of 1700 convicts transported from Gloucestershire before 1842 a slightly higher proportion – 45, or 2.6 per cent – were colliers and coal miners from the active coalfield to the north of Bristol or from the Forest of Dean. About 15 per cent came from counties with coalfields, but very few from Durham or Northumberland.[12] Most of those from Lancashire, Yorkshire or Warwickshire were likely to have been factory workers rather than miners.

As almost half the convicts transported to New South Wales and Van Diemen's Land were agricultural or general labourers, they could be usefully employed as miners in the primitive pits of the time. Many were sent to Newcastle or the Tasman peninsula for punishment rather than because of their previous occupation. As the Australian Agricultural Company began to develop the Hunter coalfield as a commercial concern they sought experienced miners.

The role of convicts as coal miners was limited. There were then few steam-driven factories or railways, and steam power was mainly used for mining pumps, some of which used wood. Most coal was for domestic heating or cooking, and there was plenty of wood as an alternative. Mining for metals took off in the 1840s in South

Australia. The labour force was mainly brought out from Cornwall, which had an ancient history of tin and copper mining requiring a different expertise from coal mining. The Cornish dominated this type of mining for the next eighty years.

The next great surge of English miners came with the discovery of gold in New South Wales and Victoria in 1851. This coincided with the collapse of lead mining in the Pennines due to foreign competition. Many came to Victoria from Derbyshire, North Yorkshire and Cumberland. The population of the lead mining district of Alston (Cumberland) dropped from 5244 in 1831 to 3409 in 1851, and the 1851 census showed emigration and decline in the Yorkshire Pennine parishes of Askrigg, Grinton, Marrick, Sedbergh and Pateley Bridge, all of them dependent on lead mining.

Gold miners

Between 1851 and 1861 the English population of Victoria increased from 28 980 to 169 586. It was by far the most populous Australian colony, a position held until 1895 after a long depression had reduced the gold-rush wealth. During the 1850s thousands poured into Victoria from all over the world, most financing their own trip in the hope of recovering the cost by discovering gold. Assisted passages continued but were hardly necessary for Victoria, which also drew in population from Tasmania, South Australia and New South Wales. In 1856 only 4679 assisted immigrants arrived, compared with 57 326 unassisted in the same year and 36 915 in the following. Of those arriving in 1856 under the remittance system – subsidised by relatives – the majority were Irish. In 1851 the English numbered 37.4 per cent of a small Victorian population of 77 345, half of them Anglicans.[13] By 1861 the English-born had dropped to 31.5 per cent, reflecting the growth of a native-born population and the influx of Chinese, Europeans and Americans to the goldfields.

On the goldfields the English remained the largest group, and in 1857 they outnumbered those born in Victoria, Ireland and Scotland combined. By 1861 the English-born population of the Ballarat district was one-third of the total, a higher level than in Melbourne. Many were from middle-class backgrounds, who could afford the inflated fares then being charged. They brought with them radical and Chartist traditions which were to upset the oligarchic political system and establish one of the first democracies in the world based on manhood suffrage and the secret ballot.

Whether the English on the goldfields could be called 'miners' is problematic. Most who came for gold had no mining experience, nor did they remain in mining once the gold rush was over. Nevertheless, the two largest occupations in the 1857 census of the goldfields were sailors and miners. Jumping ship at Melbourne was so common that many ships remained in port without crews. It was the best way for poorer gold seekers to travel across the world. Many miners seem to have come from the declining Pennine lead fields of Yorkshire, Cumberland and Derbyshire. Gold mining was not part of the English experience, and none had such a background unless they had been in California. Those who did well on the goldfields often did so from activities other than mining.

Among the gold miners were Joseph Abbott from Birmingham and Robert Haverfield from Bideford, Devon who were involved in founding the *Bendigo Advertiser*, and James Hoskins from London who was elected as MLA for Goldfields North from 1859 to 1863, as a miners' representative. Of those who went into other occupations, William Howitt wrote *Land Labour and Gold*, published in 1855; Harrie Wood from London became a public servant in the mines department of New South Wales, and James Sellar used his gold discoveries to establish himself in Adelaide. Because of the transient nature of the diggings there was no effective trade unionism until deep mining took over. One Londoner who made a trade union and political career out of the north Queensland goldfields was William Browne, MLA for Croydon and leader of the Queensland parliamentary Labor Party from 1900 to 1904.

Coal miners of the 1880s

By 1881 there were half-a-million coal miners in England, more than twice as many as in 1851. It was from this huge reserve of experienced men that the Australian coal industry largely drew its labour. Although mining was an uncertain and dangerous occupation, many miners were prosperous enough by the 1880s to seek better wages elsewhere in the world. They were not leaving a declining industry, as did the next generation, and the practice of hiring men by the year and renting them a colliery-owned house encouraged mobility. Miners had not been encouraged by the assisted passage schemes. South Australia consistently excluded coal miners from assistance, presumably because there was no coal in the colony. But soon after assistance came fully under colonial control in the 1870s, New South Wales and Queensland departed from the limitation of passages to agricultural labourers and domestic servants. By 1891 nearly half the 7000 miners in the Newcastle district were English, dropping slowly to 20 per cent as the locally born took over. Many lived in mining villages with names taken from Northeast England.[14]

The society created by English miners in Newcastle and the Hunter had several distinct features. As on the Durham and Staffordshire coalfields, Methodism and trade unionism were dominant influences. The first Durham miners' union was created by Tommy Hepburn in 1831. It was defeated through non-union labour – but unionism was restored through the new Miners' Association of Great Britain in 1842, which covered Durham, Northumberland, Staffordshire, Lancashire and Yorkshire, the areas from which most Australian immigrant miners were drawn. Co-operative stores were founded on the model created at Rochdale (Lancashire) in 1844, but not generally followed in the rest of Australia. Soccer became a major sport, which it failed to do in most other districts. The labour movement remained politically dominant to the present. It was also unusual in not acquiring Irish Catholic character after the First World War. Newcastle and the Hunter are unique in Australia as transplanted English working-class societies which still display some of their origins after more than a century.

Several English miners prospered by leaving the industry for politics or trade unionism. The most famous was Sir Joseph Cook, the only Englishman to become a prime minister of Australia.[15] Cook was from Silverdale in North Staffordshire and, like many other English miners, was an active Primitive Methodist. He emigrated to Lithgow (NSW) in 1885, became a coal miner again and resumed his active political life. By 1891 he was elected to the New South Wales parliament for the coal-mining seat of Hartley and the newly created Labour Electoral League. He refused to subscribe to the pledge of solidarity which bound Labour MPs together. He left the party in 1894 but retained his seat for some years until transferring to Sydney and the national parliament in 1901, and to the Free Trade party. Cook continued to work for some of his earlier causes, including mining safety and temperance. He eventually became prime minister in 1912, for a little over a year. In 1918 he was knighted, was fêted on his return to North Staffordshire and given the freedom of Newcastle-under-Lyme. He was high commissioner in London from 1921 to 1927, succeeding another former miner and prime minister, the Scotsman Andrew Fisher.

Joseph Cook (1860–1947), a former coal miner and the only Englishman to be Prime Minister of Australia

Cook's passage to Australia was not caused by severe poverty but by the insecurity of an industry subject to unpredictable market forces. His father, who was killed in a mine accident in 1873, was a 'butty miner' who controlled recruitment of others into his team – a method widespread also in Durham and amongst Cornish miners – and was therefore better off than the average miner in Silverdale. The village was not depressed, having grown from 1398 inhabitants in 1841 to 5775 in 1881. Indeed, it continued to provide employment for another century, as the last colliery closed only in 1997. But strikes in 1883 and 1884 and a depression in the industry caused the newly married Cook to look elsewhere. His wife Mary's brother was working in Lithgow, and the couple duly sailed from Plymouth on the *John Elder* in December 1885.

Remarkably similar paths were followed by a group of English miners who came to work on the New South Wales coalfields in the 1880s. Like their counterparts at home they were all Methodists, all trade unionists and all achieved success as elected politicians. This was, indeed, the only route into parliament for manual workers in Britain, where two miners were elected in 1874 for Staffordshire and Northumberland. As was normal, most miners began work at less than twelve years of age and were consequently poorly educated. The brothers John and George Cann, from Northumberland, were both Primitive Methodists. John came to the Illawarra coalfield at Port Kembla in 1887 and George to Lithgow in 1900. John was elected as Labor MLA in 1891 and George as a Federal MP in 1910. Like several other British-born Labor MPs, John was expelled in 1916 for his support for conscription. George remained as a Labor MLA and was not expelled until 1927 during the leadership of Jack Lang.

Others whose lives were very similar included Alfred Edden from the Nottinghamshire coalfield, who emigrated to Newcastle in 1879. He too joined the new parliamentary Labor Party of 1891, where he remained until 1917. He was also a Methodist, and was expelled by Labor in 1916 as a conscriptionist. John Fegan from Lancashire came to New South Wales in 1883, was also in the 1891 parliamentary intake, was also a Methodist and, like Joseph Cook, left the party in 1894 over the solidarity pledge. William Turner, a Methodist from Durham, came to Newcastle from Victoria in 1873 as a mine foreman. He was elected before the creation of the Labor Party as a 'working man'. The most influential English miner, James Curley, made a career in the union, being an MLA only briefly. He too was a Methodist from Durham, and was secretary of the Newcastle miners' union for twenty-seven years. Matthew Charlton, although born in Victoria, was the son of a Durham miner and became a coal miner himself at Lambton (NSW), a union official and, from 1922 to 1928, Labor Opposition leader in the Commonwealth parliament. All these men were moderate, even conservative, and set their mark on coalfield politics. Although the Communists eventually gained control of the union in the 1930s, this was in a time of depression after the first generation of miners' leaders had passed on.

The last major emigration by coal miners was in the 1920s, and assisted passages were abolished because of world depression in 1930. About 8000 miners emigrated to Australia between 1921 and 1929, of whom half were English and the rest from Scotland and Wales. Shipping lists for 1921 to 1929 show that few miners arrived before the general strike of 1926, which lasted over six months on the coal fields but only nine days elsewhere. The strike was called by the Trades Union Congress in defence of miners' wages in a declining industry. The *Euripides*, sailing in January 1927 as the strike ended, carried 68 miners and their families.

As before, coal miners from Northumberland and Durham accounted for nearly two-thirds of the English total in the 1920s. Others were from Yorkshire, Lancashire and Staffordshire. Few came from the Midlands coalfields of Nottinghamshire and Derbyshire, now almost the only ones still operating in Britain. Their unions had generally opposed the strike and formed a breakaway union which survived until the Second World War. The smaller coalfields, such as Kent, Shropshire and Gloucestershire, sent few. All have now ceased to exist.

The Ministry of Labour Schedule of Depressed Areas of 1929 listed 17 districts in Durham, 10 in Northumberland, 10 in Lancashire, 4 in Cumberland, 3 in Yorkshire and 2 each in Staffordshire, Gloucestershire and Derbyshire. All the depressed areas in England were coalfield districts, with a few coal-exporting ports such as Workington and South Shields. Most miners coming to Australia between 1926 and 1929 were leaving pit villages where the mine was closed and there was no prospect of employment. Coal mining picked up during and after the Second World War and many Poles and young men were recruited to the newly nationalised industry. Shortage of labour led to mining wages being much higher than the national average, whereas between the wars they had dropped below those for manual workers even when work was available. There was no longer a financial incentive to emigrate.

Appleyard's sample of assisted emigrants in 1959 shows that both the Northern region and Tyneside within it were slightly under-represented and that less than 3 per cent (including Scotland) were miners, well below their workforce representation. Full employment in mining was maintained by transfer schemes which reduced the desire to emigrate, such as the National Coal Board Inter-Coalfield Transfer Schemes of 1954 to 1959 and 1962. These provided jobs and housing in the Midlands mainly for miners from the Northeast.

The long story of English mining is now almost over. Before long-term depression struck in the 1920s there were one million coalminers in Britain. In 1950 there were still 700 000. By 1968 this had dropped to 400 000, fewer than a century before. Today the National Union of Mineworkers has less than 20 000 members and its main function is the payment of pensions. By 2003 there were only 5000 working coal miners left in fifteen pits. The last Durham pit closed in 1993. Even the new deep Selby coalfield is now closing.

It was so mechanised that it employed only a few miners sent in every day from South Yorkshire, and its coal was moved by conveyor direct to the neighbouring power stations. Australian mining is also highly mechanised, employing men at high wages in many remote locations. They are not primarily recruited from England, many being Finns, Yugoslavs or from other European migrant groups. Underground coal mining in Newcastle and the Hunter is sustained by the descendants of those who came from Durham, Northumberland and Staffordshire, as well as Scotland and Wales, a century ago.

Artisans

Until 1824 English law forbade skilled workers to emigrate, although many did. It was also illegal for others to 'seduce' them to emigrate. The rationale was that those apprenticed and educated at English expense should not take their skills to foreign countries, particularly the United States. But as international movement was relatively free, especially within the British Empire, this prohibition could not be sustained. The terms 'artisan' and 'mechanic' described those with some skills, often including an apprenticeship. Artisans often worked with ancient skills, some of which were being replaced by mechanisation. The term 'mechanic' was then used for those with more modern skills.

The insistence of the immigration authorities on supporting agricultural labourers and domestic servants made recruitment of skilled artisans problematic. These were often well paid in England, and in times of economic depression went to work in North America or Europe in large numbers. There were certainly some artisans among the convicts, as the quality of many public buildings in New South Wales and Tasmania suggests. Once the convict system ended, however, the need for skilled workers in the building trades remained acute. There was a growing need for engineers for mining pumps and, by the 1850s, for railways. There was not, however, a large textile industry to absorb the many immigrants who came from Lancashire during the depressions of the 1840s and 1860s.

Loans were available to 'mechanics' and 'artisans' from the 1820s. In 1833 the Colonial Office issued instructions for loans 'to persons who are able and sufficient workmen in some of the ordinary Mechanical Arts; as for instance, to Blacksmiths, Carpenters &c. and the advance will be further confined to Men who are married and intend to take their wives with them'.[16] Funds would be provided from the revenues of New South Wales and Van Diemen's Land and from the private funds of 'such Emigrants as shall appear likely to earn the means of repaying that aid, and to become useful Settlers'. No family was eligible for more than £20, and a return should be endorsed by 'two respectable Householders' and the minister of the parish or a justice of the peace. This endorsement claimed that the applicant was 'a competent workman, and likely to maintain himself in the Colony to which he wishes to go'. Repayment of the debt would be strictly enforced by the laws of the colony.

The United Kingdom commissioners for emigration reported that 397 families had been given loans to sail to New South Wales and 422 to Van Diemen's Land between 1825 and 1832. These were all headed by craftsmen such as shoemakers, carpenters and brick-layers. In 1833, 782 immigrants were assisted to Van Diemen's Land by loans or bounty payments, of whom 21 were carpenters, 35 joiners, 20 masons, 22 clerks and 23 milliners. A large part of the residue were farmers and labourers (104) and servants (83). South Australia complemented the Poor Law assisted system of the 1830s, because it was initially developed by a private company able to sell public land to cover the cost of immigration, under the scheme developed by Gibbon Wakefield. In 1834 emigrants approved for Adelaide were mostly carpenters, bricklayers, stonemasons and smiths. South Australian immigration was drawn largely from England and Cornwall. Nearly half the marriage partners recorded in Adelaide between 1836 and 1841 were from London and Southeast England, and there were almost one-third more from the rest of England, especially the Southwest.[17] In 1866 nearly one-third of the population had been born in England, the largest denomination was Anglican, and Methodists greatly outnumbered Catholics.

Artisans and mechanics were economically and socially above labourers, and they organised to maintain their differentials. They were the first to form trade unions in the eighteenth century, and the apprenticeship system limited access to their occupations. Some skilled building workers, such as carpenters, also became unionised. At various times the assisted passage schemes were modified to recruit such workers, notably during the early stages of building Adelaide in the 1840s. Artisans and mechanics, especially engineers, often travelled internationally at their own expense and with infor-mation and support from their unions, who advised on wages and conditions overseas.

Skilled employment in England expanded during the nineteenth century with the building boom caused by the population explosion and by the spread of railways and the metal trades. The textile industries, too, had many grades based on skill. All tended to be unionised. These trades were the basis of membership of the Trades Union Congress, founded at Manchester in 1868. The higher grades of skilled workers have been termed the 'aristocracy of labour' because of their ability to achieve middle-class living standards. Most were ineligible for assisted passages before 1900. Many came at their own expense or were brought out by employers. They were, however, much sought after from 1947 and generously assisted.

Trade unionism

Artisans and miners had a strong tradition of trade unionism in England, which many brought to Australia. Farm labourers were harder to organise because of the nexus between farmers, land-owners, the clergy and the Poor Law guardians in the rural areas. The 'revolt of the field' in the 1870s not only organised many of them but encouraged emigration to Canada and Australia. The skilled artisans organised themselves first, both in England and Australia. Through the apprenticeship system they had a degree of control over the supply of workers which was denied to the unskilled labourers. They also had reserves built up through union funds and friendly societies which could tide them over a strike. A major objective of the early unions was to maintain standards by excluding the less skilled, who would inevitably lower wages. Elizabeth Gaskell has a good fictionalised account in *North and South* (1855) of how Irish labour was brought in to break a strike by a Lancashire textile workers' union. Unsurprisingly, many Australian unions also objected to the effects of mass migration, not just from China but also from Britain. Unions consistently criticised immigration, and supported the White Australia policy for almost a century. As Sir Arnold White told the British Select Committee on Colonisation in 1890, 'the attitude of the labouring classes to those of their own class at home was as hostile as it was to the Chinese'. This was a trifle unfair, as the Australian unions had raised large sums to assist the dock strikers of London in the previous year. Many union activists were recent immigrants with feelings of solidarity for those they had previously worked with. But they feared the loss of the benefits they enjoyed in Australia due to labour shortages.

As in many other areas the early influences on trade unionism came from both the English and the Scots and, in South Australia, from Cornish miners. The Irish were less important until the twentieth century and never had the dominant position in the unions which they were to enjoy in the Australian Labor Party. Among the earliest unionised groups were the printers of Sydney in the 1840s. Nor was this surprising, as one of the oldest continuously viable English unions was the London General Trade Society of Compositors, founded in 1824. The arrival of large numbers from England during the gold rush of the next decade gave a boost to unionisation. The Chartist movement had overlapped with trade unionism. The first British attempt to organise on a national scale, the Grand National Consolidated Trades Union, had been formed in 1833.[18] While this had disintegrated, the working classes in England were moving from destructive rioting against new machinery to forming more lasting organisations. These focused on wages and conditions and, as friendly societies, encouraged savings for burials, unemployment and, eventually, emigration.

English unionism had been inhibited by the *Combination Acts* between 1799 and 1824 but was recovering rapidly as convict transportation drew to a close. A spinners' union was set up in Lancashire in 1829, a builders' union in 1832, a miners' association in 1841 and the Amalgamated Society of Engineers in 1851. Members of the ASE travelled out on the *Frances Walker* in October 1852 and created an Australian branch which, through several manifestations, eventually became part of the Australian Manufacturing Workers' Union. Engineers were part of the skilled 'labour aristocracy' who could command high wages. Their English unions did not admit unskilled factory workers for almost a century.

Textile factory trade unionism had little relevance to colonial Australia. But building, engineering, printing and mining were all unionised in England and soon became so in Australia. The model in both countries, based on trades rather than industries, led to a proliferation of distinct unions, many of them small or based only in one State. In both countries this has now been lost sight of in the many amalgamations of the late twentieth century. The largest British union of all, the miners', remained a federation of distinct organisations until 1945. The textile unions also remained fragmented by trade for over a hundred years. In Australia this fragmentation was preserved by the industrial arbitration system which gave awards to specific organisations. Ironically, both in Britain and even more so in Australia, amalgamation in recent years has gone along with substantial drops in membership.

Trade union leaders from England were particularly prominent among the coal miners, as indicated above. Those in other trades were more varied in their origins, religions and political views. Many became politicians in the days when the Labor Party in parliament was predominantly drawn from trade union officials. One of the earliest, with a special place in union history, was Tom Smith, born in Leominster, Herefordshire. He was a skilled stonemason, active in his union before leaving England in 1849. Employed on the many grand buildings put up in Melbourne during the gold rush, he became president of the Masons' Society in 1855, a skilled workers union which still had a few members in Melbourne a century later. In the following year he moved the historic resolution for an eight hour day, which was granted by the University of Melbourne contractors on whose buildings the masons were working. This achievement was probably the first time in the world that the day was divided into 'eight hours work, eight hours sleep and eight hours recreation' – which became an international slogan for the Socialist International in the 1880s and was the theme slogan for May Day. In 1903 the monument to '888', now opposite the Melbourne Trades Hall, was unveiled by another English trade union leader, Tom Mann.

The efforts of Victorian trade unionists following this victory were such that John Rae in 1891 referred to the Australian colonies as 'those parts of the Empire where the lot of labour is perhaps in all the world, the happiest'.[19] But despite the existence of several socialist societies, Australian labour was not radical:

> The working class of Melbourne is probably the most powerful and the best organized working class in the world ... they might if they chose march to the Parliament House with a red flag, and install the socialist State tomorrow. But they do not choose ... The world goes very well with them as it is, and they will not risk the comforts they really enjoy to try any sweeping and problematical solutions ... The labour movement where it is most advanced and powerful, is steering furthest and clearest from socialism'.[20]

Almost immediately, the depression of the 1890s hit Melbourne very hard and reduced the lead over Sydney which it had enjoyed since the gold rush. But Rae's judgement remained sound and undoubtedly reflects the moderate and parliamentary influence of many English immigrants.

Not all English unionists were so moderate. The impact of two radicals, Tom Mann and Tom Barker, was marked although neither remained permanently in Australia.[21] When he arrived in Australia in 1902 Mann was already very well known in England as a member of the Amalgamated Society of Engineers, the Social Democratic Federation and the Independent Labour Party. He remained in Australia for eight years, travelling all over the country but having most influence in Melbourne and Broken Hill. He organised the Victorian Socialist Party and was involved in the Broken Hill strike of 1908. On returning to England he became general secretary of the Amalgamated Engineering Union. Mann moved between various socialist ideologies, being typical of many self-educated radicals of the time.

Tom Barker, born in rural Westmorland, came to Australia in 1914 after several years of political activity in New Zealand. An active member of the Industrial Workers of the World, he was subject to the persecution that the IWW suffered during the First World War and was eventually deported to Chile in 1918. Unlike Mann he eventually made his peace with the British Labour Party. After a very adventurous life he was briefly mayor of the London borough of St Pancras. John Kilburn, from Middlesbrough, was active in several small Marxist groups in New South Wales and chaired the socialisation committees set up within the ALP in 1930 but dissolved by Jack Lang in 1933. Other radical unionists included Jim Healy, from Manchester, general secretary of the Waterside Workers' Federation from 1937 to 1961 and Communist Party member. Healy emigrated to Queensland in 1925. Despite his politics he was probably the most respected Communist in Australian history.

Trade unionism was served by many who came to Australia as industrial workers from the late 1870s until 1890. Once the colonies got full control of immigration they broadened the intake to include miners and industrial workers in preference to agricultural labourers and domestics. Many English immigrants in the 1880s had already been active unionists before coming to Australia. Among them were Fred Bramley (Staffordshire), president of Melbourne Trades Hall Council and MLA for Carlton (Vic) 1892–1904; John Billson (Leicester) of the Bootmakers' Union and MLA for Fitzroy (Vic) 1900–24; Thomas Bavister (Sheffield), MLA for Canterbury

(NSW) 1891–98; Fred Flowers (Staffordshire), MLC in New South Wales in 1900; Thomas Martin Davis (Worcestershire), seamen's organiser and MLA for West Sydney 1891–98; Robert Hollis (Derbyshire), railwayman and MLA for Newtown (NSW) in 1901; Antony Ogden (Yorkshire), a bounty migrant to Queensland who organised several Townsville unions; and Bob Solly from Kent and Newcastle-on-Tyne, who organised the boot workers of Melbourne and became MLA for Carlton 1908–32. These were all moderate Labor men. Bavister left the Labor Party over the solidarity pledge in 1893, and Flowers and Hollis left in 1916 over conscription. All came from English industrial districts and were founders of parliamentary Labor in New South Wales, Victoria and Queensland. Unusually, Emma Miller from Chesterfield, a Derbyshire coal mining town, was an Australian Workers' Union outback organiser and suffragist in the 1890s, and a delegate to union and party conferences at a time when these were almost exclusively male gatherings.

The moderate and reformist traditions of many English unionists were maintained by the next generation, most of whom arrived in the 1920s or later. Albert Monk, from Waltham Abbey on the Essex outskirts of London, came with his family to Melbourne in 1910 at the age of ten. His father was an industrial worker, but Monk followed a path which became increasingly common for union officials. He worked his way through various clerical positions in trade unions, becoming president of the Australian Council of Trade Unions (ACTU), the Melbourne Trades Hall Council and the

Albert Monk (1900–75) led the trade union movement during post-war immigration

Australian Labor Party (Victoria) by 1939. He was secretary of the ACTU from 1943 until 1969. Monk was a moderating influence in a movement torn between Communists and Catholic Actionists for most of his time in office.

The same could be said of Charles Crofts, Charles Oliver and John Ducker. Crofts, from Bethnal Green (London) was a sheet-metal worker before preceding Monk as secretary of the ACTU from its foundation in 1927 until 1943. Like Monk he was opposed to the Communists, who were at the height of their influence in the unions. Equally anti-Communist was John Ducker from Hull, who combined political work in the New South Wales Labor Party with unionism through the Sydney Trades and Labor Council, the Federated Ironworkers and the ACTU. Ducker was one of the most influential members of the party in the 1960s but never ran for national office. His allies included Charles Oliver of the Australian Workers' Union, who emigrated from England in the 1920s. English unionists became so prominent in some areas such as the Latrobe Valley (Victoria) that critics in the 1960s often spoke of 'the English disease' and 'Pommy shop stewards'. Other concentrated areas of English manufacturing workers, such as Whyalla or Elizabeth in South Australia, were less militant. The shop steward movements which were so powerful in England in the 1960s were generally less developed in Australia.

4
CLASS AND EQUALITY

The rich man in his castle,
The poor man at his gate,
God made them, high or lowly,
And order'd their estate.

'All Things Bright and Beautiful', English hymn
of 1848

The English had lived in domestic peace for many years, had a common language and an established religion and, many believed, a constitutional system which guaranteed more individual freedom than was common in Europe. They also had a well-defined class system, which lingered on far longer than in many other modern societies and is still very obvious to Australian visitors. Industrial and urban change greatly affected this system but did not destroy it. The monarchy and aristocracy continued long after most other societies in Europe and the Americas had become republics. The House of Lords remained as a glorious anomaly which Liberal and Labour governments promised to abolish or reform but usually only modified, until the hereditary principle was finally abolished in 1999.

Land ownership remained extremely unequal. It maintained the wealth of those like the Duke of Westminster, still the richest man in England in 2003 and, like several other dukes (Bedford, Portland, Devonshire), landlord of much central London property inherited from his ancestors. As industrialisation increased, landowners like Lord Londonderry and the Earl of Halifax with coal beneath their fields were able to draw on considerable royalties. The leasehold system was widely used in London and other cities to retain ultimate ownership in the hands of the landed aristocracy, as was the tenant farmer system in rural areas. By the 1880s it was estimated that only 4000 families owned the majority of agricultural land and that over 40 per cent of land in England was owned by 1300 people.

The young Victorian novelist Benjamin Disraeli – later to be Conservative prime minister – famously remarked in his 1845 novel

Sybil that 'the Privileged and the People formed Two Nations'. He had in mind the huge and widening gap between the aristocracy and the labouring classes. Yet the class structure was more complex than he allowed. The contemporary works of Charles Dickens were already illuminating the insecurities of the middle classes. Imprisonment for debt, the experience of Dickens' father, was not abolished until 1869. Until the *Companies Act* of 1855 introduced limited liability, shareholders could be held responsible for all the debts of bankrupt companies. In London a growing army of impoverished office workers were coming to outnumber the hordes of domestic servants. Between the unskilled and illiterate labourers and the wealthy land owners and plutocrats, there were layers of small business owners, clerks, teachers and skilled artisans who saw themselves as socially superior to those beneath them but also feared falling down into their ranks.

This was the large class that Disraeli enfranchised in 1867, realising that they could be the backbone of the Conservative Party. Many had good reasons to emigrate, but colonial policy declined to assist them. There were large and expanding intermediate classes between the rich and the labourers. Napoleon dismissed the English as 'a nation of shopkeepers', and there was great scope for them in Australia as the gold rushes created an effective demand for more goods. The professions remained very small but mercantile employees were in increasing demand. Few were eligible for passage assistance but they managed to come nevertheless. There was considerable snobbery in England towards those engaged in 'trade', but in the colonies wealth brought power and prestige however it was gained.

The original features of feudalism – serfdom, military obligations, fortified castles, monasteries and control over movement – had all perished through the series of wars and revolts between the fifteenth and seventeenth centuries. But they were replaced by a relatively uniform pattern. Each village had a squire, who occupied the largest house and often employed the largest number of servants and labourers. Each village had its church, with the parson often appointed by the local squire and supported by compulsory tithes on property. Most farmers were tenants on land owned either by the squire or, more commonly, by a large landowner who was also a member of the hereditary aristocracy. He frequently held the post of Lord Lieutenant of the county, which had social and judicial importance. Some still do. The main distinction in land ownership was between 'close' villages where all the land and the village itself were owned by a single family, and 'open' villages where ownership was more varied. Still today, many villages are wholly owned by a single landowner. During his days of affluence, English migrant Alan Bond followed in this tradition, owning the Oxfordshire village of Glympton between 1988 and 1990. Lordships of the manor are still bought and sold, though most have no economic or political significance.

By 1788 the process of modernising feudalism without abandoning its traditional basis in church, squire, landed aristocracy, tenant farmers and landless labourers was almost complete. The enclosure of common lands was becoming normal, requiring Acts of parliament which the landowning and aristocratic parliamentarians were only too willing to pass. The large commons and waste lands on which villagers fed their domestic animals were disappearing fast by the end of the eighteenth century, with a consequent decline in rural wellbeing. The notion that unfarmed waste land should be developed regardless of its previous use was important in allocating land in Australia, which had been hunted and gathered over by Aborigines for tens of thousands of years.

Land was increasingly tied up in private ownership, with the labouring class obliged to work for others, including tenant farmers. These were, themselves, liable to pay rent and to respect their superiors who leased them their farms. Agricultural labourers were the largest English social class until 1914, together with domestic servants many of whom were their wives and daughters. Many rural labourers were illiterate until the 1860s. Moreover, they were tied to their parishes by the Poor Law system and its laws of settlement, created in 1601 and reformed in 1834. This was administered by 'overseers' usually drawn from local farmers before 1834 and from farmers and shopkeepers, as 'guardians' in the larger Poor Law Unions, after that. The laws of settlement were not seriously modified until the 1860s, which was followed by considerable migration from villages to towns. Many young men had moved by then nevertheless, but it was more hazardous to do so for those with families or for the elderly.

Rural labourers, the largest social class and the backbone of assisted emigration for fifty years or even longer after 1831, were locked into hierarchies which rested on deference to betters and threats of withholding employment or welfare if that was not forthcoming. Male labourers did not get the vote until 1884 in most rural and many mining areas, well after farmers and other property owners and urban male householders. But voting was open until the ballot was introduced in 1872, and electors were well advised to vote for the preferred candidate of their landlords. Elected control of rural districts based on the Poor Law Unions was not introduced until 1894. In many country towns, local municipalities remained under the control of small cliques, including those beholden to the regional aristocracy. Even a large city such as Liverpool was in the political control of the Earl of Derby, whose mansion was at suburban Knowsley Park (now a safari theme park). It remained a Conservative stronghold until 1945.

Escaping the class system

Of the several ways of escaping these limitations, most involved leaving home. Recruitment to the army or navy was widespread. Many from such backgrounds eventually arrived in Australia as immigrants, convicts or in military stations, which did not close until 1870. Most transported convicts tried outside the United Kingdom were from the military or the navy. Despite many military victories, there was little respect for the common soldier. Their commander at Waterloo, the Duke of Wellington, described them in 1831 as 'the mere scum of the earth'. Areas close to the sea also recruited, sometimes violently, to the merchant navy, one of the largest in the world. Districts with seafaring traditions, such as Devon, Sussex, Kent or Hampshire, were strongly represented among English immigrants in the nineteenth century. The largest former employment on the Victorian goldfields in the 1850s was for miners and seamen. Seafarers were not highly regarded. Former First Lord of the Admiralty, Winston Churchill, memorably described naval traditions as 'rum, sodomy and the lash'. By the end of the nineteenth century British merchant ships were increasingly being manned by Chinese and Indians, one of the factors precipitating union support for the White Australia policy.

The rapidly growing industrial and mining areas increasingly represented an important escape from rural life, especially for those in the North and the Midlands. These areas did not provide many immigrants until the 1880s, except at crisis times like the Lancashire cotton famine of the 1860s during the American Civil War. Most movement away from villages tended to be over a short distance. In the South this meant towards London, in the Midlands towards Birmingham and in the North towards Manchester, Leeds and

Liverpool. The coalfields, too, recruited from local rural areas. Despite hard working conditions, severe pollution, bad health and poor housing, industrial occupations all paid higher wages than agricultural labouring. Emigration overseas to escape poverty and the rural class system was numerically less important than these internal movements.

A resentful society?

While rural romantics saw the English village as a cohesive and happy society, this was only true for those with particularly benevolent squires and parsons. Labouring families often faced repression based on fear of losing employment and homes. Well into the 1940s many lived in 'tied cottages' which went with the farm on which they worked and from which they could be evicted if not employed by the farmer. While many villages had alms houses built and paid for by paternalistic landholders in the past, in others the fear of old age in a distant workhouse was often a further incentive to deference. Perhaps even more important was the expectation that the labouring classes should be grateful and obedient. As the satirical rhyme put it, 'Bless the squire and his relations and keep us in our proper stations'.

The agricultural trade union leader and Liberal politician Joseph Arch recalled the refusal of his mother to accept soup from the rectory because of the expectation that charity should be gratefully received. He describes the class divisions when taking communion in the local Church of England: 'First, up walked the squire to the communion rails; the farmers went up next; then up went the tradesmen, the shopkeepers, the wheelwright, and the blacksmith; and then, very last of all, went the poor agricultural labourers in their smock frocks'.[1] Many members of Arch's union were organised to South Australia and to Queensland in the 1870s and 1880s. The writings of Flora Thompson in *Lark Rise to Candleford* suggest the deep resentments which this enforced deference created in rural Oxfordshire as late as the 1930s.

While never as extreme as in Ireland, English rural unrest simmered away between 1788 and the 1880s, by which time England was a predominantly urban society. From the Captain Swing rising of 1830 to the 'revolt of the field' which created agricultural trade unionism in the 1870s, there was persistent grumbling from 'Hodge' – the typical labourer. This was controlled by transportation in

1830, by Poor Law assisted emigration from 1831 to the 1850s, and by free passage schemes funded by the colonies – especially Queensland – in the 1880s. All offered escape from the countryside without resort to the polluted and congested industrial cities.

Emigration was often seen in this period as a safety valve. From the early 1870s a long-term depression set in for English agriculture, which could not compete with the vast new areas opened up in North America, Argentina and Australia. This was an underlying factor in the mass emigration of the 1880s to Queensland. Rural living standards did not rise as markedly as in the towns. On some reckonings, farm labourers were worse off for most of the nineteenth century than they had been a hundred years before. The relatively modest aims of rural labourers are summarised in the 1872 rule book of Arch's original Warwickshire union:

> Its object is to elevate the social position of the farm labourers
> of the county by assisting them to increase their wages; to lessen
> the number of ordinary working hours; to improve their
> habitations; to provide them with gardens or allotments; and to
> assist deserving and suitable labourers to migrate and emigrate.[2]

Urban discontents

Those who did move into the towns were also incorporated into a class system, if one in which they were better able to organise resistance. The labour of women and children was widely used until Factory Acts began to restrict hours and conditions. Workhouse orphans were particularly favoured during the early years of industrialisation, as there were no limitations on working ages and no compulsory education. Women made up the bulk of the cotton textile labour force, and continued to do so in Lancashire until the 1960s. Women and children worked in the mines until the 1840s, and miners as young as ten were recruited until the end of the nineteenth century. Fines and punishments were imposed in the factories to discipline a workforce used to the more relaxed rhythms of rural labour.

Class structures in the industrial areas were determined by wealth, skill and education rather than by hereditary privilege. Employers normally lived close to their factories, although mines were often managed on behalf of distant landlords who owned the royalties accruing to the land above the coal. Many of these restrictions and controls were little different from those in the villages. *Master and Servant Acts* bound workers to their employers over a contracted period. They were introduced into and implemented in the Australian colonies, though with less effect. Fines were imposed in the factories, and many workers were obliged to use shops owned by their employers. Child labour remained normal in the countryside after being controlled in the factories. As late as 1867 the *Agricultural Gangs Act* set a minimum age of eight for working in the fields. Despite bad working and housing conditions, industrial work had the advantage of higher wages and liberation from the restrictions of village life. Factory workers and miners could also improve their skills, and there was much geographical mobility later in the century, including emigration. The greatest benefits went to the so-called 'aristocracy of labour', including railway engine-drivers, engineers and ship builders. What outsiders and theorists saw as the 'working class' had numerous gradations, often protectively organised through trade unions.

Those who emigrated or were transported to Australia could not fully escape a class-divided society. Convict society maintained its particular distinctions – between convicts, their guards, convicts emancipated or freed by servitude, and the small official society centred around the governor. As free immigrants began to arrive they were divided between the entrepreneurs, usually from well-connected families or prosperous yeoman farmers, and the workers they brought with them or sponsored for assisted and bounty passages. Many of the early settlers attempted to create villages on English lines, for example at Camden and Kameruka in New South Wales and at Woolmers in Tasmania. These properties still exist but never expanded. Labour was too mobile to create larger settlements around them.

Society became much more fluid with the mass migration to seek gold in the 1850s. From then until the depression of the 1890s there was considerable social mobility and population movement, both contributing to a much greater degree of equality than was possible in England. But it also led to a more effective organisation of labour and trade unions. These inspired the division between manual workers, the urban middle classes and employers which characterised Australia for the next two generations. In rural areas this was often cut across by resentments against the perceived exploitation of the rural economy by the growing cities.

Middle-class and professional emigrants

The great majority of convict and assisted migration to Australia in the first formative century was from the working classes and the poor. Yet it would be wrong to see Australia as a proletarian society from which the middle classes emerged by merit. It was a 'land of opportunity' for the professionals and entrepreneurs even more than for the labourers. It earned the title 'the workingman's paradise' by the 1880s because of its high wages, trade unionism and relative egalitarianism. But as William Lane pointed out in his novel *The Working Man's Paradise* of 1892, poverty and inequality persisted. They were made worse by the strikes and depression of the 1890s, which also wiped out English immigration for the next decade to everywhere but Western Australia. Slum conditions in Sydney and Melbourne were as bad as in many English cities, especially because of the lack of basic services such as sewerage. However, housing outside these limited areas was generally better than in England.

Many of those who did well in Australia were of humble backgrounds and would have found it harder to succeed in England. But even among the convicts, people such as Francis Greenway had middle-class origins. Those who did consistently well usually ran stores or had mail concessions from government. About half the English who came to Australia before 1900 paid their own fares or were assisted by employers and charities outside the state systems. They came from those occupations and professions which were specifically excluded from such schemes. Free passages were granted to approved clergymen from 1848. Otherwise, professionals could pay their own way, as many lawyers and doctors did. In 1861 the London parish of Islington was criticised by a British parliamentary select committee on poor relief because 'we should not send out a clerk to Australia, we should send out working men'. This distinction between those who worked with their hands and those who sat around in offices echoed down the Australian labour movement for the next century-and-a-half.

A picture of the enterprising immigrants who did well from the gold rushes is contained in the family history of Edward Byrd of Newcastle-under-Lyme, which he wrote in 1900. Born in 1828, he sailed to Adelaide in 1853 with his brother Thomas, who had been a draper in his native town. They brought with them 'bales of various merchandise, such as ready made clothing, shawls, dress goods, Nottingham lace, also four Iron Houses and one Iron Warehouse ...

William Farrer (1845–1906), scientist, developed Australian wheat varieties

so constructed as to take easily to pieces and pack away in a ship's hold ... We found a profitable sale for all we took on our own account'. Moving to Melbourne, they went to the goldfields where such goods were in great demand, eventually returning to England in 1859.[3] Many who remained founded considerable fortunes by the same enterprise. Retail and wholesale trade was the basis for social advance, whereas in England it was looked on with contempt by those who derived their social position from inheritance and land.

Clubs, schools and the army

The English upper class was bound together not simply by wealth but by many relationships and institutions. Many who became newly rich in the nineteenth century were scorned by established society. Anthony Trollope's *The Way We Live Now* (1875) paints a telling picture of the fate of a self-made European Jewish businessman, welcomed into society when successful but repudiated and forced into suicide as he failed. On the other hand, impoverished upper-class families were sometimes willing to mend their fortunes by marrying rich Americans, as did Winston Churchill's father Randolph.

Intermarriage within a small range of families was common in sustaining the solidarity of the English upper classes, but less of an option in Australia where the range of suitable partners was limited. Relationships between social equals were maintained by membership of exclusive clubs, modelled on those of London. The most influential was the Melbourne Club, founded in 1838, and the Adelaide Club and the Weld Club in Perth also provided interchange between male members of the local élites.

Attendance at private schools, modelled on the English public schools, perpetuated these relationships in later generations. The English public school system had been substantially reformed from the 1830s on lines developed by the headmaster of Rugby, Thomas Arnold. Old schools like Eton, Harrow and Winchester revised their practices, discipline and curriculum. Many of the great public schools were previously in a scandalous condition, as described in *Tom Brown's Schooldays* by Thomas Hughes in 1857. Many new schools were founded on similar lines, and some town grammar schools changed their status by charging high fees and taking in boys from a wider area. Some girls' schools were created, notably Cheltenham Ladies' College, although they could not lead on to the exclusively male university, political or military careers.

Reform of the schools along Christian and sport-centred principles was probably the most important factor in maintaining the solidarity of the upper classes and extending their influence into the richer elements of the commercial classes. Eventually these schools began to dictate what was truly 'British' or 'imperial'. They were held up as a norm by publications like the *Boy's Own Paper*, most readers of which would never attend them. Some specifically trained for the army, such as Sandhurst, or for the Indian colonial service, such as Haileybury. The most politically influential school was Eton, attended by more British prime ministers than any other.

From the all-male boarding schools, many would pass into the all-male Oxford and Cambridge universities and then into the all-male civil service, the armed services, parliament or the clergy. This uniquely English phenomenon only recently lost its influence. The last Etonian, indeed the last from an English public school, to be prime minister was Sir Alec Douglas Home in 1963–64. Tony Blair went to the less prestigious Scottish school, Fettes. The civil service became socially broadened after reforms in the late 1940s, although the Foreign Office and diplomatic service remained what socialist Professor Harold Laski once termed 'a nest of aristocratic singing birds'.

Australians were quick to copy the English system of schools and clubs, but politics and the public service were much more open to male society as a whole than in England. The universities and the armed services continued to recruit from Britain until well into the 1960s, as did the private schools and the Anglican church. Anglican schools formed on the same basis as in England included King's School (Parramatta), Melbourne Grammar, Geelong Grammar and St Peter's (Adelaide). But other schools were oriented towards the Presbyterian, Catholic, Baptist and Methodist denominations and eventually towards Jewish and Greek Orthodox clienteles. Some state schools such as Perth Modern, Sydney's Fort Street and Melbourne High also maintained similar standards without limiting their intake to those who could pay. Among many heads of schools brought out from England were Sir James Darling of Geelong Grammar and Elizabeth Archdale of Abbotsleigh.

Bishop Perry (1807–91) established the Church of England in Victoria and founded Melbourne and Geelong Grammar schools

The British armed services were strongly influenced by the class system. Officers purchased their commissions until well into the nineteenth century, especially those in the cavalry who had to maintain their own horses. Scandalous incompetence during the Crimean War (1853–56) eventually led to the reform of this system but without ending the public school and upper-class domination of the military leadership. The navy was less élitist, as witness the elevation of the ploughman's son, James Cook. The entire military leadership in Australia before the withdrawal of British troops in 1870 was drawn from the army in the United Kingdom, India or elsewhere in the British Empire. They were of varied background, but the English among them included Archibald Bell from Cheshunt, Hertfordshire, who served with the New South Wales Corps from 1809 and became a magistrate; James Brumby from Lincolnshire, a private in the Corps who established himself as a landowner in Tasmania; Henry Bunbury from an aristocratic Cheshire family, after whom the Western Australian town is named; William Cox from Wimborne, Dorset, who supervised the road across the Blue Mountains in 1814 and became a landowner in the areas opened up; Charles Sturt, the explorer from a Dorset family stationed in India; and many others. Another explorer, John Oxley from Kirkham Abbey, Yorkshire, was a naval officer, arriving in Sydney in 1808. Nearly all these officers were well connected socially, and acquired land and property in the early days of settlement. Service in India was common, as it was a requirement for higher promotions in the British Army.

The British connection with the services continued after 1870 and Australians served under British command in New Zealand and South Africa. During the First World War the Australian Imperial Force (AIF) was commanded by William Birdwood between 1914 and 1918, who served at Gallipoli and in France. He was from an English official and military family stationed in India and was educated at a public school, Clifton College (Bristol), and at Sandhurst. He made a triumphal tour of Australia in 1920, and after his retirement in 1930 was created Lord Birdwood of Anzac and Totnes.

Two English soldiers with less distinguished backgrounds were 'Breaker' Morant and 'Simpson'. Harry Morant, from Bridgwater, Somerset, emigrated to Queensland in 1883, aged nineteen. Serving in the Boer War he was court-martialled and shot in 1902 for killing prisoners.[4] Like 'Simpson' he posthumously became an Australian hero, and although English, is still held up as a martyr to English military oppression. Serving at Gallipoli under his given name, John

*Lord Birdwood
(1865–1951)
commanded the
Australian Imperial
Force from 1914 to
1918 at Gallipoli
and in France*

Simpson Kirkpatrick from South Shields, Co. Durham, rescued the wounded under fire with his donkey. His eventual death made him the most honoured soldier to serve with the Anzacs. Neither Morant nor Kirkpatrick were officers or of traditional officer class.

The formation of élites

Many English immigrants were seeking not only more money and better food but also a more egalitarian society. Others wanted to recreate the classes they had left behind or even to rise socially from relatively humble origins. As a self-consciously egalitarian society Australia has been hostile to the concept of social hierarchy and élites. In recent years the very word 'élite' has become one of political abuse, being contrasted to that of the 'ordinary Australian'. English society, with its many social gradations and snobberies, has been consistently pilloried as antipathetic to basic Australian values. This has been especially true for the class distinctions surrounding official appointments and the membership of exclusive clubs. Yet while many – perhaps most – were escaping a system they resented, no society with such a large English component was likely to be without class distinction. The system of clubs and schools set up in the major cities by the mid-nineteenth century was clearly designed to bind together an upper class with access to power and wealth. Many had come from similar backgrounds in England rather than emerged from the ranks of the humble immigrants.

Measurement of classes and élites is difficult in a society where such gradations are consistently denied. The modern authoritative source, the *Australian Dictionary of Biography*, serves as a good guide to who has been important over the past two centuries. In its more recent volumes, which extend to 1980, there has been a determined effort to include people who would not be seen as élite or distinguished. This is less true for the years before 1939, when English immigrants were more prominent. Nevertheless, the *ADB* remains an excellent guide to most of those who did well in Australia over the past two hundred years, even if it includes some who did not and some who went elsewhere.

In nineteenth century Australia the ideology of egalitarianism was not strongly developed. Many wanted to be recognised for their achievements. Class distinctions were maintained between convicts and free settlers, assisted and self-funded immigrants, established families and newcomers, Protestants and Catholics, labourers and professionals. Large volumes were produced about prominent persons, who subscribed to them and thus made them profitable. To some extent these were self-described élites, but they are a major indicator of who was important and where they came from.

The largest such volume was Alexander Sutherland's *Victoria and its Metropolis*, published in 1888 to commemorate the centenary of British occupation. Incidentally, it also recorded the careers of the many Victorians who had arrived during the gold rush of the 1850s. Of 6500 recorded, one-third had been born in England and one-quarter in Australia. The English were most preponderant in Bendigo, where they made up 47 per cent of the entries, and in Melbourne at 41 per cent. They were weakest in the north of the State towards the Murray, where there were as many Irish and Australians, and in the Wimmera, which had a large German population. The English were otherwise spread fairly evenly throughout Victoria, outnumbering the Australians, Scots and Irish.

More than twenty years later James S. Battye, in the *Cyclopedia of Western Australia* (1912), found that one-fifth of his self-selected élite of 1500 had been born in England. Neither in Victoria nor later in Western Australia did the English heavily outnumber others. In

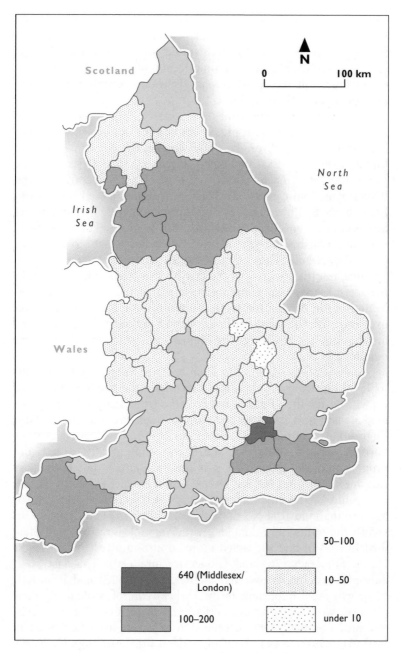

County of birth of Australian Dictionary of Biography *entries, 1788–1980*

Victoria they shared their dominance with the Scots and Irish, in Western Australia with Australians who had come to the State in the gold rush of the 1890s. Both studies suggest that the élite was relatively representative, in ethnic terms, of the adult population as a whole. But regionally it was disproportionately drawn from London and the Home Counties.

In Victoria, of Sutherland's self-selected English-born total of 2200, 30 per cent were from London and the Southeast, 9 per cent each from the North or the Southwest and 8 per cent from the Midlands and the East combined. But more than twice as many came from Scotland as the 10 per cent of Scots recorded in the United Kingdom census of 1871. Scots outnumbered those from London, the Southeast and the Southwest combined. This may reflect Sutherland's own Glaswegian birth, but is more likely to suggest that the English were secondary in Victorian society to an extent unusual elsewhere. The domination of Londoners among the English remains, but the élite role of the English was less significant than in the rest of Australia. Some might attribute the strength of intellectual life in Melbourne to the superiority of Scottish education over English! The southern English and Londoners were, however, most strongly represented in Melbourne, while the Scots were dominant in the Western District.

Analysis of the *Australian Dictionary of Biography* from 1780 to 1980 illustrates the regions from which the English élite were drawn. By far the largest number came from London and its immediate and now suburbanised surroundings. From a total of 2400 English-born entrants over two centuries, 753 or 31 per cent were born in London, Middlesex and Surrey. This greatly exceeds the proportion of the English living in that area at any time in the past two hundred years. Other Home Counties such as Kent (128), Hampshire (72), Essex (50) and Sussex (49) were well represented, as were the industrial North, with Yorkshire (157) and Lancashire (159); the industrial Midlands, with Warwickshire (62) and Staffordshire (44); and the much more rural Southwest, with Devon (121), Somerset (76) and Gloucestershire (70). This last area, although it contains two major cities, Bristol (28) and Plymouth (24), was most important in the earlier years of settlement when pioneers were bringing out agricultural labourers. The far North also produced many who succeeded in Australia, from Northumberland (51), Durham (45) and Cumberland (35). Although the North had a greater population than the Southeast by 1841, its contribution to élite formation between 1780 and 1980 was only half that from the Southeast. This bears out both earlier attempts to list the élites and the statistics of assisted emigration before 1900 and even in modern times. English Australians have more often come from the gentle south than the rugged north.

This distribution underlines the spread of English recruitment to the élites, and their relatively urban background. The cities of Birmingham, Liverpool, Manchester, Newcastle, Portsmouth and Leeds are well represented. But many others are not, such as Bradford, Derby, Nottingham, Leicester, Wolverhampton and Stoke-on-Trent. This suggests, as do the figures for assisted immigration in the nineteenth century, that Midland England was less likely to produce emigrants to Australia than were the seaports and coastal districts. Apart from those from London and the three major industrial and mining areas, very many English immigrants came from villages and small towns in the first century of settlement. While there is a considerable shift northwards by the 1880s, many of the 'founders' of Australia came from the southern counties. And London has always maintained its strong influence, whether through convicts, free emigrants, the professional classes or the leaders of society.

The English as an upper class

Australians developed a very ambivalent attitude towards the English. They were often seen as poor, subservient and dirty. But they were also resented as superior, condescending and arrogant. This exchange was reported between an Australian and his public-school educated English migrant neighbour in 1965: 'I suppose you think you're better than me?' ... 'Yes, I do, as a matter of fact.'[5] Another equally puerile exchange was recorded by Alan Richardson during interviews in 1966: 'They always call me a Pommy b... because they resent us reminding them that they still have chains on'.[6] This sort of exchange was hardly friendly banter. The English were well known for their xenophobia. They brought it to Australia, where it was often turned against them.

Such attitudes suffer from the silliness of stereotyping English and Australians over the entire two centuries of settlement. The English were governors, warders and convicts; slum dwellers and business-men; working class and farmers; trade unionists and clergymen. However, they did have certain advantages such as being early settlers, as forming the core of the professional and administrative classes, and as inheriting the imperial system and the glory which went with it. Conservative English attitudes and institutions were made their own by Australian conservatives. Humble and even convict origins were obscured by the socially aspiring. As in England, the upper classes adopted and assimilated people from a variety of backgrounds. Australia has never had a national ruling class comparable to that in Victorian England. But it did have a range of localised élites who were only too willing to adopt similar lifestyles and cultures and to glory in the English inheritance. London was their capital city and the 'cultural cringe' their approach to anything which came from there. These colonial pretensions were not the fault of the English as a whole, many of whom regarded them with amusement.

The English class system was formalised at its summit by titles drawn from the Middle Ages and by more recent awards often given to public servants in recognition of their service to the state, such as the Order of the British Empire or the Royal Victorian Order. At the pinnacle of this system was the Royal Family, based on hereditary principles and confined to communicants of the established churches of England and Scotland. Apart from Queen Victoria's son, the Duke of Edinburgh, who came twice between 1867 and 1869, royalty did not visit Australia in the colonial period. It did so with increasing frequency after Federation. Only the Duke of Gloucester, as governor-general between 1945 and 1947, established residence. Most English governors or governors-general were barons of the first or second generation, with the exception of Lord de L'Isle whose family is unusual in predating the Wars of the Roses. Recency of ennoblement did not prevent the various government houses becoming social centres for the Anglophile social set, a phenomenon which has only recently disappeared as Australians have replaced British appointees.

Australians were normally incorporated within the English honours system in its lower ranks as barons and knights. Lord Bruce and Lord Casey were both politicians who, like many in England, were created as barons and thus eligible to sit in the House of Lords. Far more common was the award of knighthoods or membership of the Privy Council. It was long the policy of the Australian Labor Party that its members should not accept these honours. This was consistently ignored in Tasmania, but in 1976 the trade union leader Jack Egerton was expelled from the Queensland ALP for accepting a knighthood recommended by the National Party State government.

Until the 1970s there was, then, the appearance of an 'upper class' of knights. This was superseded with the creation of an Australian honours system by the Whitlam Labor government. Except for Queensland, conservative State and Commonwealth governments discontinued the recommendation of English honours despite complaints from their supporters. However, the award of a knighthood was more an historic anomaly than recognition of either power or wealth. It has now disappeared with the creation of the Order of Australia.

Australia has not had a ruling class in the narrow sense understood in nineteenth-century England. It did, however, create the impression of having one through the various government houses and their social circles, which enjoyed their greatest significance before 1914. The upper classes tended to be defined in terms of their access to government house, where the incumbent was normally British and had an English or Scottish title. Before 1856, more than half the colonial governors and their executive councils were English and three-quarters were Anglicans. Of 53 English-born, 23 were from London and the Home Counties, a proportion which held for colonial premiers between 1856 and 1901. In contrast, elected political leaders included a growing number who were born in Australia.[7]

If the English were to be found at the core of the upper classes in colonial Australia, they always had to share this role with the Scots and with Irish Protestants. As an early democracy, Australia gave political power to the less well bred to a far greater extent than did Victorian England. The hold of the English landed classes on the British parliament did not fade until after the First World War and the rise of the Labour Party, whereas large landowners have not been important in Australia except in the Legislative Councils. After Federation they largely ceased to count in national politics at all. The ALP came to power years before British Labour and was consistently more working class and trade union based until the 1970s. Scots in the conservative parties and Irish in the Labor Party outflanked the English and their descendants and sometimes outnumbered them. The institution of parliament was unmistakably of English origin, but many parliamentarians were not. There is a marked contrast between the importance of the English-born and descended before Federation and their limited role afterwards. Between 1914 and 1966 there was only one prime minister of predominantly English descent – Sir Earle Page, who was very briefly a 'caretaker' in 1939.

Political positions, including those nominated from London, were as often in the hands of the Scots and the Irish as the English. This was even more true of elected positions after the adoption of manhood suffrage in the late 1850s. Elected politicians were not drawn from the established upper classes to the same extent as in England. Nor were they, or the nominated governors, predominantly English or of English descent. They could more accurately be described as 'Anglicised'. Governor Macquarie and Governor-General Lord Dunrossil were both native speakers of Scottish Gaelic, and Billy Hughes of Welsh. But they were very exceptional, as were the two Jewish governors-general (Isaacs and Cowen) and one colonial premier (Vaiben Solomon of South Australia). The social and political élites were largely assimilated to the practices and attitudes of their English counterparts, but were not necessarily of English origin. Irish Catholics were more coherently organised than the English and took leading roles in the Victorian Protectionists before Federation and in the ALP after the conscription split of 1916. They were not welcome in the conservative parties until after the split in the Labor Party of 1956, but have now become a quite significant element. Scots and people of Scottish descent have been very influential in both the urban and rural conservative parties, reflecting their economic success. While education at an Anglican school often led to élite membership in later life, this was less usual than in England. The Presbyterian Scotch College in Melbourne has made a greater contribution to élite formation than any one of the Anglican schools.[8]

A land of opportunity?

A central belief in immigrant societies is that they offer far more opportunities for social advance than did the 'old country'. This was certainly a major theme of the thousands of English immigrants who arrived in the 1950s and 1960s. Earlier generations had tended to stress higher wages and better food. Certainly Australia has been a land of opportunity for many immigrants. The remarkable passage from refugee to millionaire by many European Jews is outstanding. The success of Greeks, Lebanese and Chinese from poor villages in under-developed countries has also been a source of pride to entire ethnic communities. But these triumphs have been much less notable for the English, given their numerical predominance in all waves of migration from 1788 into the 1970s. The rise and fall of the humble sign painter, Alan Bond, were equally spectacular

– a variant on the old Lancashire saying, 'clogs to clogs in three generations'. Those who came out from England as convicts, or as rural labourers, or as refugees from the Poor Law, or as orphans, occasionally did very well. Most did not and are forgotten. They were a major element in the 'backbone' of Australia – but backbones are always hidden.

One advantage which some families of English descent have enjoyed was the early arrival of their ancestors at a time when English domination was more important than it later became. Early arrivals were in a strong position to acquire land, the basis for wealth, power and influence in a pre-industrial society. Much investment in other economic activity came from companies located in London, which sent out staff to manage their affairs. The higher education system and the churches also favoured expatriate professors and clergymen. Even the Catholic Church was initially staffed by Benedictines from England before the Irish influx of 1838 quite rightly changed the ethnic character of its leadership. The Church of England was established in New South Wales by two Yorkshire evangelicals, Richard Johnson and Samuel Marsden, and continued to recruit its leadership from England for nearly two centuries.[9] It did not elect an Australian-born primate until 1978. The Methodists were led by the Rev. Irving Benson from Hull, as

*Rev. Samuel Marsden
(1765–1838),
a founder of the
Church of England in
New South Wales*

superintendent of the Central Methodist Mission at Wesley Church, Melbourne, from 1933 to 1967. Both he and most leaders of the Anglican church were enthusiastic Anglophiles.

There were many advantages in being English during the formative years of settlement. Early land ownership consolidated such dynasties as the Hentys, the Archers, the Drake-Brockmans, the Manifolds and the Macarthur-Onslows. The situation was often less secure for those building their wealth from commerce or industry. The ancestors of Kerry Packer, media owner and for several years the richest man in Australia, had tenuous convict links through the original family from Reading. None of this family had any connection with the media. The rival newspaper owners, the Fairfaxes, had their origins in the newspaper industry in Warwickshire. But their local founder, John Fairfax, was bankrupt and penniless when he arrived in Sydney on the *Lady Fitzherbert* in 1838.[10] He was, of course, fortunate in arriving in a city now big enough to support regular newspapers with no competition from anywhere else. His development of the *Sydney Morning Herald* from 1842 as one of Australia's leading newspapers was due to hard work and initiative rather than the patronage connections so important for some of the landed families. His Warwickshire rival, Henry Parkes, failed to build his Sydney newspaper, the *Empire*, over the same period but succeeded in politics instead, which John Fairfax did not.[11]

John Norton, of humble origins from Brighton, was also in the right place at the right time. He arrived in Sydney in 1884, when it was already a major city with an organised labour movement and a large potential readership for something less elevated than the *Herald*. Norton was active in the labour movement but made his fame and fortune by buying *Truth* in 1896. As in England at the same time, the newly educated working class was ready for a popular paper which also campaigned on social issues without being too political. Today that era has almost passed in both countries, and *Truth* is no more. During its lifetime it was published throughout Australia.

Apart from the media, other avenues to economic success lay through retail trading and alcohol. The major Australian stores – David Jones, Myers and Mark Foys – were not founded by Englishmen. Marcus Clark, from Liverpool, founded the Sydney store which expanded under his son, Sir Marcus, who was a staunch Anglophile and leader of the Royal Empire Society and the Royal

Society of St George. Grace Brothers also had humble beginnings in Sydney, with a hawker's licence granted to Joseph Grace from Buckinghamshire in 1883. George Coles also began as a hawker in Victoria during the gold rush. Anthony Hordern, from a wealthy Staffordshire family, arrived in Sydney in 1825 with very little, setting up a drapery store which eventually became Anthony Hordern's and Son in 1869 on the Haymarket site which it occupied for a century.

Wealth acquired through commerce, retailing and the media did not carry the same prestige in England as that based on land. This did not matter to the same degree in Australia which, like the United States, saw no need to glorify a distant past with which its citizens had only remote connections. But unlike America, it was prepared for a long time to accept honours and distinctions from elsewhere and to regard another country as the 'fount of honour'. Commercial wealth and political power were inherited to a limited extent. But they had to be worked for, and there were just as many failed English entrepreneurs as successful ones. Recent wealth has been accumulated by many who are not English at all, and this 'new wealth' is also sometimes insecure. What most English immigrants probably preferred was security and comfort within an English-derived culture, rather than the roller-coaster of success and failure at business. Most English immigrants in recent years have been young to middle-aged parents who came for the future of their children in a less class-defined society.

The massive intake of English immigrants over two centuries was for most of them a transfer from one social system to its local equivalent. Workers remained workers, professionals remained professionals, landowners remained landowners. The 150 years of assisted passages ensured the recreation of a working class from a small cross-section of its English counterpart. The English were less well educated than the Scots for at least the first century; less politically influential than the Irish for several generations; not very socially mobile or enterprising. Apart from the major depressions of the 1890s and the 1930s they were normally better off economically than if they had remained in working-class England. But the differentials between the two countries have narrowed since the 1960s. The supreme irony for many English immigrants is that the friends and relatives they left behind often have the same material goods and the same basic lifestyle which they worked so hard to achieve. They do not have the same climate or class system – and never will.

5

FROM COLONIES TO COMMONWEALTH

When our Colonists visit England ... the dominating thought in their hearts as
the white cliffs of Kent face them, or they are warped into Liverpool's landing
stage, is that they are back again in the family – 'they have come home'.
Journal of the Waifs and Strays Society, London, March 1913

The separate colonies of Australia were all peopled and developed
by immigrants, with the largest number being English. Unlike North
America there was very little ethnic variety from place to place,
despite the vast distances between the colonial capitals.The colonies
were all managed from London through local governors until the
1850s. Supervision of assisted immigration remained with London
until the 1870s, on the basis that only British subjects would receive
passage money. This was supervised by the Colonial Land and
Emigration Commission, which was not wound up until 1872.[1] By
the time the colonies became effectively self-governing – which was
not until 1890 in Western Australia – their inhabitants were overwhelmingly British, with a growing majority of these being English
by birth or recent descent. When immigration policy passed into the
hands of locally elected governments, these naturally responded to
their constituents by favouring the existing policy of reserving
Australia for the British. As the United States was always more
attractive to the Irish, and as the ratio between the English and the
Scots greatly favoured the former, the English component in Australian immigration steadily increased. It was, however, being replaced
by the Australian-born, who constituted the majority by 1880.

The English who came to Australia in the first century were
building a predominantly English society, with an important Scottish
and Irish population. The English language, English law, English
constitutional systems, English élites and rulers, and the need to
answer to London and to be loyal to Queen Victoria and the Empire,
all reinforced the English sense of having moved within a single

society. The 1880s in Queensland and New South Wales, and the 1890s in Western Australia, saw the last great bursts of English migration to this 'English' society. Between 1881 and 1891 the English-born population of Queensland more than doubled, and 40 000 were added to New South Wales. The greatest impact of all was in Western Australia, where English numbers rose from 9000 to 25 000 between 1891 and 1901.

But these waves of migration from England were too late to change the basic fact that most Australians had been born in the country and that growing numbers were looking towards an end of the colonial system through federation and a single government

TABLE 1: English-born percentages of the total (non-Aboriginal) population in the nineteenth century

Colony	Year	English-born (%)
New South Wales	1846	30.2
	1861	24.0
	1891	13.3
Victoria	1851	37.4
	1857	36.0
	1861	31.5
	1891	13.8
South Australia	1861	35.4
	1866	31.6 (with Wales)
	1891	14.9
Queensland	1868	25.5 (with Wales)
	1881	16.0 (with Wales)
	1891	19.6 (with Wales)
	1901	13.8 (with Wales)
Tasmania	1881	14.7
	1891	11.7
Western Australia	1870	28.9
	1901	13.8

Notes: Figures refer only to those born in England (including Cornwall), unless Wales is specified. Aborigines were counted in some colonies sometimes, but rarely affect the totals.

Sources: Colonial censuses for the stated year.

for the continent. This movement was led until his death in 1896 by the most famous of all English immigrants of the time, Sir Henry Parkes. Even in Western Australia the English-born proportion was only 14 per cent. In Queensland it was the same. Elsewhere, English immigrants were coming into a society with well-formed characteristics of its own and, especially through the new labour movement, some fairly critical attitudes towards the 'old country'. The English who arrived in large numbers between 1880 and 1914 were not fundamentally changing it as their predecessors had done. It is, perhaps, not surprising that during this period the mildly derogatory term 'Pommy' began to be used, instead of 'new chum'. The *Australian National Dictionary* cannot trace it back further than 1912, nor is anyone really sure of its origins. The Scots and Irish were not Pommies – the English were.

Building Queensland

Queensland had only a limited convict population at the Moreton Bay station, which closed in 1839. It was opened up to immigrant settlement in 1842. Some settlers came up from New South Wales, but the importation of English agricultural workers was as marked as in the southern colonies between the 1830s and the 1860s. An English labourer, writing in the National Agricultural Labourers' Union journal, summarised the attractions of Queensland:

> I never enjoyed better health. This is a beautiful country. We never have any snow, but we have what the poor men at home very seldom, if ever, get – plenty of good beef and mutton ...
> I now live well and can have a pound in my pocket, and that is more than I could at home ... Here we can put it by, and soon get a piece of land and be our own master ... I can live well on 9s. a week and have beef three times a day. I wish all my fellow-labourers were here. Do not stop to be crushed down by the farmers and the gentleman stewards. Come out here and be free: where there is no slavery – where you can be your own master.[2]

This is a good summary of what made Queensland so attractive to English countrymen and women in the 1880s, when mass recruitment began – good food, good health and independence.

Queensland established agents in England in 1884, at London, Leicester, Crewkerne (Somerset), Malvern, Reading, Southport

(Lancashire), Taunton, Winchester, Dunstable (Bedfordshire), Manchester, Barnstaple (Devon), Plymouth and Grimsby. The majority were in rural areas. Charles Lucas told the United Kingdom Select Committee on Colonisation of 1889 that 'the Queensland government selects its emigrants by agents who go throughout the country districts'. As full control of immigration policy had passed from London to Brisbane, the government was no longer limited in its choice of occupations. It had huge resources of public land to sell and enjoyed a major economic boom in the 1880s.

The movement of immigrants to Queensland was one of the first concerns of the colonial government set up in 1859. It was unhappy that there were few direct sailings to Queensland, making it hard to attract those who had landed in New South Wales. Following precedent, Queensland set a quota system based on the relative proportions of the English, Scots and Irish in the United Kingdom population. Between 1861 and 1901 this meant that 58.5 per cent of all assisted arrivals were from England and Wales. Many were given completely free passages. Queensland also operated a land grant system, whereby 18 acres of land to a certain value was allocated to new arrivals or to those paying their fare. While some of this was sold off, the policy intention was to create a class of farmers, and preference was given to those with agricultural backgrounds. The passage of immigrants was monopolised by the Black Ball Line of Liverpool, which was already engaged in transporting immigrants to Victoria for the Colonial Land and Emigration Commission.[3] All Black Ball Line vessels were sailing ships, taking an average of 86 days between Liverpool and Melbourne in the 1860s. Its *Marco Polo* was the largest ship carrying passengers to Australia by 1852. The Black Ball Line had four hundred agents in the United Kingdom, far more than the CL&EC or the Queensland government.

On securing the exclusive passage contract in 1861, Thomas Mackay of the Black Ball Line declared his aim:

> to further the interest of the colony as far as we could by
> fostering a continuous and healthy stream of emigrants
> comprising capitalists, farmers with moderate means, well-to-do
> trades men, as well as the ordinary working classes.[4]

This aim liberated Queensland from some of the restrictions imposed by the British authorities, including those on non-British

The Marco Polo *of the Black Ball Line was the largest and fastest emigrant sailing ship of the 1850s and 1860s*

immigrants. It also increased the scope for passengers paying full fares to occupy cabins rather than the usual steerage dormitories. Among the first free passages granted were to 1781 unemployed cotton textile workers from Lancashire with their families, during the crisis caused by the American Civil War in 1863. The shipping contract laid down that half must be landed in North Queensland, to develop remote towns.

The Black Ball Line moved its sailings from Liverpool to London and Plymouth by 1864, which probably increased the numbers coming from southern England. But economic conditions caused cancellation of the contract in 1866, the last sailing to Queensland was in 1871, and the company then went bankrupt. Sailing ships were already being replaced by steam and a new contract was arranged in 1880 with the British India Steam Navigation Company, the great majority of whose ships also left from London or Plymouth. This began a massive boom in migration to Queensland under the legislation of 1882. These ships were faster than the Black Ball Line and better managed. Matrons were supplied by the British Ladies' Female Immigration Society and passenger conditions were carefully supervised. This avoided some previous problems, including the 'rude and dissolute habits' of navvies brought out in 1865 and tensions between English and Irish passengers in 1863, 1872 and 1885. The company was advised not to fill up empty places at the last minute, a practice very common since the start of assisted migration in the 1830s.

A special effort was made to attract Scots, and the Catholic Church organised to attract Irish immigrants. But England was now quite dominant over the United Kingdom. The English population of Queensland increased by 51 000 between 1871 and 1891 to a level of 77 000, while Scots rose only by 14 000 and Irish by 22 000. Queensland drew its immigrants from the same regions that had supplied the southern colonies, namely London, the Southeast and the Southwest. It also drew in more from the Eastern agricultural counties than had been prepared to come thirty or forty years before. London and Middlesex were well represented, as usual. But the slump in English agriculture in the 1870s persuaded many to emigrate from Norfolk, Lincolnshire and Somerset. As the coal mines at Ipswich were developed, miners were brought out from Durham, Staffordshire and Lancashire, as in New South Wales.

Queensland was less urbanised than the southern colonies and continued to seek rural labourers. Between 1879 and 1888 there were 107 483 overseas immigrants to Queensland, including children. Of these, all but 8000 received some form of government assistance. Their occupations were predominantly unskilled: 24 148 farm labourers (who received free passages), 21 011 domestic servants, 7455 general labourers, 2655 carpenters and 1541 miners. But pauper emigration had died out. Only 100 had been sent out from England by the Poor Law Board to all the British colonies in 1860, due to the success of schemes funded from colonial resources. By 1888 the UK Select Committee on Poor Law Relief was told that 'the colonies ... would object to any considerable emigration of paupers' and 'there was a strong prejudice against state-aided emigration' in the colonies. In other words, Australia was now deciding who should come, which continues to be true to the present day.

The main Queensland occupations in 1891 were farmers (20 364), labourers (11 603), servants (9299), sugarcane growers (8799), pastoral workers (8748), gold miners (6293), farm servants (6150) and clothing workers (4982). There were only 4 professors, as the university had not yet been established, and 1151 school teachers, many of whom had come on free passages.The immigrant input from England thus fitted the campaign for a White Australia – to replace Asian and Pacific Island labour. The government wanted to recruit those with no knowledge of or interest in the cities. 'The pure farm labourer – one who has never worked off a farm – is the best class of emigrant for the Colony', argued the official report of 1885.[5]

Despite this, the English, as elsewhere, settled in the small but growing coastal towns. They made up 23 per cent of the population of Brisbane and Townsville, and 21 per cent of Rockhampton by 1891. But they were also found in the remote outback. The Marathon and Aramac census districts were the heartland of Australian sentiment and symbols. The shearers' strike of 1891 was largely within their bounds and the Australian Labor Party claims to have been founded under the 'tree of knowledge' at Barcaldine in the same year. These districts became a stronghold of the Australian Workers' Union, the location for the writing and first performance of 'Waltzing Matilda' and the home base of Qantas and site of the Stockmen's Hall of Fame. Yet there were 919 English-born there in 1891, making up 20 per cent of the predominantly male, manual population, of whom 44 per cent were Anglicans.[6]

Of those who came to Queensland in the 1880s some moved south, like William Angliss. Born in Dudley, Worcestershire, he had lived in London and New York before arriving in 1884. Moving yet again to Melbourne, he began business as a local butcher, went on to export meat once freezer shipping developed, and eventually became the richest and most influential person in Australia's expanding meat industry. Joseph Collings, from Brighton, arrived in Queensland in 1883. Afer a long career as a union organiser and Labor politician, he became a Senator and wartime Minister for the Interior, 1941–45. Richard Dowse, from Portsea, Hampshire, arrived in 1885. He had a distinguished military career, serving in the Boer War and on the Western Front throughout the First World War. George Griffiths of Bristol arrived earlier, in 1870, and developed the windmills for pumping water which became typical of farms all over Australia. Two prominent socialists, William Lane from Bristol and Henry Boote from Liverpool, arrived in Queensland in 1885 and 1889 respectively. They were among many thousands influenced by trade unionism in England. Many of them laid the foundations for the election of the first labour government in the world, in 1899, and the forty years of Labor Party rule in Queensland between 1915 and 1957.

The male working-class English immigrants who arrived between the 1880s and 1914 were better organised and more politicised than most of their predecessors. Urban males had been granted the vote in 1867 and rural labourers in 1884. The trade union movement had been centralised through the Trades Union Congress, formed in Manchester in 1868, although many craft and local unions were not affiliated. Union membership rose from 1.5 million in 1893 to 4.1 million in 1914. Moreover, much of this increase was among less skilled workers from whom many of the immigrants were drawn. Coal miners had elected several of their officials to parliament, and the trade union movement had a regular lobbying function and close relations with the Liberal Party. The idea of a distinct labour party was canvassed from the 1860s but did not reach fruition in England until 1901, partly due to the strength of Liberalism but also to the Conservative loyalties of many unionists in Lancashire. In that respect Australia was well ahead of Britain. The idea of a distinct labour party was sustained by the immigrants of the 1880s, who found that manhood suffrage and the organisational weakness of non-labour parties provided more fertile ground for success.

The shift to Commonwealth control

The Colonial Land and Emigration Commission dissolved in 1872 in recognition of the total control over settlement now exercised by the self-governing colonies. From then until the *Empire Settlement Act* of 1922, the United Kingdom government had no official interest in emigration. This left the colonies free to choose who they wanted rather than having to respond to instructions from London. It became possible to support non-British immigrants, as did Queensland for Germans and Scandinavians in significant numbers, and was no longer necessary to limit recruitment to rural workers. New South Wales no longer did so, and Victoria did not assist immigrants any more because of the great population surge created by the gold rush. In the 1870s New South Wales recruiting agents were located mainly in the north of England, whereas the Colonial Land and Emigration Commission had focused on the south. Apart from Bristol and Plymouth, agents were in Newcastle-on-Tyne, Bishop Auckland (Durham), Guisborough (North Yorkshire), Bradford, Leeds, Sheffield and Manchester.[7] These were all mining and industrial locations, appropriate to a colony with a growing coal industry in the Hunter and Illawarra and a manufacturing base in Sydney. Queensland and Western Australia continued to recruit farm workers, which was appropriate to their stage of development.

Immigration languished with the depression of the 1890s but recovered rapidly in the years before war broke out in August 1914. This was a period of considerable industrial unrest on the English

Advertising on the building site of Australia House in London in 1910

coalfields and railways, with rapidly rising numbers of trade unionists in both England and Australia. Armed soldiers were sent against
miners at Featherstone in Yorkshire in 1893, leading to two deaths.
In the same year Lancashire cotton workers went on strike. In 1897
about 50 000 workers were locked out of engineering works in a
dispute with the Amalgamated Society of Engineers. By 1901 some
major British unions were ready to form the Labour Party, and it
adopted its present parliamentary form in 1906 following the
Liberal landslide victory. In Australia industrial unrest was also
marked, leading to the creation of arbitration systems, which also
favoured trade unionists in the granting of awards. The unstable
conditions were doubtless a major factor in persuading many from
industrial areas to emigrate. Between 1909 and 1913 the total of
assisted emigrants to Australia rose to 150 554. But between 1914
and 1920 the war greatly reduced international movement, except
for soldiers proceeding to the battlefields.

The Commonwealth assumed responsibility for assisted immigration from March 1921, leaving reception and settlement to the
States. However, the States retained the right to select and nominate
in general and the Commonwealth undertook not to endorse assisted
immigrants without State approval. Western Australia retained con-

siderable influence over its intake. The British government agreed to provide matching finance under an agreement from 1922 to 1928, leaving immigrants to find about £11, which could be advanced as a loan. By 1923 loans equalled grants, with equal amounts subscribed by the British and Australian governments and an equal responsibility to write off losses. These were considerable from Western Australia where immigration was tied to land settlement in schemes which ultimately proved disastrous. Under this system 115 435 assisted immigrants arrived between 1921 and 1925, the great majority being English. Demand exceeded the willingness of the States to absorb new immigrants and was further expanded by industrial unrest surrounding the British general strike of May 1926. The return of Britain to the gold standard in 1925 at an unrealistically high exchange rate was permanently damaging for many export industries, including coal and textiles, with consequent rising unemployment.

Despite the demand from industrial and mining workers, the States were still asking the Commonwealth to select farm labourers and domestics as in the past. In 1925 Victoria wanted 200 to 300 farm workers and 100 domestics a month; New South Wales 100 farm lads and 100 domestics; Western Australia 100 farm workers and an 'unlimited' number of domestics; and Queensland 75 farm lads and 50 domestics. Altogether, the aggregate annual demand for farm workers and domestics was over 7000 a year, or one-third of

Young emigrants at Australia House in London in the 1920s

the total assisted intake. This added to the unskilled working class, with disastrous results when the depression came in 1929. Pressure for rural workers came mainly from the conservative parties which dominated Victoria and South Australia. But the ruling ALP in Queensland and Western Australia also rested on rural voters to a large extent. Consequently, urban and industrial immigrants tended to be attracted to New South Wales, where the English-born population rose from 126 000 in 1901 to 193 000 in 1933. Only Western Australia increased as rapidly, and some States actually recorded a decline.

Rural settlement

The idea that immigration was needed to supply rural workers and 'fill the empty spaces' flourished long after England had become a predominantly urban society. Scotland was equally urbanised, although past agricultural success obscured this fact. Irish immigration dropped off in the 1890s and never recovered. The Irish were free to emigrate to Britain, or to the United States, being unaffected by the American national quotas introduced in 1924 to limit immigration from southern and eastern Europe. While rural workers still came to Australia from England, increasing numbers were being selected and trained from urban backgrounds. Ex-servicemen in England were encouraged after the war to take up small holdings or chicken farms, many of which failed. The Australian situation was even more acute. Not only were many immigrants unfamiliar with agriculture, but what little they did know was unsuited to Australian conditions.

The Empire settlement strategy involved agreements between the Commonwealth, the States and the British government to fund and encourage settlement by immigrants on undeveloped land.[8] Agreements were signed with Victoria in 1922 and with New South Wales and Western Australia in 1923, and further agreements in 1925 with all States except New South Wales, now controlled by Lang's Labor Party. Low interest loans were payable by the Commonwealth to the States. One-third of the immigrants to be assisted and settled with their families had no capital. Those assisted were to sail directly from Britain. Assistance was restricted to British subjects, both for nominees and nominators, under an Australian Cabinet decision of 6 July 1925. Reacting to criticism at increasing numbers of foreigners entering after the United States restrictions, the Commonwealth

The Agricultural Workers' Union deplores the need for rural families to emigrate after the First World War

issued a statement in January 1925, claiming that 'the present proportion of the British population represents 99% of the whole' and there was little possibility of this dropping very much.

Western Australia was by far the greatest beneficiary, being allocated £9 million out of £12 million. Land was available in the south, especially around Busselton and Pemberton, with expenditure needed on roads, railways and drainage. Western Australia was ruled by Labor for about half the years between 1920 and 1930, and by the Nationalists for the other half. Both agreed on the need to people the State through immigration and to put those immigrants on undeveloped land in the Southwest. Nationalist Party premier, Sir James Mitchell, was so keen on developing dairy farms that he earned the title 'MooCow Mitchell'. The group settlement scheme was the direct responsibility of Western Australia rather than of the Commonwealth.

The most detailed analysis of these settlement schemes is by Geoffrey Bolton in *A Fine Country to Starve In*. It is not a happy story. As Bolton puts it:

the prevailing belief was that every man should have a chance to be a farmer, whether he had lived all his life in the bush, or whether he was a newly arrived London clerk ... In choosing bush life, such a man showed himself more deserving than the parasites in the city, because he was attempting to add to the real productivity of Western Australia.[9]

The idea of Greater Britain, which had originated in the 1880s, had been revived credibly by the imperial sacrifices in the First World War. Many thousands of English immigrants were attracted to the group settlement schemes. Most regretted it in due course.

The basic problems were lack of agricultural experience among the immigrants, poor services, lack of decent housing, arduous clearance of forests, and a general indifference to the well-being of the settlers once they had arrived. Information available in England was very inaccurate. Trying to turn urban English immigrants into pioneers was grossly mistaken. When the schemes began to fail, official remonstrances and resentments turned against the immigrants. Yet conditions in the forests of the Southwest were quite different from anything likely to be experienced in England. In the end, the collapse of the world economy in 1929 finished things off. Western Australia had the highest unemployment in Australia, there were riots in Perth and, by referendum in 1933, two-thirds of the voters sought to secede from Australia altogether. No scheme of settling English immigrants on uncleared Australian land had much hope of success. But the Western Australian experience should have buried the idea altogether. It looked like rational planning, but it was ideologically driven by the idea that wealth came from the land and that rural life was superior to urban.

The failures of the 1920s did not completely discourage the idea of Empire settlement. Following an Empire Migration Development Conference in London in 1937, nomination of United Kingdom settlers was resumed in March 1938, again under the Empire Land Settlement Scheme. But the outbreak of war eighteen months later ended this plan and, coincidentally, the practice of trying to turn English urban workers into Australian farmers.

The network of voluntary societies

Voluntary and charitable societies had a role in encouraging and organising emigration from England from the early efforts of Caroline Chisholm in the 1850s well into the period of mass emigration after the Second World War. Their rationale was that life in the colonies was healthier and morally superior to slum life in England. Young people, in particular, needed to be 'rescued' by sending them out to pioneer the Empire. Most such societies had a Christian motivation and were supported and subsidised from the resources of the major churches. They were dominated, like many other charities, by established middle- and upper-class patrons, and preferred those they were organising to go to country areas where life was cleaner and healthier.

This corresponded well with the interests of Australian rural employers, who were trying to stop the drift from the land that set in by the depression of the 1890s and escalated after the First World War. Rural interests were well represented in colonial and State parliaments and the conservative parties. For much of the period between the depressions of the 1890s and 1930s they influenced the practice of taking town youths from England and trying to turn them into rural labourers and, eventually, farmers. These efforts were often well intentioned. But there were echoes of the Poor Law philosophy of a century before in trying to solve the social problems of England while rationalising emigration as a great service to those sent away. One effect in Australia was to sustain the belief that English immigrants were lucky to have come, were poorer than Australians, and should be grateful for charity.

Had Australia continued to prosper into the 1930s most immigrants would have adjusted and done well. But it did not and the impact of the 1929 depression was even more devastating than on urban England. When mass immigration began again in 1947 many of the concepts developed in the 1920s – charitable concerns, immigrant poverty, manual employment, direction to the bush – were applied to European Displaced Persons but no longer to the English. Rural group settlement was abandoned altogether, and only advocated by B. A. Santamaria's Catholic Rural Movement for immigrants from southern Europe.

The range of charitable emigration societies is illustrated in the report of the Empire Emigration Conference of October 1927, which lists twenty-six 'private overseas settlement agencies and friendly societies' and fifteen 'juvenile migration societies'. Nearly all had their headquarters in London and were Christian or patriotic. Exceptions included the Board of Guardians for the Relief of the Jewish Poor, the Jewish Colonization Society, the Kent Committee of Empire Settlement (Tunbridge Wells), the Liverpool Selfhelp Emigration Society and three Scottish and two Birmingham juvenile homes and orphanages. Some organisations were quite small, but the Salvation Army had emigration offices in Liverpool, Bedford, Southampton and Plymouth as well as in Scotland and Northern Ireland, and a regular shipping service from Liverpool to Australia. The New Settlers' League, funded by the Australian Commonwealth, was also represented.

The Church Emigration Society gave advice, passage assistance and introductions only to Church of England members.[10] Unlike many groups which had a strong interest in Scots, it was almost exclusively concerned with English emigrants. It was established in 1886 under the patronage of the Archbishop of Canterbury and a range of Anglican clergy, including all the Australian bishops. The numbers assisted to Australia were modest until the years before the First World War. From 1886 until 1915 the society sponsored 1675 to Australia. Like other charities it sent more to Canada.

Two other agencies concerned only with English emigration were the Central (Unemployed) Body for London and the Kent Colonizing Association. By agreement with the British Ministry of Labour, recruitment took place through the network of labour exchanges set up in 1909 for those seeking work. This close link between emigration and unemployment was more attractive to England than to Australia. It was inspired by precisely the same motivations as had encouraged pauper emigration a century before.

As part of the Land Settlement agreements, the Commonwealth set up the New Settlers' League of Australia in 1921. This was an advocacy and settlement organisation, funded initially by the Commonwealth and then jointly with the States. Subsidies were also paid to the Fairbridge Farm School, the YMCA and the Salvation Army. The New Settlers' League continued into the late 1950s, when most of its functions were assumed by the Good Neighbour Council. It co-operated closely with the Big Brother movement, founded by Sir Richard Linton in 1924, which until 1982 brought English teenage boys to Australia to work on farms. The Big Brother movement's journal in the 1920s, *The New Australian*, created the name subsequently appropriated for non-British immigrants after 1947. New Zealand-born Sir Richard Linton was a conservative politician and later agent-general for Victoria in London. His patriotic and Anglophile views fitted well with the dominant thinking between the wars, but became less fashionable by the 1970s.

The Millions Movement was closely associated with Big Brother. It continued into the 1950s as predominantly the voice of employers and enthusiasts for the Empire. Big Brother was extended privileges which were not finally ended until 1983, including virtually free office space at Australia House in London and a regular subsidy towards expenses. When it lost official sponsorship, Sir John Pagan was not only president of Big Brother but also of the New South Wales Liberal Party, which did not endear the movement to the incoming Hawke Labor government. In response to the loss of Commonwealth support, Big Brother launched a campaign accusing the new government of discriminating against British migrants – but to no avail.[11]

Child and youth migration

Children and youths had been emigrating to Australia since the nineteenth century under the auspices of a variety of charitable and religious organisations. Many arrived as convicts or as workhouse paupers. An Act to appoint guardians for child migrants was passed in Western Australia as early as 1839. More than 1000 boys from Parkhurst prison were transported between 1842 and 1853. Many of the early immigrants were under the age of twelve which, when free primary education was introduced, came to be a dividing age between childhood and adult life, although not strictly observed until the end of the century. The Dreadnought scheme was developed in New South Wales from 1911, using a training camp at Scheyville. Its origins were in money raised to fund a new battleship for the British Navy, some of which was redirected towards bringing out young British men.

Child migration had become institutionalised by the 1920s. Barnardo's had sent a group of Londoners to Western Australia in 1883, and in 1921 they sent boys to Sydney in co-operation with the Millions Movement. Girls followed in 1923. By 1926–27 assisted immigrants to New South Wales included 988 farm lads, 148 Barnardo boys and 43 Wembley Scholarship lads.[12] The migration of youths and children in the 1920s was organised through a number of voluntary agencies including the Catholic Church, the Salvation Army, Barnardo's and the Big Brother movement. The Salvation Army chartered the *Vedic* to make regular sailings from Liverpool between 1925 and 1929.

All these schemes aimed at taking youths from the cities and employing them on farms after some training either in England or Australia. This was furthered by the founding of Fairbridge Farms

An emigration recruiting poster, 1925

at Pinjarra (WA) in 1913 and at Molong (NSW) in 1938. Western Australia was the main beneficiary of child migration between the wars, with 1140 arriving at Pinjarra between 1921 and 1939. Pinjarra was supported by the British government under the *Empire Settlement Act* and by the government of Western Australia. Molong also received public funding, and took in 135 children before the war ended official immigration. The Fairbridge homes were non-denominational but had close links with the Anglican Church and most of their inmates were English. This explicitly imperialist scheme also operated in Canada and southern Africa. Unlike some of the orphanages maintained by the churches, Fairbridge farms seem to have been quite humane, though committed to turning their charges into rural workers rather than expanding their horizons.[13]

Conflict and variety

In conflicting attempts between 1880 and 1930 to define Australian national identity, English immigrants often played an ambivalent role. The conservative alternative to the nationalists and socialists continued to emphasise the importance of the British Empire and the sacrifices made at Gallipoli and in France as part of an imperial army. Prominent among those promulgating this view was Sir Ernest Scott, professor of history at Melbourne University from 1913 to 1936. Scott was born in Northampton of humble origins and came to Melbourne in 1892 aged twenty-five. While not a reactionary imperialist he saw Australian history as explicable only from a knowledge of English history. Many of the most enthusiastic imperialists and Anglophiles in the 1920s were Australian-born, like Charles Bean, who developed the Gallipoli legend in his official war history. Born in Bathurst of a British Indian family, Bean was educated at English public schools and Oxford.

A renewed interest in the Aboriginal people was largely due to the work of two English immigrants, Baldwin Spencer from Manchester and Radcliffe-Brown from Birmingham. Spencer came to Melbourne in 1887 at the age of twenty-seven, as foundation professor of biology. His lasting influence came from his work in the Northern Territory and his field work reports, *The Native Tribes of Central Australia* (1899) and *Native Tribes of the Northern Territory of Australia* (1914). While his work is now regarded as rather reactionary, he also advised the Northern Territory government on welfare provisions and laid the foundations for Australian anthropology. Alfred Radcliffe-Brown has a wider reputation, based on work undertaken in Western Australia from 1910 and in the South Pacific, and was foundation professor of anthropology at Sydney University from 1926 to 1931, when he left Australia. With his colleague Bronislaw Malinowski, he is regarded as the founder of the social anthropology approach which was dominant in British universities for many years.

Australia's mass immigration in the 1880s, between 1910 and 1914 and from 1920 to 1930 was predominantly from England, as immigration from Ireland declined rapidly after 1890, from Europe remained limited in the absence of public assistance, and from Asia was ended under White Australia. Public debate centred not so much on immigration (as White Australia was broadly accepted) as on national identity and loyalty. English immigrants were very varied and their attitudes and influence were not uniform.

Just to give two extreme examples: the insane bigamist and serial killer Frederick Deeming, from Ashby-de-la-Zouch, Leicestershire, who was 'better known than Ned Kelly' though hardly as popular when he was hanged in 1892; and shy and gentle May Gibbs, originator of the highly popular and very twee gumnut babies. Gibbs

was born in Sydenham (South London), came to Australia at the
age of four in 1879, but returned to England to study and practise
art. Her children's illustrated books were very successful and are
still regarded as a uniquely Australian art form. Australia was
attracting an extremely varied English input by Federation in 1901.
The *Immigration (Restriction) Act* of that year did nothing to affect
this, as it was directed against non-Europeans. English immigrants
were encouraged where others were discouraged.

There was considerable debate about the character of Australia
and its relationship with Britain and the British Empire between
1880 and 1930. Those who upheld that connection were encouraged
by a wave of patriotism following the First World War. This was
fanned by the Returned Services League (originally the Returned
Soldiers, Sailors and Airmen's Imperial League of Australia), which
was largely appropriated by political conservatives. On the other
side of politics were those who wanted to weaken the imperial
connection. This debate continued right through the Menzies era,
1949–66, then faded rapidly. The republican referendum of 1999
provoked a late, and perhaps final, revival.

Despite the arrival in the 1920s of many thousands of working-
class English immigrants who had little to thank England for, the
equation of 'Englishness' with conservatism was probably at its
strongest between the wars and immediately post-war. Australian
national identity developed on the basis of distinguishing the society
from England – both aristocratic, snobbish England and poverty-
stricken cloth-cap England. The idea that the English establishment
was trying to unload unwanted English workers was a significant
element in the debate – and not entirely mistaken.

Building the empire by relieving poverty

The Empire Settlement policy had three major objectives: to alleviate poverty and unemployment in Britain; to people the imperial
empty spaces with young and productive emigrants from Britain;
and to provide capital to expand the infrastructure of undeveloped
areas within the Empire. The major Australian beneficiary was
Western Australia, the last of the colonies to gain self-government
and the last of the States to build up its population from overseas. It
thus followed in the footsteps of Queensland in the 1880s, but with
less immediate success. The English-born population rose by only
17 500 between 1921 and 1933 and then declined, not reaching the

same level again until the mass migration of the early 1960s. Many had gone back to England during the depression while others had moved to the east. The failure of the group settlement schemes and the significant reliance on child and youth migration underline that the immigrants of the 1920s were among the least fortunate of those attracted and organised through public planning during the twentieth century.

Elsewhere, immigration from England was substantial in the 1920s, negligible in the 1930s and confined to evacuees and refugees from the Empire between 1940 and 1946. The overseas-born population reached its lowest proportion at the 1947 census. With deaths from previous generations, the ending of new arrivals and returns to England during the depression, English-born numbers were less in 1947 than in 1921 nationally, and in all States except Western Australia. Numbers rose in the two Territories, largely due to the expansion of Canberra, but were only 1500 in all. Western Australia had lost 13 300 since 1933, Queensland had fewer than in 1886 and Victoria less than in 1854, but New South Wales maintained its numbers rather better, reflecting the arrivals of the 1920s from London and the coalfields.[14]

The slogan 'populate or perish' applied not only to Australia as a whole but particularly to the gradually declining English core of the immigrant population. The absence of effective immigration since 1930, the shock of Japanese destruction of the British Empire in the East, and rigid adherence to the White Australia policy presented policy makers with a crisis before the war was over. Their first instinct was to look towards Britain once again, and the first post-war immigration programme of 1946 focused on British ex-servicemen and their families. By then, 80 per cent of the United Kingdom population lived in England. This was reflected in the British intake from the 1940s onwards, even though the Scots were still more willing to move.

The natural tendency to look back to previous decades meant resurrecting the idea of 'empire settlement'. But that had depended on the British belief that unemployment had become endemic and threatened social cohesion, that children and youths could be treated as farm fodder and that imperial loyalty would inspire the 'better types' – and especially ex-servicemen – to move within the Empire. Many things had changed since 1920, however. There was no longer a fear of social and industrial unrest, as discontents had expressed themselves through the election of a Labour government in 1945 with an exceptionally large majority. Unemployment had disappeared during the war and did not reappear significantly until the 1960s. Massive reconstruction kept the housing industry active, while the need to export coal and to build ships sustained the two most depressed industries of the 1930s. Farm labourers had declined in numbers but agricultural production had increased in the face of enemy threats to shipping lanes. Most importantly, the new Labour government abolished the remnants of the Poor Law, replacing it with a variety of pensions and the National Health Service. Skilled labour was in short supply and the government had no incentive to encourage it to leave.

This left only two major influences on the desire to emigrate: the housing shortage and the fear of a return to pre-war conditions. The British government continued to subsidise assisted passages for twenty-five years, but on a modest scale, leaving Australia with the main responsibility. There was sufficient residual imperialist sentiment in the Conservative Party, which regained government under Winston Churchill in 1951, for them to look benignly on the peopling of the Commonwealth (as many reluctantly now called the Empire). In Australia these sentiments were still strong, as suggested in 1954 by the triumphal tour of Queen Elizabeth, the first visit by a monarch in history. Most Australians could not contemplate Asian immigration. They had shown by their ambivalence towards European Jewish refugees in the late 1930s that they were unenthusiastic about foreigners of all types. In the majority view, it was the English or nothing. But it did not turn out that way.

6

BRINGING OUT BRITONS

Ours is a British country and we have a degree of kinship with the 'old country' which we do not have with other countries, no matter how highly we regard individuals from those other countries.

Athol Townley, Minister for Immigration, Citizenship Convention 1957

The first shiploads of post-war British immigrants began arriving late in 1946. They were mainly ex-servicemen and women or building tradesmen and their families.

There was full employment in Britain but rationing persisted in some items until 1952 and was imposed on bread, which had never been rationed during the war. Those from Scotland, Wales and the northern English depressed areas feared a return to pre-war unemployment, and the Labour Party had won its landslide victory in June 1945 by appealing to that fear and promising that unemployment would not return. A similar promise of 'homes fit for heroes', made by Prime Minister David Lloyd George after the First World War, had proved illusory. But it was mainly post-war exhaustion which drove the earliest arrivals. The *Orion* arrived in Sydney in July 1947 from Tilbury with 173 assisted migrants, including dentists, nurses, architects, farm workers, electricians and building tradesmen. A painter and decorator claimed that 'red tape and regulations are strangling British ability and will to work. It is heartbreaking to try to bring up a family in England now ... English people are pessimistic about conditions for the next five years'.[1]

Queensland was recruiting dentists, and one of them similarly argued that 'after seven years of rations [his sons] need sunshine and proper food'. An electrician from Cheshire said that 'ex-servicemen are fed up with battling on under wartime shortages and regulations into the indefinite future'. Eleven Yorkshire weavers, brought out by a Marrickville factory, claimed that 350 girls had answered the company's advertisement in a Leeds newspaper. Their motivation was reminiscent of earlier generations in stressing the absence of a basic wage and the tradition of piece-work in the Yorkshire mills. But this was not just history repeating itself. English assisted emigrants were more skilled than in the past, and their motivating concern with lifestyle rather than basic economic problems strengthened as Britain recovered from the wartime shortages. Numbers actually rose as English conditions got better in the 1960s. But so did numbers going back.

Between 1947 and 1976 the English-born population of Australia increased by nearly 500 000 – more than in any other thirty-year period before or since. Over 80 per cent of English arrivals had received assisted passages under a variety of schemes. By the 1960s these were no longer confined to those with particular skills. The only limitations were on those with disabilities or chronic illness (true since the 1830s), with criminal records or not predominantly 'European' in appearance, descent and culture. The last restriction was lifted in 1973, but by then English immigration was tapering off, never to recover. Although it was rarely stated, assisted passages were still designed to attract those with few resources. Qualifications were recognised under the *Tradesmen's Rights Regulation Act* of 1946, but this was not universally valid for State registration in some occupations and did not apply to non-British qualifications.

The United Kingdom immigrants arriving between 1947 and the 1980s were overwhelmingly urban, and 82 per cent were English. They were also disproportionately from London and the Southeast. While recruitment was country-wide, only the Northwest, including Manchester and Liverpool, was also 'over-represented'. In the first three years – 1946 to 1949 – about 48 000 left England for Australia, of whom 46 per cent were from London and the Southeast and 12 per cent from the Northwest. This pattern was maintained into the 1980s as assisted passages were discontinued and numbers dropped off. Between 1975 and 1981 those from the Southeast were 44 per cent of the total, half of them from London. All other regions were under-represented. The Northwest picked up again in 1982 and 1983 but dropped behind in 1984, the first year in which there were no longer any assisted passages. By then the English component of the British had risen to 88 per cent, and the Southeast English to 53 per cent of the English total. Numbers had dropped from 36 605 in 1982 to 11 192. All the industrial areas had dropped far behind, except for the West Midlands (Birmingham). Scotland, too, declined heavily. The abolition of assisted passages effectively ended emigration to Australia from industrial Britain and relocated it, in smaller numbers, to the prosperous London and Home Counties. Perhaps unwittingly, the peopling of Australia from the English working classes had drawn to a close after nearly two centuries.

Assisted passages

The assisted passage schemes were at their zenith in the 1960s. Migration offices were being maintained in London, Birmingham, Manchester, Bristol and Leeds as well as in Scotland and Northern Ireland. Every State, as well as processing personal and employer nominations in Australia, had an immigration office in London. The official 1968 pamphlet *Assisted Passages to Australia* shows a miserable family in raincoats contrasted with another 'down under' in open shirts enjoying the sunshine.[2] A picture inside shows 'a former RAF man and his family relaxing near Perth' in their bathing costumes. A suburban street with several cars, trees and front gardens completes the appeal. There is no suggestion that wages and conditions are better in Australia, but some indication of this was available in separate pamphlets, *Employment in Australia* and *Wages, Prices and Taxes in Australia*. Nor is there any rhetoric about Australia being a British country or part of the Commonwealth. The White Australia policy is not mentioned, although it still breathed faintly. Essentially the appeal is to lifestyle and opportunities for children.

Official information sought to reassure intending emigrants that they would be welcomed. Unfavourable comment had been appearing in the British press for some time from those who had returned. Some opinion polls showed that the favoured English destination was New Zealand. Emigrants also went to South Africa and Rhodesia (Zimbabwe), but only Canada consistently competed with Australia. The greatest attraction, apart from the sunshine, was that it cost very little to get there. A husband, wife and any number of children under nineteen could fly or sail for only £20. They were assured that conditions would be comparable to those for regular passengers. This was essentially true by the 1960s, after problems with ageing ships such as the *Moreton Bay* in the previous decade. Applicants had to be 'healthy and of good character' but preferably under fifty-one if married and forty-six if single. There was no age limit for those joining close relatives or for dependent parents joining their children. This was considerably more liberal than current

An advertising poster for the post-war assisted passage scheme

regulations, which make it very difficult for retired or elderly relatives to come to Australia.[3] Regulations began to be tightened under the Whitlam government (1972–75), when visas were required for all arrivals other than New Zealanders.

The cost of passages was increased to £75 per family in 1973, but this was not a serious disincentive. While there was no means test, assistance was designed, as always, for those who could not otherwise afford to come. On personally blocking an application by an English businessman in 1967, Minister Billy Snedden said that 'people of affluence are not entitled to an assisted passage'.[4] His officials claimed that local officers used their discretion because 'a rigid means test is hardly appropriate'. Assisted passages perpetuated the practice of bringing to Australia working-class immigrants with limited resources. By the late 1960s many were able to realise assets by selling their home, which had been rare in the past. Others arrived with quite negligible savings.

As in the past, emigrants could be sponsored by relatives, employers, charitable organisations or the Australian government.

The United Kingdom government still made a small contribution of about £150 000 annually, but withdrew this in 1972. Under the Commonwealth Nomination Scheme, accommodation was provided in hostels and an obligation to remain for two years was imposed. This was the most problematic policy area as there was much discontent with the hostels. Those who returned early were not often prosecuted but jeopardised their ability to come back to Australia. Passports were retained as a precaution. More fortunate were those with relatives ready to accommodate them. After 1957, Bring out a Briton committees throughout Australia became sponsors, as did churches. The most generous provision was for single men and women. and couples without children. They did not need sponsorship if under forty-six, able to find accommodation and having £25 each on arrival, equivalent to a week's wages for a skilled worker.

Most emigrants were not found employment, but this was not a problem as the level of unemployment rarely rose above 2 per cent between 1947 and 1974. Even better for many was employer nomination for groups of workers and their families based on job availability and accommodation. BHP was most active in this area, bringing many English steel workers to Newcastle and Wollongong and especially to Whyalla, which still has over 10 per cent British-born residents. The South Australian government provided housing in the new outer Adelaide suburb of Elizabeth, where motor manufacturers were also located.

The South Australian Housing Trust visited the English new towns in 1954 and 1956, having followed their planning principles closely in creating Elizabeth in 1954. By 1958 the trust had an office in London. This recruited for the Migrant House Purchase scheme which, to those who could raise £1000 as a deposit, gave an assisted passage and a house within one week of arriving at Elizabeth. Consequently, by 1966 two-thirds of the Elizabeth population was either British-born or had a British-born parent. A survey conducted in 1986 found that 29 per cent of voters in the electorate of Bonython (mainly Elizabeth) were English-born, with the largest number being from London and the Southeast, followed by the Northwest (Manchester, Liverpool and Lancashire) and the Midlands (Birmingham). Nearly all had arrived between 1950 and 1980.[5]

Many problems faced by immigrants in the past, in Australia or elsewhere, were avoided by careful planning. Applicants for assisted passages were interviewed at a convenient location to ensure that

*An English building
worker in Elizabeth
(SA) in 1958*

they knew what they were doing and were otherwise suitable. Immigrants were transferred to their new homes free of charge, were
eligible for most welfare services (other than the age pension) on
arrival, were entitled to vote after six months and to register as
Australian citizens after twelve. All this was the culmination of more
than a century of experience. These generous arrangements were
confined to British subjects normally resident in the United Kingdom,
and mark the high point of state planning to build the population
on an English base. The great majority of British immigrants in the
1960s were assisted and the great majority of those were English.
They were not, however, uniformly happy. About one-quarter left
Australia within a few years, some complaining loudly.

Bring out a Briton

The post-war decision to recruit European refugees and then Europeans in general was seen by many as threatening the 'traditional'
basis of immigrant intake. 'It is my hope that for every foreign
migrant there will be ten people from the United Kingdom' said

Arthur Calwell, Minister for Immigration, on 22 November 1946. This promise was regularly repeated and regularly unfulfilled. The Opposition leader, Dr Herbert Evatt, consistently attacked the Menzies government for not keeping a high British element in the migration programme. In 1958 he called vehemently for a level of 60 per cent to be maintained:

> We believe that we can pursue a systematic immigration program and yet bring a much higher proportion of our kinsmen from Britain. They have the first claims on us ... In Australia and New Zealand British stock was vitally important and should have preference.[6]

This was the official policy of the ALP at the time.

The Anglican archbishop of Sydney, Howard Mowll from Dover, had argued in the previous year that 'the Church of England must continue to press for a due proportion of English people in the total intake of migrants if Australia was to retain the traditional character of its national and religious life'. Later in 1957 he urged active Anglican organisation for the Bring out a Briton campaign as a way of 'strengthening our British and Protestant heritage'.[7]

English children arriving on the Fairsea *in 1956*

The Bring out a Briton programme of 1957 was designed to counter such fears. Intending migrants could be nominated by any individual or organisation as well as by the Commonwealth. This conformed with guidelines laid down by Harold Holt as Immigration Minister the previous year: 'As long as they fulfil our normal health and character requirements all available British migrants will be accepted by the Government subject only to the limitations imposed by the availability of shipping berths and accommodation'.[8] Two or three very large passenger liners left Tilbury or Southampton for Melbourne and Sydney every week, being gradually replaced by air travel in the mid-1960s. European shipping lines were drawn into this system, cutting a week off the normal five. No disabled applicants were accepted, leading to several publicised cases, nor those of 'non-European' origin.

This was the era of the 'ten pound tourists' who could get to Australia for that modest sum, bringing their children with them for nothing. The great majority were English. All six States had Agents-General offices in London whose windows, like those of Australia House at the end of the Strand, were full of enticing advertisements to come to Australia with government assistance. This concentration in London was probably a factor in the predominance of emigrants

Prospective emigrants view the Australia House window in The Strand in 1962

from London and the South. Otherwise, England was well covered, and most potential emigrants were within 100 miles of an immigration office. Several voluntary societies also nominated immigrants. In 1960 Apex sponsored 400 from Britain, who arrived on the *Orontes*.

There was a high rate of return by those without family or organisational sponsorship who were sent to hostels by the Commonwealth. One attempted solution was to grant priority under the 'Nest Egg' scheme to those who could bring £500 – then a reasonable deposit on a house, especially in smaller cities. Another was to allocate public housing, which until the late 1960s was available only for Australian or British citizens. South Australia still has the highest level of public housing of any State. From 1967 the Commonwealth started building custom-designed hostels. Eventually the main beneficiaries were not the English but refugees from Vietnam.

The hostels[9]

Since the days of Caroline Chisholm it had been recognised that arriving immigrants, many of them penniless, needed temporary accommodation until they got a job. The colonial authorities eventually built some in the capital cities. The largest, most spacious one, still extant, is Yungaba, built in Brisbane in 1883. The oldest, Francis Greenway's former convict barracks, still stands in Macquarie Street, Sydney. The churches and charities sponsoring young immigrants in the 1920s maintained their own homes. The size of postwar immigration necessitated hostels on a much greater scale, especially as there was an acute housing shortage. The challenge was met for the 171 000 Displaced Persons by using former army camps, of which the largest were at Bonegilla (Vic) and Bathurst (NSW). These were later used for southern Europeans, and Bonegilla did not close until 1971. In general, English immigrants were not placed in the same hostels as Europeans, and they complained if they were. As Labor Senator Jim Ormonde put it in 1967, 'The Nissen huts were introduced into Australia to house displaced persons ... These migrants are not refugees. They come from decent homes in England'.[10]

Nissen huts left over from the war were treated as temporary accommodation, and were still in use twenty years later. Most hostels were hidden away in swampy industrial outer suburbs, with views of the gas works, oil refineries or power stations. Some, such as Altona in Melbourne, close to an oil refinery and other noxious factories, would probably not satisfy current health regulations. The Commonwealth claimed that State regulations, including health inspection and fixed prices, could not apply to their properties. They are still maintaining immunity from State inspection for the detention centres used for asylum seekers today.

One of the worst hostels was at Finsbury (SA), formerly a camp for Displaced Persons. The first rent strike and organised protest was held there in November 1952 by the Federal British Migrants' Association. They were legally represented by Don Dunstan, future State premier. The strike spread rapidly to Melbourne, gaining support from the ALP and some unions. The minister for immigration, Harold Holt, alleged Communist influence:

> I would advise them that we have accumulating evidence of the manner in which the Communist party is trying to exploit them for its own purposes ... The hostels were intended to provide

A large family at the Finsbury (SA) Hostel in 1963

transit accommodation and the more enterprising of the
migrants have moved through them rapidly. Unfortunately the
proportion of less enterprising people is progressively increasing
and with it the volume of complaints.[11]

The protesters had, of course, been selected and nominated by the
Commonwealth government through Holt's department. Threatened
evictions were not carried out and an official enquiry was set up.
The use of old wool stores as hostels provoked more protests in
mid-1953, which were met by evictions in Sydney.

By 1965, after a series of well-publicised complaints, officials
were talking of improving matters. A new hostel was to be built
near Sydney airport, and another in the industrial Melbourne suburb
of Springvale. A Department of Labour spokesman told a parliamentary committee:

> Australia must improve its hostel accommodation standards
> if it wants to continue attracting and keeping migrants.
> Despite improvements these hostels still had the kind of
> accommodation provided to meet the emergency period
> immediately after the war.[12]

Twelve years before, Harold Holt, minister for immigration, had told
the 1953 Citizenship Convention that 'hostel life does not appear to
suit the British temperament and it is an experiment that we are not
anxious to expand or to continue indefinitely'.[13] Holt was responding to the first of several organised protests against hostel conditions
and charges. It took twenty years from the start of post-war immigration before there was major change. By then, hostel conditions
had become an important reason for leaving Australia.

Knowing all this, the Department of Labour, through its ancillary
Commonwealth Hostels Ltd, expanded the hostel system to take
in Commonwealth sponsored immigrants during the 1960s. This
led to a crisis in 1967, when about 13 000 English immigrants
were living in twenty-eight hostels. In January 1967, 400 residents
in Melbourne's Preston, Maribyrnong, Brooklyn and Altona hostels
organised a rent strike. At Broadmeadows the protest committee
criticised 'appalling conditions', while a Coventry immigrant, John
Dixon, said, 'all we want is to get out of here and have our own
home, but this tariff increase makes that hope still slimmer'. Every
hostel in Victoria was protesting. Labor Senator George Poyser lent

his support, attacking conditions as an 'utter disgrace to Australia … The Metropolitan Board would be horrified at the primitive drainage and sewerage'. A Cheshire production planner claimed that 'seventy per cent of the families in Brooklyn will end up going back home still broke'. Unlike other protests led by Scots, the Melbourne activists were predominantly English.[14]

The protracted Melbourne dispute, during which some rent strikers were charged, gained support from the Federal Opposition and the media. The *Age* editorialised that 'these recurrent complaints are a dismal commentary on establishments which give migrants their first glimpse of life in Australia'.[15] Eventually, Opposition leader Gough Whitlam raised the issue in parliament in mid-February. The Combined Hostel Tenants' Committee of Melbourne distributed information to the British media and petitioned Prime Minister Harold Wilson. Discontent spread to Sydney, and private discussions were held with the British High Commissioner. With the crisis escalating, the government announced plans to house future migrants in flats, to build new hostels and to close Brooklyn hostel in Melbourne. Complaints to England and the involvement of the Opposition meant the protest could not be ignored as others had been. More British migrants were leaving and fewer were arriving. The government was especially sensitive to the fact that 20 000 migrants had left Australia during 1966–67, the majority of them English.

Going home

Australia assisted immigration for 150 years because it wanted settlers who would remain, work and form families, and who were of the same race and culture as the majority. Distance from England ensured that most did remain. Cost-conscious politicians and public servants were never anxious to spend money unless it served the aim of building the labour force and the population in general. The belief that life in Australia was much better than in England became part of the national myth. It was usually true, and acknowledged to be so by many English immigrants. As shipping gave way to air and incomes rose it became more practical to make return trips. As entry to England was always open to those born there (and still is) increasingly rigorous passport and visa systems were not an obstacle. By the 1960s, at the height of English immigration, it was no longer imperative to stay in Australia for life. Assisted passage money was repayable for anyone returning before two years, on the assumption that this was a minimum period to overcome initial doubts and problems. Otherwise, Australia did not impose any restriction on those wishing to leave nor England on those wishing to return.

Many had returned over the years, including convicts, free settlers and former assisted immigrants. Those who succeeded often went back in triumph to their native place, as did Joseph Cook to Newcastle-under-Lyme in 1918. However, from the 1920s onwards a new and less welcome phenomenon emerged: the returning English who criticised Australia and left because it did not match their expectations. Australians not only developed the 'cultural cringe' of worrying about what England thought of them, but also the 'chip on the shoulder' of being unduly sensitive to criticism from emigrants who did not find it a perfect paradise. As more and more English poured into Australia between 1950 and 1970 a small but vocal minority of them scratched at this sore point. Over several generations Australians had absorbed the idea that people came because it was better than their own country and stayed for the same reason. Consequently, they should be grateful, especially if they had been paid to come on a scale unknown to any other immigrant society.

There is evidence from the correspondence pages of the newspapers in the 1960s that the English were puzzled by this attitude and that Australians were outraged by the ingratitude of those who complained and eventually left. As about one in five English immigrants did leave within a few years, this was not just a minor irritant. Essentially the English thought they were doing a favour by coming – and Australian propaganda had encouraged this view – whereas Australians thought they were doing immigrants a favour by letting them in. It was especially hurtful that the English remained the favoured settlers both in public opinion and in public policy. Yet they seemed to complain the most, simply because they could speak English and use the media. As a Ukrainian delegate said to the 1965 Citizenship Convention:

> if the European migrants could speak English as well as the
> English migrants, they probably would grumble more than
> the English people. By the time they learn sufficient English
> to be understood they are already satisfied in this country and
> do not grumble'.[16]

A case which attracted much attention, although very untypical, was that of the Robsons from Thornaby, North Yorkshire. Apart from being the birthplace of Captain Cook's mother, this crumbling industrial slum had little to recommend it. Yet it was home to Kenneth and Elizabeth Robson, who wanted to go back there on the day they arrived by air in Sydney in 1965. Finding a large cockroach at Villawood hostel, they fled into hiding and demanded to be repatriated. It emerged that they had decided their voyage was mistaken about half way across the world.[17] This bizarre episode allowed critics full rein to talk about the unsuitability of some assisted immigrants. Unfortunately it also obscured the more concrete reasons for departure which were increasingly preoccupying the research capacity of the immigration department and led to the Dovey report two years later.[18] These reasons included Australian attitudes towards immigrants, hostel conditions, failure to accept qualifications, lack of suitable employment, poor school standards and the general complaint of misleading information from Australia House. The Robson story died when they decided to remain after all.[19]

Publicised incidents, like the Robsons' complaints and the hostel strikes, raise the question of whether more care might have been taken in selection and information. In his interviews with intending and returning immigrants, Appleyard notes their lack of preparedness and basic knowledge.[20] Mrs Robson had never been further from Thornaby than Stockton, less than a mile across the Tees. Some of those interviewed thought that Australia was as far away as France or Spain. These amazing responses suggest that some of those selected and assisted were every bit as insular and uninformed as the agricultural labourers of more than a century before.

Accusations of incorrect information were regularly laid against Australia House and its local officers. These were refuted by presenting printed material with accurate facts about prices, wages and housing. But to people who left school at fourteen or had their education disturbed by the war, these statistics might have conveyed very little. Nor was there any record of what enthusiastic recruiting officers might have told applicants. The official objective was to bring out as many British migrants as possible, and staff in overseas migration posts understood that.

Some of the hostels were undoubtedly run in a scandalous and authoritarian way. Most were quite unsuited for families from modern English housing built after 1918. Those in Melbourne were so unattractive that in 1958 Prime Minister Harold Macmillan was shown Nunawading, the only one considered likely to impress. This did not stop some of the English inmates from complaining to him.[21] At Wacol (Brisbane) in 1967 protesters went even further by writing to the Queen.[22] It is hardly surprising that return rates were much higher for Commonwealth nominees living in hostels than for those looked after by sponsors and relatives under the Bring out a Briton schemes. A lot of money was wasted by short-sighted savings, and a lot of goodwill was dissipated. Many people were strongly encouraged to come to Australia who should have remained in England and waited for the return of good times, which eventually came for most of those left behind. No doubt those who did stay in Australia settled down as satisfied and comfortable Australians in the full employment economy which did not end until the early 1970s.

Settling and assimilating

Despite the high return rate and considerable disillusionment, most English immigrants remained in Australia. They dispersed throughout the country, with concentrations in Western and South Australia. Virtually none of the eight hundred local authority areas have no English immigrants, which is not true for any other overseas-born group. This means that the English have had to integrate into a very wide variety of situations. As Australia is an exceptionally urbanised and metropolitan society, this has most frequently meant settling into the suburb of a major city. This was, perhaps, the easiest transition for them to make, as most would previously have lived in the suburbs of a large city or urban area.

However, many English had lived in smaller towns, and might have found Australia's metropolitan centres rather spread out and inconvenient, especially as public transport was less developed in Australia than in England in the 1950s and 1960s. Many new suburbs were poorly serviced, as it was common to build houses before sewerage and made streets, which is not the case in England. The density of population, and hence of activity, was usually much less than in England, producing an eerie quiet during the day which those left at home might have found disconcerting. The similar English phenomenon of 'new town blues' produced sometimes serious psychological reactions among those moving from London to planned towns such as Milton Keynes. Considerable efforts were made by the South Australian Housing Trust to avoid this by adopting the English concept of neighbourhoods in Elizabeth, and in 1962 they claimed to have solved the problem.[23] Elizabeth did develop an active community life. But it was 30 kilometres from central Adelaide, almost as far as the English new towns around London were from the city. Many English settlers found themselves far from the city centres and the beaches because of the need to buy cheaper housing in the first few years.

Where they lived

English immigrants added more than 400 000 to the population between 1954 and 1981. Of these new settlers 86 000 were in South Australia and almost 90 000 in Western Australia. Nearly half chose the two States which had made the most consistent efforts to attract them. By 2001 there were more than 130 000 English in the Perth region. Unlike South Australia, the Western Australian government had not attracted immigrants with public housing, which was often allocated to Aborigines. Less than 5 per cent of housing in Perth was publicly owned by 2001. In Adelaide nearly 9 per cent was publicly owned, and public rental levels in Elizabeth were still at 44 per cent in 1991.

There was a contrast between English concentration in Elizabeth and Noarlunga in South Australia, and the wide spread of the Perth English along the south coast to Rockingham and inland towards Gosnells and Armadale. These were areas with high levels of home ownership and low levels of public housing. The English experience in Perth and Adelaide has been rather different. In Perth they live in property-owning suburbia; in Adelaide in districts with high unemployment and considerable poverty. This is no doubt a factor in Perth remaining attractive to English immigrants into the present, whereas Adelaide has ceased to be. The Perth suburbs favoured by the English had some unemployment and few of their inhabitants had qualifications beyond trade certificates. But they did not face the serious social problems experienced in Elizabeth as industries closed down.

In Sydney and Melbourne the English population is more socially varied, with many middle-class immigrants rather than the predominantly working class assisted immigrants elsewhere. There is a strong English concentration around Sydney Harbour in affluent areas like Mosman and Manly. In Melbourne there was substantial English settlement in the developing suburbs along the Maroondah Highway, such as Ringwood and Croydon, and into the Dandenong Hills. Public housing was insignificant in these districts. It seems to have played little role in English settlement in either city, except in North Frankston on the southern fringes of Melbourne. The more usual pattern was for immigrants to take private rented housing in Bondi or St Kilda before buying a house, or to live in hostels. The Nunawading hostel in Melbourne may have influenced settlement along the Maroondah Highway. But most other hostels used for the English were in industrial areas in which only small numbers settled – mainly in Melbourne, in Sunshine and Broadmeadows. In Sydney there was some English working-class settlement in the newly developed outer district of Campbelltown. In neither city have large numbers of the English settled near industry or in areas favoured by non-British immigrants.

Brisbane did not attract as many English immigrants as the other cities. It was not heavily industrialised and public housing was confined to two areas – Inala near the former Wacol migrant hostel, which catered for Aborigines and Indochinese as well as the English, and Logan City, with rather more English settlement. Logan City, like Elizabeth, Campbelltown and Frankston, suffered from high unemployment and social disadvantage by the 1990s. After Brisbane, the second largest number of English living in Queensland are on the Gold Coast. Most arrived in Australia before 1981 and many have retired there.

In Melbourne, Sydney and Brisbane English settlers were so widely spread that it is hard to generalise about them. On the whole they favoured the newer suburbs, except for the well-off around Sydney Harbour. This usually meant new houses, often of better quality than those they left behind in England. However, public services were not as good and there were many problems of social isolation. Women missed their mothers and were more often anxious to return than were men. Most of the English settled comfortably into Australian suburban life – the area in which 'Neighbours' is filmed was favoured by many English families from the 1960s. It was certainly better than Coronation Street.

Concentrated English settlement in the rest of Australia mainly reflects recruitment to particular industries. The most obvious example is at Whyalla (SA). This isolated steel and shipbuilding town was developed by BHP to take advantage of the iron ore deposits at Iron Knob. As BHP ran down its manufacturing activities and workforce, Whyalla began to decline and to lose population. By the 1980s its empty houses were being used to house Vietnamese refugees. The Latrobe Valley in Victoria was hailed as the

The Cockney Pearly King and Queen visiting Australia in 1963

'Australian Ruhr' because of its large brown coal reserves tied into power generation. But this promise was not fulfilled. Towns like Morwell became quite disadvantaged, though not as drastically as neighbouring Yallourn, which was demolished altogether. Modern technology drastically reduced the labour needs of electricity generation, and brown coal extraction and other industries did not take their place.

The Kwinana oil refinery in Western Australia and its associated new town, Medina, also attracted many English workers, and was the scene of protests and discontent in 1964, prompting an enquiry by the State immigration minister.[24] Many were planning to return to Britain from what some called 'the Pommies' graveyard'. This provoked a heated correspondence in the *West Australian*, with one correspondent, a Londoner, deploring 'the gross misrepresentation and false statements about our fine town and State by a few dissatisfied migrants who have failed to adjust themselves'.[25] Most objections of those who eventually sailed away on the *Aurelia* were against social isolation, inadequate housing, lack of apprenticeships and failure to recognise British qualifications. Medina was

35 kilometres from central Perth, isolating it like Elizabeth as a raw new 'Pommy ghetto'.

The experience of Elizabeth has been detailed by Mark Peel in his excellent study *Good Times, Hard Times*. As he says, 'most in the early days were happy to be out of England, happy to be in a place where you had a decent house, a yard, an indoor toilet and a proper bathroom, a bit of space and a bit of privacy'.[26] Elizabeth was held up as a model new town and living conditions were at least as good as in the contemporary English new towns, though the physical environment is arid and hot and the beach promised to English immigrants by Australia House is a long way away. Held up as a model, 'by the 1980s Elizabeth was more of an embarrassment than a showplace'. Its two major employers, the Weapons Research Establishment and General Motors-Holden's, were still there, but half the factories built in the 1960s had closed twenty years later and unemployment had reached 17 per cent. Elizabeth was indisputably a working-class town where half the population had left school by fifteen and 55 per cent of men were in manual, craft, process and labouring jobs. As Peel argues, 'its disadvantage is new, the poverty of postwar suburbs savaged by restructuring and recession ... a lot of people find themselves left behind, their factories closed and their jobs gone'.[27] That the same could be said for many of the English manufacturing areas from which Elizabeth drew much of its population was hardly consoling.

Who were they?

As in the past, most English immigrants were chosen from wage-paid workers and their families. Most remained at that social level. While there was no specific means test for assistance, it was assumed that most could not afford the fare. In 1986, when immigration had tapered off, there were 880 891 English-born in Australia, of whom 78 per cent were in the working ages of fifteen to sixty-five. Of these, half had left school by fifteen. Three-quarters were wage or salary workers and almost 9 per cent were unemployed. Less than 3 per cent were employers. Occupationally, only 10 per cent were managers and administrators and 21 per cent professionals or para-professionals. This middle class was marginally below the level for the Australian-born. Immigration selection had determined that most would be in the manual or clerical working classes. More than one-third, mostly men, were tradespersons, plant and machine operators or labourers and related workers. Less than one-third, mainly women, were clerks, sales and personal services.

Nineteenth-century English immigrants had a large component of labourers and domestic servants. In the twentieth century the major occupations were factory workers and white collar wage earners. Many of the English women were in 'community services', which were usually poorly paid and often unskilled. Essentially this population was 'English' in every sense of the word. It did not differ markedly from the Australian-born but was certainly a wage-earning, moderately educated working-class population. Despite including many who had been settled in Australia for years, there was little evidence of social mobility into the middle classes.

The British made up 76 per cent of English-speaking immigrants in 1986 and almost 90 per cent in South Australia. Well over half had arrived between 1957 and 1981. Apart from trade certificates they had few qualifications. Two-thirds of the English-speakers claimed English ancestry but only 36 per cent were Anglicans. Of those born in England, 48 per cent were Anglicans and only 10 per cent Catholics. Those who had 'no religion' or did not state a religion numbered 27 per cent, while 98 per cent spoke only English. There was only a small representation of the Islamic, Hindu or Buddhist religions, or of languages such as Hindi, Urdu, Tamil or Bengali, despite substantial settlement from those backgrounds in England.

The White Australia policy operated throughout the period of mass English immigration and was applied to anyone not of predominantly European appearance. As late as 1970 Australia denied assistance to a West Indian-born electronics engineer, St Clair Allen, his French wife and their children, solely on racial grounds. This provoked the British Race Relations Board to charge that the implementation of Australia's immigration policy might be illegal under the *Race Relations Act* of 1968. This created a storm of protest from the Australian high commissioner, the minister for immigration, the Opposition spokesman Fred Daly and the Victorian minister for immigration, Vance Dickie, all claiming the absolute right of Australia to determine who could come. Dickie stated quite unashamedly while in London that 'ninety-nine per cent of all people of dark blood, even if only one member of their family has dark blood, who apply for the assisted passage, will be refused'. A spokesman for the Commonwealth minister, Phillip Lynch, said, 'it is a matter of general policy to grant assisted passages only to persons of European descent'.[28]

This controversy was especially acute as Britain was introducing immigration regulations restricting the settlement rights of many Commonwealth citizens, including Australians. Within two years, with the election of the Whitlam government, racial discrimination in selection was ended. Daly had already been removed from his 'shadow' role by Whitlam in 1971. St Clair Allen and his family emigrated in 1971 with financial support from wellwishers, which could have been achieved without bad publicity had the bureaucracy been more flexible.

Exceptional migrants

While most of the English melted into the skilled working and white collar classes, a few achieved prominence. The best known was Alan Bond from west London.[29] In 1950 he came to Australia with his mother as a twelve-year-old assisted immigrant on the *Himalaya*, and later became an apprentice signwriter. By 1982 his Bond Corporation was the biggest company in Western Australia, based mainly on property speculation. His yacht *Australia II* won the America's Cup in 1983, a unique victory for a non-American contestant, greeted with public joy by Prime Minister Bob Hawke. His bankruptcy in 1992 began a downward spiral, leading eventually to his imprisonment for fraud between 1996 and 2000. Bond

Londoner Alan Bond, at the height of his business career

was a local hero in Western Australia during the boom years of the 1980s, which later saw the collapse of several other major businesses. For several years he was the best known of all the post-war assisted immigrants from England, and one of the richest men in Australia.

From a different background, David Hill was sent out to Fairbridge Farm at Molong (NSW) from Barnardo's in the 1950s. He went on to head the New South Wales railways and the Australian Broadcasting Corporation from 1986 to 1995. He then became chairman of the Australian Soccer Federation. Peter Shergold from Crawley, Sussex came to Australia at the age of twenty-five in 1971 after education in England and the United States. He was the innovative first director of the Office of Multicultural Affairs in 1987, going on to a highly successful public service career. This culminated in 2003 when he became secretary of the Department of Prime Minister and Cabinet, conventionally regarded as heading the Commonwealth Public Service.

Barbara Porritt was fêted as the millionth post-war migrant when she arrived in 1955 from Redcar, Yorkshire with her husband.

Painter from Liverpool and Mayor of Brighton (SA) in 1963

The millionth migrant, Barbara Porritt, and Immigration Minister Hubert Opperman in Geelong in 1955

A series of celebrations and meetings with public figures were arranged to mark this event, planned months before by the Immigration Department and Australia House in London. This also emphasised the continuing importance of English immigration. The family was originally located in the brown coal complex of the Latrobe Valley in Victoria, where English and other immigrants made up much of the workforce. They eventually moved to Canberra. In almost fifty years another four million immigrants have come to Australia. But none were as effusively welcomed as the Porritts.

The end of an era

Its steady decline makes it difficult to say when the era of mass English immigration drew to a close. From 1 January 1975 British immigrants and visitors were required to have visas to enter. All English non-citizens now needed a visa to enter, including a re-entry permit, however long they had lived in Australia and whether they retained the vote or not. Only New Zealanders retained the right of almost free entry, which the English had enjoyed for 150 years. New Zealanders did not get assisted passages either, but their proximity made this irrelevant. One decisive date was 1983, when the Fraser government ended assisted passages for all except refugees. Another was the withdrawal of citizenship rights for the unnaturalised in the following year, and the distinction made between 'citizens' and 'non-citizens' for immigration purposes. The latter included British subjects from outside Australia who had not become naturalised. The British media mistakenly attacked these changes as meaning that British citizenship would need to be renounced by immigrants, which was quite untrue but may have discouraged some. A further discouragement arose from the fear of conscription for the Vietnam War.

The ending of assisted passages and distinct privileges for the British (essentially the English) by 1983 had several rationales. Such special treatment was incompatible with the principle of 'universal' intake following the end of the White Australia policy in 1973 and the official adoption of multiculturalism between 1973 and 1978. As Whitlam said when visas for the British were introduced, 'preferential treatment ... is wholly inconsistent with the Australian Government's non-discriminatory immigration policy'.[30]

Migrant protests and discontents had produced several bad-tempered exchanges in the Australian and British media, with damaging consequences for the high immigration targets, which ranged between 100 000 and 170 000 for all but one year between 1955 and 1974. One enterprising English businessman, Simon Goodman, made a living from organising travel for returning migrants.[31] Questions were asked in the British parliament and the Scottish National Party called for a boycott of the immigration programme.

Three areas of concern were the hostel strikes, the White Australia policy and claims that the 'English disease' of industrial militancy had been introduced by immigrant shop stewards. Ian Sinclair, a Country Party minister in the Fraser government, claimed in August 1977 that 'British-born unionists had imported industrial disruption into Australia' and thus 'imported the British disease into the Australian trade union movement'.[32] This upset everybody, from English union officials to Bob Hawke of the ACTU. Unusually the British High Commission, presumably in consultation with the British Labour government, issued an official refutation, showing that industrial disputes took far more working days in Australia than in Britain.[33]

Australian responses to criticism were both defensive and offensive, and relied to some extent on satisfied immigrants who refuted the criticisms of their compatriots. At the 1965 Citizenship Convention a delegate from the Queensland Good Neighbour Council claimed that 'British migrants we are getting now are prima donnas. They come from a welfare state and expect the most'.[34] The contradictory view, that the English were both spoiled and impoverished, echoed old resentments. Bad publicity in England created by the hostel strikes and by returning migrants probably damaged the programme and certainly concerned officials and ministers. Return rates to Britain remained high, and about 12 000 English migrants went home in 1970.

Equally important was the realisation that the days of importing labour for manufacturing industry were over. Much attention has been paid to the role of southern European and later Asian immigrants as 'factory fodder'. Many undoubtedly were, as previously in the United States and Europe. But it has been forgotten that the English immigrants also filled this role, if at a higher level of skill and language proficiency. Most English assisted immigrants in the 1950s and 1960s had left school by sixteen, had trade qualifications or none at all, and went into industrial, manual or basic clerical employment. Because so many English immigrants came as university teachers, doctors or other professionals, the predominantly working-class character of the mass intakes tends to be discounted. But, as in the previous 150 years, assistance was being given to those who would add to the Australian working class. In the technologically changing economy of the 1980s they were no longer needed. Fear of an 'Asian' invasion also declined as Indonesia stabilised and China was recognised.

English assisted immigration finally disappeared because the arguments for maintaining it were no longer persuasive. It had also become accepted that the large wastage and dissatisfaction caused by unselective immigration from England were a drain on budgets which could better be spent on settlement and services for non-English-speaking immigrants. The secretary of the immigration department in 1981/82, John Menadue, makes it clear in his memoirs that dismantling White Australia also meant limiting English access to places so easily available in the recent past.[35]

7

THE ENGLISH
INHERITANCE

The crimson thread of kinship runs through us all.

Sir Henry Parkes, born in Warwickshire, speaking
at the Federation conference, Melbourne, 1890

In English-speaking Australia it is always hard to determine which influences came from English ideas, practices and institutions, which came with English immigrants and which were passed on by them to their descendants. It is also very difficult to disentangle what is undeniably 'English' from other influences from the English-speaking world, which now includes the United States to a far greater degree than was true a century ago. Because of the regional and class divisions in England it is also hard to establish what constituted a common English culture, even within a limited period of time. This becomes more difficult over time as England changed from a rural to an urban and then a metropolitan society and from semi-literacy to universal education.

The English 'fragment'

Forty years ago an attempt to determine the founding influences on Australia and other settler societies was made by two American academics, Louis Hartz and Richard Rosecrance. Their basic proposition was that the social and political character of 'new societies' was largely determined in the early years of settlement by the fragment of 'old societies' represented by the first settlers. With others they studied the United States, Canada, South Africa, Latin America and Australia. Rosecrance argued for Australia that:

> the cultural fragment of British society implanted in Australian soil
> in the first half of the nineteenth century has retained a remarkable

distinctiveness and fixity. Its lineaments are still discernible and its influence largely undiminished. Australian society today has umbilical connections with the egalitarianism of the gold fields, the struggles of the exclusives and emancipists, and even the sullen resentments of the early convict settlements ... The Australian social adult of today is prefigured in the social embryo of yesteryear'.[1]

This is a very interesting justification for studying the years between 1788 and 1860 and relating them to the 1960s and early 1970s when Rosecrance was writing. In the intervening century, as he acknowledges, Australia had moved from being an immigrant society to one dominated by the locally born majority. That majority was still overwhelmingly of British origin, with an English-descended majority within it. The impact of post-war migration was yet to be seen and is still remarkably mild on political institutions and majority myths and attitudes. Australia was on the verge of declaring itself multicultural and of ending the White Australia policy. Many changes since the early 1970s must also be taken into account in assessing Rosecrance's analysis. The strength of the Labor Party and the trade unions, and state regulation of the economy and industrial and social relations, have been subject to steady erosion since then. Australia is not yet the free market society of American ideologues, but it has moved strongly in that direction since 1974. The influence of the 'fragment' seems to have waned.

It is obviously hard to generalise about a society which has increased its population 1.5 times since the early 1970s and no longer draws its immigrants mainly from the United Kingdom. Looking further back, the 'fragment' theory is more attractive and worthy of serious consideration. But like most attempts to generalise about changing societies it needs greater depth and complexity. It assumes a common 'British' implant, whereas there are good reasons for supposing that the large Irish component was different from the English and Scots in many ways, including its religion, its lower literacy and skills and its political attitudes towards Britain and the Empire. Nearly all the Irish Catholics came to Australia either as convicts or assisted immigrants, which was not true for the English or the Scots. It concentrates on the convicts and the gold rush immigrants, whereas overall the assisted immigrants with their large English majority were more important numerically through to the 1880s.

This theory sees the 'fragment' as predominantly from the lower classes, but overlooks that these classes were also the great majority in the United Kingdom. The substantial unassisted migration, which was also largely English, sustained the skilled artisan and non-manual classes. Indeed it could be argued that this stratum was more liberal and radical and had more political influence than the less well educated. What was different in Australia was the absence of a well-organised and stratified social hierarchy, sanctioned by history and the church and enforced by the Poor Law and the local magistrates. The large number of English convicts and immigrants who had lived under and often resented that system often felt liberated in Australia.

Rosecrance quotes, but disagrees with, the English Victorian statesman Charles Dilke that Australian society was English 'with the upper class left out'.[2] Essentially Dilke was right. Attempts to create a 'bunyip aristocracy' in the 1850s were simply laughed at. This did not stop generations of prominent Australians from accepting British honours, including a few peerages and a plethora of knighthoods. But it did not make them an upper class. Political and bureaucratic power rested on mass democracy from the 1850s, which was not the case in England. Social prestige depended on wealth, often recently acquired, despite the veneer of social distinction surrounding the rural squatters and the Government Houses. The professions were open to competitive talent, although this was modified by middle-class recruitment from the United Kingdom. To some extent English social gradations were reproduced by the distinction between assisted immigrants and those who paid their way. But social fluidity was marked, especially in colonies such as Queensland and Western Australia which did not have major population inflows until the second century of settlement. Periodic economic crises also made the position of the rich more insecure than it had become in England by the end of the Victorian era.

The middle classes as an element in political formation are somewhat dismissed by Rosecrance, with the exception of radicals coming during the 1850s gold rush in the aftermath of English Chartism. These were certainly of great importance in gaining the franchise and thus cementing parliamentary systems with popular support. But Rosecrance regards this influx as something of an exception to his generalisation about convicts and immigrants. While there was certainly a planned and deliberate transfer of manual workers from England to Australia, there was also a large flow of qualified middle-class people, farmer settlers and established or potential entrepreneurs. Those who came without state assistance often equalled the numbers paid to come, especially in Victoria from the 1860s onwards. Scots were prominent among these free settlers but the English normally formed a higher proportion of the unassisted. The great majority of Irish Catholics, in contrast, came with public funding. Rosecrance's use of the blanket term 'British' obscures these differences, and the varied immigration experiences of the six colonies. Some, like Queensland and New South Wales, attracted large numbers through public assistance. Others, such as Victoria, South Australia and Tasmania, did not. Western Australia was a different story altogether.

Rosecrance sees the character of the settlers as an explanation for two features of Australian development – reliance on the state and the absence of a conservative political force. This overlooks the quite different potential for private enterprise in the provision of utilities such as railways, water and eventually electricity in Australia and Britain. This was almost wholly determined by the very sparse distribution of the Australian population and the absence of developments such as roads, drainage and forest clearance which had been created in England over centuries. State provision of welfare and education was not as developed as in England, where the Poor Law (for all its faults) and the Church of England schools were well established at the parochial level. Nor was local government well developed in general by English standards. The colonies were divided into counties and parishes, but these were simply legal devices for describing the location of landed property and had no governing function. Many had almost no population. Local government emerged mainly between the ending of the gold rushes and the depression of the 1890s. Outside the major cities it was very limited, as suggested by the Western Australian practice of calling such authorities 'road boards'.

In many societies it is undoubtedly true that practices, beliefs and attitudes are handed down through the generations despite intervening political, economic or social influences. Witness to this persistence can be found in the revival of religion in post-Communist Russia or of democracy in post-fascist Italy, Germany or Spain. Certainly, many features of Australian society, including of course its language, can be traced to influences brought out from England over the past two centuries. But there are also corrosive effects from the passage of time as well as contradictory and conflicting traditions. The English were numerically dominant during the first century and their descendants during the second. But they were not alone. Many ideas came through the English language, including those from the United States which influenced the Commonwealth constitution of 1901. England was the site of conflicting political ideologies – liberalism and conservatism, statism and *laissez faire*, socialism and private enterprise. Unlike most of Europe there was little ethnic or religious conflict in England. But there was plenty in Ireland, and this influenced at least one-quarter of the Australian population.

The messages were always mixed. Rosecrance is comparing Australia with the United States and seeing a strong state, growing welfare provision and a powerful labour movement as distinguishing features which he attributes to the recruitment of convicts and immigrants from the working classes. An effective labour movement might also be traced to the mass English immigration of the 1880s, which he largely ignores. It is necessary to ask how lasting these influences have proved to be in the forty years since he wrote. The Labor vote has been sustained – as in England – but at a lower level than in the past. It now relies to a significant extent on non-British immigrants in the major cities. The trade union movement, in contrast, has declined quite rapidly to a level now below that in the United Kingdom and not much above that in the United States. The industrial arbitration system, which gave the unions a central role, has been progressively dismantled. Australia is still more socially egalitarian than England (but not than Canada or the United States) but is economically more unequal than in the recent past. Ideologies decrying the welfare state and social engineering have replaced the consensual social democracy of the 1940s and 1950s. While it is true that some of this has also happened in England, it does raise the question of how lasting and universal has been the inheritance which Rosecrance traces to early English influences.

The political English

Democracy was not widely accepted in English political circles during the founding decades of the Australian colonies. It was associated with the French Revolution of 1789, which Britain had resisted by warfare in alliance with the major European despotisms. Its American version was similarly rejected. Yet democratic ideas were not new in England. During the Civil War (1642–51) the

Levellers had demanded manhood suffrage, only to be suppressed by the Cromwellian Protectorate. A limited degree of democracy existed in some Nonconformist sects such as the Quakers, Congregationalists and Presbyterians, and this tradition was continued by the Methodists. All chose their clergymen and preachers, rather than having them imposed by the state or the landed gentry as in the Church of England. All forms of Australian democracy until the 1890s were defined as excluding women, as was true in England until 1918, except for some local government boards. While women got the Australian vote well before it was granted in Britain, they were slower to secure elected office. Hard though it may be to swallow, Margaret Thatcher became the thoroughly English prime minister in 1979, an achievement still well out of sight in Australia.

The origins of colonial democracy lie in the demands of the local pastoral, mercantile and land-holding classes for a say in administration. This was initially granted by adding to the councils advising the governor. 'Unofficial' members joined the 'officials' nominated by the governor. This model continued to be used throughout the Empire for over a century but was soon replaced by elected assemblies in Australia. Elections on a property franchise followed in New South Wales by 1843. The franchise in England had been extended by the *Reform Bill* of 1832 to male owners of property of a certain value. This limitation gave an impetus to movements calling for manhood suffrage, most notably the Chartists. Such demands, periodically raised in England at least since 1800, reflected the growing wealth and population of the Northern and Midland industrial cities. Parliamentary representation remained heavily biased towards the rural south. Voting was by open declaration until 1872, fifteen years after the secret ballot was introduced in Australia. The House of Lords was, of course, limited to hereditary male peers.

The Chartist movement was the first mass working-class political movement in the world.[3] It had more influence in Australia than in Britain because it met with less resistance. The numbers coming to Victoria in the 1850s simply swamped the conservative establishment around the governor and the Legislative Council. While the Irish element at the Eureka Stockade in 1854 was predominant, Chartist leaders usually came from England. Chartism had been a mass movement in the northern industrial regions, where it overlapped with trade unionism. The six Chartist demands were: manhood suffrage, annual parliaments, 'one vote one value', abolition of property qualifications, secret ballot and payment of members of parliament. None of these has been fully achieved either in Australia or anywhere else. But most were instituted in Australia well before the United Kingdom, including manhood suffrage, the secret ballot and payment of parliamentarians.

English immigrants naturally took an important role in Australian politics before Federation. Between 1856 and 1901 there were 213 English members of both houses of the New South Wales parliament, of whom half came from London and the Home Counties. There were 240 in the Victorian parliament between 1859 and 1900, of whom 54 were from London and the Home Counties. In New South Wales the English outnumbered the Scots and Irish combined, but the opposite was the case in Victoria. Between 1855 and 1900 only two Victorian premiers were born in Australia, compared with seven in England, five of them from London and the Home Counties. In New South Wales during the same forty-five years three premiers were Australian-born and five English, three of them from London and the Home Counties. In Tasmania five were locally born and eight English. As elsewhere, five were from London and the Home Counties. The story was similar in Queensland between 1859 and Federation. Four were Australian-born, including Andrew Dawson who in 1899 briefly headed the first Labor government in the world. Four were English, of whom only John Douglas was born in London.

In South Australia, where Irish and Scottish influence was weak, five were Australian born, including Vaiben Solomon, the only Jewish premier in Australian history. Ten were English and two Cornish. London was less well represented than elsewhere but Thomas Playford, a Baptist from Bethnal Green, held the office for two periods between 1887 and 1892 and was the grandfather of Sir Thomas Playford, Australia's longest serving premier from 1938 to 1965. Western Australia did not become self-governing until 1890 and its first English premier was Sir Cornthwaite Rason from Somerset in 1905.

English-born politicians were very common before Federation, normally calling themselves 'Liberals'. Apart from those from London and the Home Counties, however, they were relatively under-represented compared with the Scots. Of those who became colonial premiers Sir Henry Parkes was by far the most important.

Robert Lowe was an unusual Australian politician in coming from a leading Anglican family in Nottinghamshire and attending a public school and Oxford university.[4] During his stay in Sydney

Robert Lowe, Viscount Sherbrooke (1811–92), served in the
New South Wales parliament and United Kingdom government

from 1842 to 1850 he served in the Legislative Council, agitated against the revival of transportation and for responsible government and state school education. Lowe was a strange combination of liberal and conservative, being strongly opposed to manhood suffrage. On his return to England he served in Gladstone's 1868 Liberal government as chancellor of the exchequer, ending his political career in the House of Lords as Viscount Sherbrooke. Apart from his radicalism, which eventually offended Queen Victoria, Lowe was an unusual Australian politician because of his establishment origins and his service in the colonial and imperial parliaments.

More typical were Sir Henry Parkes and Sir John Robertson, premiers of New South Wales. Parkes emigrated from Warwickshire in 1839 under the bounty system.[5] Coming from a farming family and being employed as a general labourer and later apprentice in Birmingham and London, he was well qualified within the limits

Sir Henry Parkes (1815–96), Premier of New South Wales and 'Father of Federation'

set by assisted passage schemes. Parkes was more radical than Lowe, whom he supported politically, having a Chartist background. He, too, opposed the renewal of transportation, but, unlike Lowe, also supported manhood suffrage. Parkes was an unsuccessful businessman but a highly effective journalist and politician. He dominated New South Wales politics from his first period as premier in 1877. From 1890 until his death in 1896 he was identified with the movement for a federation of the Australian colonies.

Sir John Robertson came from an East London family which was well connected, unlike the humble origins of Sir Henry Parkes. Robertson established himself in the bush and is best remembered for his land reforms between 1859 and 1861, and 1882 and 1884. These greatly expanded the ability of small selectors to secure freehold land and to develop agriculture and rural settlement. All three politicians, like many others from England, located themselves at the liberal end of the political spectrum. Few Australian politicians were prepared to call themselves conservatives. Unlike Britain and Canada, no major Australian party has ever been prepared to adopt

*Sir John Robertson
(1816–91),
London-born
Premier of
New South Wales*

that description. Opposition to the convict system, electoral appeals to the common people, and reliance on parliament as the means of reform characterised the political legacy brought from England rather than the conservative and aristocratic inheritance or the more radical objectives of socialists.

In the national parliament elected in 1901, 10 of the 36 Senators and 14 of the 75 Representatives had been born in England or Cornwall. Eleven Senators and 23 Representatives adhered to the Church of England and there was a good representation of Methodists, Congregationalists and Baptists.[6] Within the political parties, nine Protectionists, eleven Free Traders and three from the Labor Party (including the Welshman Billy Hughes) had been born in England, and there was a large Scottish contingent in all parties. Indeed Scots on the conservative side and Irish on the Labor side were to be more prominent in Australian politics than those of English birth or descent.

Many English politicians in the colonial period began their careers as liberals or radicals. Once formed in 1891, the leagues which went to make up the Australian Labor Party also drew in many English. In the first Labor caucus of 35 elected in New South Wales in 1891, nineteen were English, with nine from the North and four from the Midlands. Of the 13 Labor members elected in Queensland in 1893, seven were English, with three from the North. They were not always happy with their radical commitments. One major test was the imposition of the solidarity pledge in 1894, which bound New South Wales Labor MPs to vote together in a caucus. Joseph Cook left on this issue. The second major test was over conscription in 1916. Those Englishmen who left or were expelled from the ALP included W. A. Holman, premier of New South Wales; W. H. Carpenter, MLA for Fremantle; W. O. Archibald, MHR for Hindmarsh; Senator G. Henderson of Western Australia; Senator W. Senior of South Australia; and W. Webster, MHR for Gwydir. Of the 22 Commonwealth parliamentarians leaving the party over this issue in 1916, five were English and one Cornish. All were Protestants. This defection marks the turning point in Labor history which replaced English and Scottish domination by Irish-descended Catholics.

The frequency with which colonial governments were replaced meant that the number of premiers in the nineteenth century was greater than in the twentieth. A major contrast between the number of English heads of government before and after Federation was compounded by the near-monopoly of the Australian-born over politics after 1920. Almost alone, W. A. Holman, premier of New South Wales between 1913 and 1920,[7] was elected for the ALP before being expelled because of his support for conscription. Nearly all other English-born premiers were from the conservative side of politics, to which Holman eventually moved. Sir John See from Huntingdon was premier of New South Wales from 1901 to 1904; Sir John Bowser from London of Victoria in 1917; Sir Hal Colebatch from Herefordshire of Western Australia in 1919; J. W. Evans from Liverpool of Tasmania from 1904 to 1909; and Frank Wilson of Sunderland of Western Australia from 1910 to 1917. More recently, Sir Charles Court established a stronghold in Western Australia between 1974 and 1982. He was born in Brighton but came to Australia as a baby. Apart from him, the only English-born premier in recent years has been Mike Rann of South Australia, born in Eltham (London) and elected in 2002 for the ALP.

The parliamentary representation of the English in recent years has been relatively equitable, after a long period of decline following 1920. This reflects the entry into politics of many who arrived in the boom years between 1950 and 1970, and is marked in areas of considerable English settlement. In Western Australia in 1990 there were 10 English-born MLAs, of whom nine were from the ALP. With 11 per cent of parliamentarians in a State where 11 per cent of the population were born in England, this was unusually equitable. The Commonwealth parliament in 1997 contained 12 English-born members, or 5.4 per cent when the English proportion nationwide was just under 5 per cent. As in Western Australia the majority represented the ALP. This was equally true of the ethnic background of politicians a century before. New arrivals from England in the 1880s were elected for Labor around 1900, just as new arrivals from the 1950s and 1960s were elected in the 1990s. One difference was that Labor politicians in the 1990s were more likely to come from southern England rather than, as in the 1890s, to be manual workers from the industrial North.

The English input into politics created certain traditions which are now viewed as classically Australian. One was the insistence on elected parliaments based on manhood and then universal suffrage. This aspiration of the Chartists and radicals was frustrated in England by consistent opposition from the House of Lords, the relative conservatism of many politicians and the strength of the Conservative Party. Most English politicians in Australia were drawn from the commercial and professional classes in the nineteenth century and more broadly in the twentieth. There was no aristocratic house, even though many Legislative Councils obstructed electoral reform. This was normally done in the interests of a political party, with Labor in Queensland and Western Australia defending rural bias because it was of benefit to them. The Chartist tradition, domesticated by Liberal politicians, was much more effective in Australia.

Australia introduced manhood suffrage in South Australia in 1856, Victoria in 1857 and New South Wales in 1858.[8] At the same time it invented the secret ballot, for years thereafter known as the 'Australian ballot' and not achieved in Britain until 1872. The most important influence on developing the ballot was Londoner Henry Chapman in Victoria in 1856. Chapman had worked with John Stuart Mill in London and was a philosophical radical rather than a Chartist. Nevertheless, while in the Victorian parliament in the 1850s he worked consistently towards several Chartist objectives. Equal electorates took much longer, but were finally achieved for most jurisdictions by the 1980s and are more rigorously distributed at the national level than in Britain.

Women achieved the vote in South Australia in 1894 and nationally at the 1903 Federal election. This predated the suffragette movement in Britain and its brutal and sometimes insane suppression by the Liberal government of Asquith. The vote was extended to eighteen year olds in 1973, several years before Britain. Payment for MPs was introduced in Victoria in 1870 and South Australia in 1885 and has always applied for the Commonwealth. This reform was not introduced into the British parliament until 1911 and has never been extended to members of the House of Lords, who merely enjoy a sitting fee.

Radicals and dissenters

Most English politicians in Australia have been in the liberal or social-democratic parliamentary tradition. While many have become more conservative with age, they have remained within the limits set by the parliamentary system and have accepted a private enterprise system tempered by reform and protection of the less privileged, and the traditions created by the Liberal and Labour parties in England. But other English political traditions, including socialism and republicanism, have influenced local political life, often quite strongly. Between the 1880s and 1914 Australia was remarkable for its radical innovations and for the attention these attracted overseas, especially in England. Many radical and socialist organisations were formed on English lines, including Fabian societies and the Social Democratic Federation. During the period surrounding Federation and the formation of the Australian Labor Party, several English immigrants had an important role in criticising conventional politics.

Henrietta Dugdale emigrated from London to Melbourne in 1852, and lived through the radical days of the 1890s and the First World War. Victoria was the last State to grant women's suffrage, for which she had been organising since 1869. Her utopian novel *A Few Hours in a Far Off Age* (1883) was in the mainstream feminist tradition of believing that many social evils would be cured when women got the vote. She was not a socialist but an outspoken critic of the monarchy, Christianity, alcohol and male domination.

The best known English radical was William Lane from Bristol. Influenced by socialist ideas in North America, Lane arrived in 1885 as an admirer of the American utopian Edward Bellamy. Lane became a labour journalist and organiser, but his utopianism led him into the ill-fated New Australia exodus to Paraguay in 1893.[9] After

*William Lane
(1861–1917),
Utopian socialist
and labour journalist*

its inevitable failure, he left for New Zealand in 1899. Although Lane is often held up as a labour hero, it should be said that he was a rabid racist and embraced imperialism during the First World War with great enthusiasm. His novel *The Workingman's Paradise* (1892) remains the best memorial of his radical days.

Two leaders of the 1889 London dockers' strike, H. H. Champion and Tom Mann, came to Australia in the 1890s. Champion remained permanently. They were quite different in their origins. Champion was from a British India family, went to a public school and joined the army as an officer. Mann started work in a Warwickshire coal mine at the age of ten and then became an engineer.[10] Like Champion he became part of the radical labour movement of the 1880s in London, and the two worked closely in the new Marxist party, the Social Democratic Federation. Champion came to Australia in 1890 and again in 1894 and Mann in

1902. Mann was active in the Victorian Socialist Party, along with Champion, and during the Broken Hill strike of 1909. He returned to England in 1910, ending his days as president of the Communist Party. Champion eventually drifted away from the labour movement and died a Christian Scientist.

Other socialists included Adela Pankhurst from the Manchester suffragette family, Frank Anstey from London, Henry Boote from Liverpool and Dora Montefiore from London. Of these, Frank Anstey had the most consistent influence and the hardest upbringing as an orphan who stowed away on a ship to Australia in 1878 at the age of eleven. He became active in the Seamen's Union and then as a labour organiser in Victoria. Anstey was an ALP representative in the Victorian and Commonwealth parliaments between 1902 and 1934 and strong opponent of conscription in 1916. Boote was a skilled compositor and one of the most influential labour journalists during the rise of the movement, working for Australian Workers' Union newspapers in Queensland and Sydney between 1894 and 1943.

Frank Anstey (1865–1940), radical Labor politician

Montefiore, from a middle-class South London family, came to Australia in 1874. She became active in the socialist wing of the women's suffrage movement, later joining both the Social Democratic Federation and the British Socialist Party. Like her friend Adela Pankhurst she became a Communist, representing the small Australian party internationally although ending her life in England. Adela Pankhurst came to Australia in 1914, after a dispute with her formidable mother Emmeline and sister Christabel.[11] She was a foundation member of the Communist Party with her husband, Tom Walsh, but became increasingly conservative. She was associated with the Australia First movement, and in consequence was interned for pro-Japanese sympathies in 1942.

These radical, sometimes eccentric, English immigrants were at the core of attempts to move on from the liberal reformism which had become the dominant ideology of Australian politics by the end of the colonial era. That their inheritance was limited was partly due to the strength of liberal traditions, but also to the wave of conservative patriotism that swept the country after the First World War. The isolation of radicals in the small and sectarian Communist Party, the suspicion that many Protestants had of Catholic influence on the Labor Party, and that party's relative disunity and lack of

Adela Pankhurst Walsh (1885–1961), suffragette, communist and conservative

competence, shifted the emphasis away from radical reformism towards much more cautious and limited goals. Working-class and trade unionist immigrants continued to come until 1930, but radical dissenters mostly remained in England. Australia was known for the strength of its unions and parliamentary Labor parties, but not for its socialist ideology.

English politicians were associated with many important changes which made Australia a fairly progressive society by the end of the nineteenth century in terms of working conditions and wages, the franchise, elementary education and economic progress. The depression of the 1890s notwithstanding, end of the century Australia was often described as 'the richest country in the world' (a term, incidentally, applied to England in the 1860s). There is a case to be argued that Australia became more conservative after 1914 under the influence of the locally born. In national politics the conservative parties were in office for forty-six of the sixty years from 1914 to 1974. Labor was much stronger in the States and especially in Queensland, Western Australia and Tasmania. But its record, except for the first few years in Queensland and during the Lang regime in the 1920s, was also quite conservative. Racial policy towards immigrants and Aborigines was distinctly reactionary. Over this period the number of English politicians faded to negligible proportions.

There had, of course, always been a conservative strand to politics, most markedly in the Victorian Legislative Council. The White Australia policy was actively pursued by the Labor Party both before and after its control by English leaders. English enthusiasm for the Empire led Australia into the First World War. What happened then and afterwards was the appropriation of English symbols such as the monarchy, the Union Jack and the Empire by Australian conservatives. Socialist attacks on capitalism necessarily meant attacks on British capitalism, as that was the dominant foreign economic interest. This was most acute in 1932 when the English-born governor of New South Wales, Sir Philip Game, dismissed the government of Jack Lang for defaulting on foreign, mainly British, debt.

Decline in English influences on Australian reformism and radicalism, and appropriation of the symbols of Empire by conservatives continued under the Liberal Party leadership of Sir Robert Menzies, which lasted until 1966. Most English politicians during this period were conservatives. Both the Liberal Party and its Country Party ally proclaimed their loyalty to the monarchy and the Empire. Conservative rule in Britain lasted from 1951 to 1964 and in Australia from 1949 to 1972. In both countries living standards rose and full employment was maintained. Enthusiasm for socialism and communism waned within the labour movements. The English political tradition seemed to be a conservative one, and a high proportion of English immigrants during this economic boom were attracted to the Liberal Party.[12]

The English at play

Australia is renowned for its sporting achievements. Most of the sports are of English origin, major exceptions being Australian Rules football, surfing and basketball. Cricket was already well established in England by 1788 but organised football codes did not develop until the 1860s. There is no more English game than cricket and Australians took to it from the earliest years of settlement when it was mainly played by army officers. The typically English division between gentlemen (who were unpaid) and players (who were paid) was not followed in Australia beyond the earliest years. Cricket is historically a southern English game, originating in Hampshire and Surrey, and many of Australia's early settlers came from cricketing counties. It was also taken up with enthusiasm by the reformed English public schools and their Australian imitators. As it involves standing out in a field for three to five days it is suited to the Australian climate on mild days. But as it has flourished from Yorkshire to Sri Lanka this may not be why Australians have been so good at it since they won the 'ashes' at the Oval in 1882. Of all sports, cricket has given Australians the opportunity to face and defeat the 'mother land' ever since. These regular mock battles, extending over a century, reached their most serious crisis in 1932. The English team adopted the bodyline tactic of aiming at the batsman rather than the wicket – not a very gentlemanly approach! This was the worst year of the depression, which many Australians blamed on English finance capital.

The next most popular and distinctive English sport is soccer. It has spread throughout the world but been resisted in all the main English-speaking societies. Different codes of football dominate sport in the United States, Canada, Australia and New Zealand. In contrast to the other three, Australia has two major commercial codes – Australian Rules and Rugby League. Until recently, under the influence of mass media companies, these were confined within State borders, with overlaps in the two Territories. These borders do

The 'bodyline bowler' Harold Larwood settled in Australia in 1954 with his family

not correspond to English settlement patterns over the two centuries and cannot be explained by them. The two States most popular with the English for the past fifty years – Western and South Australia – are dedicated to Australian Rules, as is Tasmania, which is historically the 'most English' in terms of its early settlers. Queensland, where the mass migration of the 1880s was predominantly English, is dedicated to Rugby League, as is New South Wales, where Irish influence has been at least as strong as in Victoria. The only area where there was a close correspondence between English settlement and support for soccer in the past is the Newcastle and Hunter area, colonised by English and Scottish miners more than a century ago.

As with cricket, so with Rugby football, the English made a distinction between 'gentlemen' and 'players'. Rugby, like cricket, had a strong base in the public schools and was played by amateurs. Its only popular following in England was in the Southwest. In the North it had become a working-class game, especially on the Yorkshire and Lancashire coalfields, with soccer dominating the large cities such as Liverpool, Manchester, Newcastle and Leeds. This led to the division between Rugby League, played for money, and Rugby Union, played by the public schools, which was cemented at Huddersfield (Yorkshire) in 1895. Sydney quickly followed, and by 1907 Rugby League began its replacement of Rugby Union as the most popular code.

This was very late in the day compared with the domination of Australian Rules in Victoria, which goes back to 1864. That soccer, which was organised in Australia only in the 1880s, could not compete with Australian Rules is explained by the lapse in time. That it could not compete with Rugby League is more surprising, explicable partly by the establishment of Rugby Union in Sydney by 1874.

Mass attendance at soccer games was well established in England by the 1880s. Yet the large influxes of English immigrants from then until 1914 did not displace the popularity of Australian Rules, Rugby Union or Rugby League – and likewise with mass immigration in the 1920s and from 1950 to 1980. Soccer continued as a minor code, passing largely into the hands of European immigrants from the 1950s. Popular, media and commercial investment in the two local codes was by then a powerful obstacle to changing loyalties. In contrast to England, where few public schools would touch soccer and Eton had its own game, their Australian equivalents were happy to encourage the codes played and watched by the mass of Australians.

The post-war history of Australian soccer has not been a happy one. Many good players have been sold off to European clubs as an important source of income. Periodic campaigns, most recently by English immigrant David Hill, head of Soccer Australia, have tried to 'Australianise' the game by forcing the adoption of such typically local names as 'knights', 'bears', 'wolves' attached to place names. This has antagonised many ethnic loyalists without increasing the number of 'Australians' in the crowds. Only one television channel, SBS, takes soccer seriously, although the ABC, which is often oriented towards Britain, is starting to do so. Among Englishmen important in Australian soccer is Terry Venables, who has coached both the England team and the Australian Socceroos.

With a potential English audience of hundreds of thousands it is surprising that post-war immigration did not create specifically English soccer clubs. Clubs were formed in places like Elizabeth and Perth, but were not long-lived. One recent exception is Perth Glory.[13] Its large following is mainly English and Scottish, and it is not surprising that it does so well in the city with the largest proportion of English settlers. But the team is multicultural, and appeals to Western Australian patriotism as much as the equally successful Australian Rules West Coast Eagles.

The tragedy of English food

The English who landed at Sydney Cove from the First and Second Fleets almost starved to death. They suffered, like the first English settlers at Jamestown, Virginia, in 1607 from an inability to extract familiar food from unfamiliar surroundings. The dry Sydney soil would not grow grains and vegetables. There were no local markets from which to buy food and no understanding of the skills of hunting and gathering which had sustained the Aboriginal population for thousands of years. There were no obviously edible animals and it was some time before pioneers were willing to eat kangaroo or cockatoo. Moreover, many were urban and were used to prepared food which someone else had grown. The salt meat and maggoty biscuits on which they had lived for months at sea were all exhausted and were not, in any case, either appetising or very nourishing. The first priority was to explore towards the Hawkesbury and Emu Plains, where they could develop an agriculture to replicate that left behind.

For over a century Australians pursued an English diet and sought suitable land to produce it. Eventually, agricultural industries became closely tied to the larger British export market, which reinforced the types of product available. This gradually reduced choice to foods preferred in working-class England. They turned their back on the indigenous alternative or on menus chosen by the European or Asian minorities among them. The Germans and Chinese had large enough communities to sustain their own preferences. But English food won out – a tragedy which Australians endured because they knew little else. English food was limited and unimaginative – 'good ingredients cooked to death'.

In England itself, mass-produced food was already becoming dominant in an urban and industrialised society. Laws to protect food standards were introduced in the 1890s to guard against the worst excesses of food adulteration. The diet of the rural poor was even worse. What thrilled many immigrants was the opportunity to eat meat every day – long since impossible at home. English immigrants in the 1950s appreciated liberation from wartime rationing to a generous diet of essentially English food. It was still assumed that half-starved Displaced Persons would be happy with mutton on most days. All their memoirs tend to dispel this myth.

The diet of rural England seems to have deteriorated along with living standards during the foundation years of Australia. It was mainly bread and cheese, with an onion for relish and a slice of bacon for a special treat. Tea became the favoured drink at home, but labourers were usually supplied with beer or cider in the fields. Many supplemented this from cottage gardens, but growing vegetables in them was forbidden in some villages. Unlike the Irish the English did not starve to death. But, much to the indignation of Cobbett on his rural rides in the 1830s, they were starting to turn to the potato as a staple.[14] In the North the dark rye loaf was probably more nutritious than the southern white bread, which Southern labourers saw as one of their few remaining privileges – to the annoyance of those investigating the Poor Law in the 1830s. The standard labourer's lunch in the fields was resurrected by the English catering trade in the 1950s as the 'ploughman's lunch', but with exotic additions such as Stilton cheese, ham, tomatoes and watercress.

Food was far more plentiful in Australia, and letters home almost invariably refer to this. A typical comment came in 1850 from Mary Ann Davey from Adelaide to her sister: 'There is no fear of starving here, here is very great waste of beef and mutton, it being cheap and everybody wants the best joints ... Bread and meat and tea and sugar is cheap; fruit is very dear except grapes'.[15] But food was constrained within the limited imagination of English cuisine, and the 'meat and two veg' formula was still dominant into the 1950s. Urban and suburban Australians ate similar meals to their English counterparts at home, including the traditional Christmas feast of a roast bird and vegetables followed by plum pudding. All-male banquets followed the menus and rituals of the business and political classes at home.

In the bush a simpler menu was adopted, very similar to that in the American West. Its basic ingredients were steak and eggs, damper and billy tea. Pubs and cafés in the bush and working-class suburbs followed suit, as did the growing number of Greek cafés in country towns. These were substantial meals which single men could throw together. Aborigines were given limited rations, mainly of flour and sugar, which laid the foundations for obesity and diabetes. Missing from most of these diets were fruit and vegetables, which were often supplied by Chinese market gardeners from the 1860s onwards.

English working-class food was not completely limited. One mystery is what happened to the many attempts at variety in mid-Victorian urban society. Some of these survived in Australia – most triumphantly, fish and chips. This staple of the urban working class was allegedly invented in Oldham (Lancashire) in 1861 to provide for the families of women working in the cotton mills. Another version credits London Jews with developing the traditional fried fish of eastern Europe. But this seems improbable as fish and chips was, and remains, a Northern speciality. The only fish and chip cafés ever mentioned in the prestigious *Good Food Guide* are all in Yorkshire. Despite the inroads of Chinese and Indian takeaways, fish and chips survives well in the North but has faded fast in London and the Home Counties. 'Chips with everything' now includes Asian food, and many chip shops are Chinese-run. In Australia, fish and chips has declined but, like seafood in general, owes much of its survival to immigrants from Greece. It remains popular in English enclaves such as Elizabeth.

Other delicacies have disappeared or were never adopted in Australia. A major exception is the oyster. Both London and Melbourne in the mid-Victorian period had many oyster bars catering mainly for working-class men. But the Thames oyster, centred on Whitstable in Kent, was over farmed and became affordable only to the rich. Australia was far more fortunate. This delicacy was largely monopolised by immigrants from the Greek islands. Unless in batter, Australians were once reluctant to consume sea food at all. Other Thames-based titbits disappeared from Australia, including jellied eels, whelks, cockles, mussels and winkles, though some have reappeared as tastes became more complicated in recent years. The same is true of animal products like tripe, pigs' trotters, black pudding, kidneys, liver, brains, tongues and hearts, and vegetables such as turnips and mushy peas. With plentiful mutton, lamb and beef, Australians felt themselves lucky not to have to resort to 'offal', and gave it to the cat. Despite occasional marketing campaigns they felt the same about kangaroo meat, which they gave to the dog. The myth that the meat pie was invented in Australia is hard to credit. The traditional Adelaide pie floater seems to have come straight from Cockney London to that most English of Australian cities. Pea soup and pease pudding were two working-class favourites with only limited appeal in Australia.

Part of the English culinary inheritance was to separate eating from drinking – tea in the home, beer in the pub and wine not at all. This was not true for the banquets of the rich, where imported wine was always available. But England ceased to be a wine producing country in the fifth century, when the Romans were replaced by the beer-drinking Saxons and the climate became colder. Spirits – mainly gin – were losing their appeal in England by 1800 and rum was soon replaced in Australia by beer, which had to be locally produced in case it spoiled. The proliferation of small beer houses in English villages was seen as one cause of the 1830s unrest. In both countries large commercial breweries developed to serve a growing market, although small local breweries remained important. They are still free from monopolies in some English towns, but no longer in Australia. Quite recently, English and Australian breweries have entered each other's markets, with Foster's highly successful in England as tastes move away from the traditional flat beer towards lagers.

England had many commercial breweries by the 1830s and beer houses flourished until licensed in 1869. Large hop fields were cultivated from Kent to Worcestershire to supply the basic ingredient. Crop failures on the Kent hopfields were an important factor encouraging emigration in the 1830s. William Shoobridge from Tenterden arrived in Hobart in 1822 and cultivated hops brought from Kent from 1825. From nearby Cranbrook (Kent), John Tooth founded the Kent brewery in Parramatta Road, Sydney, in 1835, where it remained for over a century.

Individual English brewers and winemakers have greatly influenced local tastes. Australia is one of the few countries in which English winemakers have been influential. Frank Potts from Hampshire arrived in South Australia on the *Buffalo* in 1836 and set up the Bleasdale vineyard at Langhorne Creek in 1850, which remains in the family. Thomas Hardy from Honiton, Devon planted his first grapes near Adelaide in 1853 and went on to develop the wine industry of McLaren Vale. Christopher Penfold from Steyning, Sussex arrived in South Australia in 1844 and developed his vineyards at Magill, near Adelaide. John Reynell from Ilfracombe, Devon arrived in South Australia in 1838 and planted his first vines at Reynella in 1841. Early English settlers in Western Australia also planted vines, although most development there was due to later arrivals from the Dalmatian coast of Croatia. European influence was important in the Barossa, in Victoria and, later, in the Riverina. Nevertheless, English pioneers were ready to try their hand at anything which made money, and their names are preserved on a wide variety of labels. Australia's largest wine market is England.

How English is Australia?

Discussion of food and drink raises the question, 'How English is Australia – or indeed England?', given that catering innovation is so strongly marked by immigrant influences. In general, Australia has liberated itself from English influences without completely abandoning the heritage. Food and drink industries have found other markets – beef in Japan, sheepmeat and flour in the Middle East, wine in England and Scandinavia and beer in East Asia. Tourists come from Japan, China and Korea, and Australians travel to Thailand, Singapore, Bali and Hong Kong. Thousands of Asian students are at Australian universities, some of which have opened overseas campuses as well. The world has opened up for Australia, and England is only one focus of attention, if still important. But England itself is now part of Europe – if with some reluctance. London is easily as cosmopolitan as Sydney. Holidaying English have deserted Blackpool and Southend for the Costa Brava and the Greek islands. Many Australians no longer have British ancestors and many English no longer have English ancestors.

Having asked 'How English is Australia?' we might also ask 'How English is England?' Both societies are changing rapidly, becoming more multicultural and globalised and moving away from 'traditional' forms and attitudes. Both still retain nostalgia for a rural past. But both are among the most urbanised societies in the world. One-quarter of Australians now live within 100 kilometres of Sydney. This is even more concentrated than the proportion of the English living within a similar distance of London. England is still more urbanised in the sense that few are more than an hour's drive from a very large city. Yet urban lifestyles based on fully serviced suburban homes, electronic information and entertainment, access to shopping malls, cinemas, universities, large hospitals and public transport are equally accessible in both countries. Considerable expense and effort is mobilised in both to ensure that these facilities are accessible to people in remote areas – although 'remoteness' means something rather different.

The greatest difference lies in the density of population, namely 2.5 people per square kilometre in Australia and 368 in England. Even Victoria, the most densely populated state, has only as many people outside Melbourne as were recorded in England's Domesday Book in 1087, on twice the territory. There are few parts of England, other than the northern Pennines and some moors and woodlands such as Dartmoor or the New Forest, where a house is not in view. These are central facts which must never be lost sight of. The English live in a congested environment in a climate which encourages indoor life. Australians do not. Banjo Paterson romanticised the difference in his 'Old Australian Ways':

> The narrow ways of English folk,
> Are not for such as we,
> They bear the long-accustomed yoke,
> Of staid conservancy:
> But all our roads are new and strange,
> And through our blood there runs
> The vagabonding love of change
> That drove us westward of the range
> And westward of the suns.

Paterson was writing a century ago about Australians, many of whom had English parents or had recently come from England. Yet there is still something to be said for his contrast. The British *Clean Air Act* of 1956 ended smoke pollution. The rapid rise in car ownership at the same time produced massive traffic congestion. Both changes took place during a decade when English emigration was at its height. While many English immigrants welcomed the space and sunshine of Australia, rather than wanting to escape close living they have usually preferred the city. Their sense of distance and remoteness is often more restricted than that of most other Australians. But their preference for the coastal cities is shared with the majority. Between 1996 and 2001 families on farms declined by 22 per cent.

Australians and English have flocked to the coast and the outer suburbs with equal enthusiasm. Indeed, part of the English inheritance has been urbanisation in large coastal cities. Far more are escaping urban congestion in England by moving into a suburbanised countryside than by emigrating. Many who do still come to Australia reproduce this behaviour by settling in semi-rural outer suburbs.

A mixed blessing?

It has become customary to assess the 'contribution' of various immigrant groups to the settler societies of North America and Australasia. An early local example was J. F. Hogan's large work

The Irish in Australia, published to mark the 1888 centenary of the landing at Sydney Cove. Applying this popular, if not entirely satisfactory, approach to the English in Australia is very difficult and arguably fruitless. The English established modern Australia and dominated it numerically, organisationally and culturally at least until the gold rushes of the 1850s. They created most of its basic institutions and attitudes up until the 1880s, when the locally born had become a majority.

The 'English' were 'contributing' to their own creation. The same dilemma arises when discussing assimilation. Of course the English appeared to assimilate more readily than anyone else. They were assimilating to themselves and their immediate ancestors. Adjustment is another matter. The English, coming from a well-developed and increasingly urban society, had to make great efforts to adjust to the raw and undeveloped nature of Australia. Today this is scarcely an issue. Both countries have living standards and lifestyles which are rather similar and becoming more so. Both speak the same language. Both watch the same television programmes and eat at the same fast food outlets. They are more like each other than it is fashionable to admit. But they are certainly not the same.

The English inheritance includes many constitutional arrangements, including the base of the government in a lower house majority; the limited powers of an appointed head of state taking legitimacy from a hereditary monarch in London; collective responsibility through a Cabinet chosen from the parties commanding a lower house majority; a legal system which accepts English precedents including those predating the establishment of the Commonwealth; electoral systems based on distinct geographical constituencies; and a public service and judiciary which are assumed to be willing to serve alternative governments without prejudice. These arrangements derive from English practice and are not universal in other representative systems, including those of Ireland, Scotland and Wales, let alone the United States.

The English inheritance also includes what has become the 'universal' global language. Whether Australian English is a distinct language is hardly worth worrying about for most Australians. Written Australian is certainly not distinct from written English or American, except for a limited number of phrasings or terms. Spoken Australian is a dialect less distinct from standard English than those of Scotland, Ireland or parts of northern England. This inheritance has been of inestimable value to Australia, giving access to a widening range of cultural, business and communication uses. While this universalising lays Australia wide open to British and American influences, it also allows Australians to travel, reside and work in more societies than would any other language. This, of course, is a very mixed blessing for the one-sixth of Australians who normally use another language. It has meant that most Australians remain monoglot and that the teaching of languages and their use in international activities has been severely inhibited. It has also meant that Australia is particularly vulnerable to American influence, which some find deplorable.

England has given Australia a workable if imperfect political system and a universal language. The inheritance of the English living within Australia is much harder to measure. Hartz and Rosecrance attempted to do so, but their analysis has not fully survived the ravages of time. Imperialists attributed noble features to the British overseas which did not necessarily fit the rather motley reality. Pluck, fair play, loyalty, cleanliness and purity were enshrined in the Scout Law and the speeches of private school headmasters. But they coexisted uneasily with the hard drinking, swearing, sometimes brutal and uncaring males of pioneering society. Nationalists have also credited mateship, the fair go, solidarity and egalitarianism to Australians, but have sometimes denied these attributes to the 'Poms', who have often been seen as whingeing, subservient and conservative. The great many Australians of English birth or descent seem to have lost these undesirable features somewhere along the path to becoming dinkum Aussies.

If the English have made any measurable 'contribution' it was undoubtedly more marked and more radical in the first century than in the second. Manhood suffrage, the ballot, the trade unions and the labour parties, while not exclusively created by English immigrants, owe a great deal more to them than local historians have usually acknowledged. But the English were also a moderating influence. They lacked a revolutionary tradition. Contemporary reports of the Captain Swing rising and the Chartist movement accept that, despite violence, the aims were modest, behaviour usually controlled and bloodshed avoided until the repression by the yeomanry and the dragoons. The rural trade unionists of the 1870s were also peaceful and deferential, despite considerable persecution by farmers and magistrates. While these rebellious movements from the 1830s to the 1880s caused a great deal of alarm among conservatives, they lacked the violent confrontation found in Ireland or even parts of the Scottish highlands, let alone in Russia, Poland, Italy or Spain.

As the English have been at the core both of the middle classes, the political and social élites and the working classes, their role in society might be seen as contradictory and confused. It is even more confused because English influence had already spread to Scotland, Wales and Ireland before 1788, and continues to do so. Immigrants from all three 'Celtic' societies have normally spoken English, particularly after the 1860s. One-quarter of Irish immigrants have been Protestants, and many English immigrants had their origins in Ireland. The Scots have been more noticeable in agriculture and rural politics, the Irish in urban politics and the labour movement. But otherwise it is safe to assume that English influence and English individuals have been of central importance in the formation of Australian society. That a distinct national character has emerged which is no longer English (or Scottish or Irish) is not surprising, as a similar process developed in the United States 150 years ago.

Basic English attitudes shared by most immigrants included the acceptance of peaceful and democratic resolution of social conflicts; a belief in 'fairness' and social responsibility towards the less fortunate; affection and even loyalty towards national symbols such as the monarchy and the flag; a preference for urban and suburban life; a lack of interest in other cultures and languages; suspicion and even xenophobia and racism towards foreigners and those seen as inherently inferior; deference tempered by resentment towards social superiors; materialist aspirations; a limited interest in religion; a limited interest in association with other English immigrants; a strong interest in competitive sport; reliance on the mass media for information and guidance; and a willingness to assimilate without accepting the whole range of Australian myths and symbols. This was a mixed inheritance which many Australians are still trying to work into a consistent pattern of national identity.

In the past the English were much less concerned with national identity than were Australians. They had no written constitution, no national day, no national flag and a national anthem which praised the monarchy but did not mention the country. None of this precluded a fairly strong but unstated identity, sustained by universal education after 1870, by the mass media after 1890 and by the searing experience of two world wars. The English saw themselves as an imperial people, ruling over others into the 1960s and never subject to others.

Recently, this unquestioning self-confidence has been seriously challenged.[16] A new form of English nationalism is in the making, with a degree of insecurity and resentment which was previously absent but has been very characteristic of Australian nationalism since the 1890s. The flag of St George is now widely displayed, which was seldom the case twenty years ago. The devolution of limited powers to Scotland and Wales has not been graciously conceded by many of the English. Above all, the incorporation of England into the European Union has stirred up considerable questioning, which makes her one of the least enthusiastic members. It remains to be seen whether the English in Australia, most of whom have been here for thirty years or more, will reflect these attitudes. So far there is little evidence that they consider themselves an alien ethnic group, whatever Australians may think of them.

8

THE ENGLISH AS 'FOREIGNERS'

Far-called our navies melt away,
On dune and headland sinks the fire:
Lo, all our pomp of yesterday
Is one with Nineveh and Tyre.

Rudyard Kipling, 'Recessional', 1897

William Wentworth waxed eloquent in 1823 about 'a new Britannia in another world'. In 1881 recruiting agents were telling East Anglian farm labourers that Queensland was 'England over the water'. They attracted more migrants to that colony with free passages than in any other decade before or since. The founder of the Salvation Army, William Booth, favoured emigration of the poor because 'it would be absurd to speak of the colonies as if they were a foreign land'. By 1966 Australia House in London was issuing recruiting material claiming that Australia was a British country 'and we aim to keep it that way'. This was in the middle of the greatest avalanche of assisted English immigrants to Australia in any decade before or since.

Yet in 1999 the High Court decided, in the contested Senate election case of Helen Hill of One Nation, that Britain was a foreign power for the purposes of section 44(i) of the Constitution. This barred those owing other allegiances from sitting in the national parliament. The section was, of course, introduced when Australians had no citizenship of their own and were, like one-quarter of the world's inhabitants, British subjects. Unlike another disqualified Senator-elect (who was not even an Australian citizen), Hill was an Australian-British dual citizen, but had failed to renounce her British allegiance to the satisfaction of the court. Section 44(i) has been the subject of several enquiries, all of which have recommended its amendment to allow dual citizenship.[1] However, as that would involve a constitutional referendum, no government has been prepared to follow this through. Those directly affected have so far been predominantly dual British citizens, as these have constituted the majority of the overseas-born elected to the Commonwealth parliament. But potentially, several million dual citizens are in the same situation should they seek a political career, at least a quarter of them being English.

That those born in England were 'foreigners' was rarely canvassed until recently. However, various bursts of nationalism, in the 1850s, the 1890s and the 1920s, have distinguished those born locally from immigrants, the majority of whom were English until the post-1945 intake of Europeans. As early as 1828 a distinction was being drawn between 'Currency' Australians – born in the colonies – and 'Sterling' immigrants, with the latter assuming superior airs which the former resented and rejected.[2] This theme echoes down the years and fuels the belief that English immigrants look down on real Australians, while the latter are superior to the former in fact. Non-British immigrants have, of course, usually been regarded as different and inferior, while non-Europeans were placed outside the pale altogether for at least eighty years. Far from the English feeling slighted by these attitudes, they often endorse many of them. A regular complaint from those placed in Commonwealth hostels in the 1960s was that they had to share these with 'foreigners'.

Slow decline

The English-born were the largest group of immigrants registered in each year between 1788 and 1996. Irish-born numbers peaked in 1891 and then went into a rapid decline. Scottish numbers continued to rise steadily until 1971, and Welsh numbers did not peak until 1991, although always being modest. Within these totals Cornish migration was heavy between the 1840s and 1870s, but then almost disappeared. Scottish Highland migration was briefly important between 1840 and 1870, but also became negligible. Scottish, Welsh, Cornish and Gaelic enclaves developed, especially in Victoria and South Australia, but gradually disappeared as they were culturally swamped by the English majority.

By the end of the nineteenth century Australia could not only claim to be white and British, but might also have rightfully claimed to be English. However, this claim was rarely made officially after self-government, as political power was disproportionately in the hands of Scottish and later Irish politicians. They were able to build on a population which was almost equally divided between those of English and 'Celtic' origins. But the 'Celts' were also seriously divided, mainly on religious lines.

Table 2 shows clearly the decline in British immigrants as a proportion of the population since 1881. It also shows that the English-born component remained relatively healthy while the Irish-born, and to a lesser degree the Scots, go into terminal decay. This reflects their comparable decline within the overall British Isles population, the Irish decline being due to falling population and the

TABLE 2: Immigrants born in the British Isles as a percentage of the Australian population, 1881–2001

Year	England	Scotland	Ireland	Wales	Total
1881	15.9	4.3	9.4	(0.4)	30.0
1891	14.5	3.9	7.2	(0.4)	26.0
1901	10.2	2.7	4.9	0.3	18.1
1911	7.9	2.1	3.2	0.3	13.5
1921	8.2	2.0	1.9	0.2	12.3
1933	7.4	2.0	1.2	0.2	10.8
1947	5.0	1.4	0.6	0.2	7.2
1954	5.3	1.4	0.5	0.2	7.4
1961	5.3	1.3	0.5	0.2	7.3
1966	5.9	1.3	0.5	0.2	7.9
1971	6.6	1.2	0.5	0.2	8.5
1976	6.5	1.1	0.3	0.2	8.1
1981	6.1	1.0	0.5	0.2	7.8
1986	5.6	1.0	0.4	0.2	7.2
1991	5.3	0.9	0.5	0.2	6.9
1996	4.9	0.8	0.4	0.2	6.3
2001	4.5	0.7	0.4	0.1	5.7

Notes: Wales is included with England for Western Australia (1881) and Queensland (1881, 1891). Ireland includes North and South.

Sources: Jupp and York, *Birthplaces of the Australian People*, (updated to 2001).

greater attractions of North America. In the twentieth century, being British in Australia normally meant being English. The 1986 census asked an ancestry question for the first time, which showed that 39 per cent described themselves as 'English', with only 15 per cent answering 'Australian' and very small numbers (3–4 per cent) admitting to being Irish or Scottish. This was partly influenced by 'hyphenated Anglos' – those of mixed English and other descent – but was rather odd. By 2001, 34 per cent were still calling themselves English, but 'Australians' had risen to 36 per cent and Irish to 10 per cent. Charles Price, using a complex system of calculating descent, gives English 'ethnic origins' as 45.3 per cent, Irish as 12.4 per cent, Scottish as 10.9 per cent and other 'Anglo-Celts' (Welsh, Cornish and Manx) as 2.9 per cent.[3]

Immigration oscillates in reaction to economic conditions, wars, and ethnic preferences and exclusions. At least half the British and Irish immigrants arriving between 1831 and 1982 were deliberately recruited through free or assisted passages, with peaks in the 1880s, just before and after the First World War and, highest of all, in the 1960s. These peaks account for the proportionate increase of the English-born in 1921 and 1971, which did not happen for the Irish, Scots or Welsh. The peak of 1971 came at the end of a massive increase in assisted passages. The Bring out a Briton and various other campaigns had been aimed at countering the largely unassisted southern European influx. Over 80 per cent of those coming were English.

Meanwhile, the Scots, Irish and Welsh were not replacing those from earlier migrations who were dying off. After the Second World War, the great bulk of British assisted migration was English, and such figures as we have show that London and the Southeast and Lancashire/Merseyside were the major sources. This marks a shift from the nineteenth century, when assisted migration from the North was less important and from the rural South more so, reflecting the official preference for agricultural labourers and domestic servants (their wives and daughters). At that time, the South was also a prominent source of 'élite' English migrants, as measured by the *Australian Dictionary of Biography*.[4] In so far as there was a clear English culture brought to Australia by mass migration, it was from southern and Anglican origins. But it was also class-divided, and much influenced by rural English subcultures which have now largely disappeared. It was also, of course, greatly modified by the large 'Celtic' immigration.

The break in immigration between the 1930s depression and world war was more marked than ever before or since. With a population of only 7.6 million in 1947, Australia was urgently concerned to 'populate or perish', and it was politically necessary to stress that any mass immigration programme would be from traditional sources. Assisted passages were essential to attracting English immigrants, as they had been since 1831. Several States, notably Western Australia and South Australia, ran their own campaigns, and one-third of all English immigrants today live in those two States, essentially in Perth and Adelaide. The English proportion of the population rose from 5 per cent in 1947 to 6.6 per cent in 1971 (see Table 2).

British and Irish settlers dropped from 8.5 per cent of the population in 1971 to 6.3 per cent in 1996, and are even lower in 2001. Still the English maintained their lead, but their lowest-ever proportion showed no signs of recovery (see Table 3). Arrivals for permanent settlement were officially consolidated into a category called 'Britain and Ireland'. From a high point of 47 per cent in 1965–70, the numbers and proportions dropped with remarkable regularity to little over 10 per cent in 1999. The English still come, which is not surprising as various aspects of the migration pro-gramme (such as English language proficiency) encourage them to do so. But they come in continuously diminishing numbers, without any public assistance or deliberate recruitment. Without remarkable and unpredictable developments in both countries, there is no reason to suppose that this decline will not continue to some irreducible minimum in the near future. The decline from 1975 to 1980 was much bigger than was caused by the ending of assisted passages in 1982.

Some aspects of permanent and temporary entry serve to keep up an English presence. The employer nominee system still favours British employees, brought out mainly by British companies. The working holiday visa system is attractive to young Britishers, who make up almost half the total of 60 000 temporary entrants a year. Britain is still a major source of tourists, the majority visiting relatives. British professional and trade qualifications are almost invariably recognised, as they always have been. But few English tradesmen and skilled manual workers now emigrate and many professionals are paid more in the United Kingdom than they would be in Australia. While there was another marked shift towards English-speaking immigrants under the Howard government, this

TABLE 3: Number and percentage of immigrants born in the British Isles, 1959–1999

Years	Total admitted	% of all immigrants
1959–65	303 750	42.5
1965–70	369 110	47.3
1970–75	252 810	41.3
1975–80	89 560	26.0
1980–85	124 340	26.6
1985–90	119 461	19.4
1990–91	20 746	17.0
1991–92	14 465	13.5
1992–93	9 484	12.4
1993–94	8 963	12.8
1994–95	10 689	12.2
1995–96	11 268	11.4
1996–97	9 674	11.3
1997–98	9 193	11.9
1998–99	8 785	10.4
1999–2000	9 037	8.4

Notes: The immigrant total includes the Migration Program, the Humanitarian Program and New Zealand permanent settlement. It excludes short-term and temporary arrivals (e.g. students and tourists). Ireland was excluded after 1999.

Sources: Bureau of Immigration Research/Department of Immigration and Multicultural Affairs, *Immigration Updates* and *Settler Arrivals.*

was drawn largely from New Zealand and South Africa rather than from England.

Shifting policies and priorities

In the 1960s there were only three important limitations on the right of English immigrants to enter Australia and settle permanently. They had to be 'of substantially European appearance', without a criminal record and free from any disability or chronic disease. Once settled, they enjoyed the rights of citizens without the need to become naturalised. They could vote after six months' residence, had no need to secure a visa or re-entry permit if they left Australia, had access to all welfare services and public housing, and could join the armed or public services without further qualification than their British nationality.

These privileges were open to other white British subjects (mainly New Zealanders) but not to anyone else born overseas. Moreover, the great majority of the English were assisted at very generous rates and were generally free to nominate their relatives to follow them. A range of welcoming services were available through the Good Neighbour Councils, sponsoring organisations such as the churches, Rotary or the Returned Services League (RSL) or local committees associated with the Bring out a Briton programme. By and large the only English immigrants unhappy with this situation were Commonwealth nominees living in hostels. They had a high rate of return and were a source of concern and annoyance to officials of the Immigration Department and Commonwealth Hostels Ltd. Otherwise, it was only the unadaptable or the unemployed who could not settle, and there were few of the latter in conditions of full employment and even of labour shortages.

Over the next thirty years the privileges enjoyed by English immigrants were steadily withdrawn, and they gradually ceased to come. While this was officially justified as equalising the status of all immigrants, it was seen by many English immigrants as equating their position to that of foreigners. Both positions are correct. Between 1973 and 1983 Labor and Liberal-National governments steadily eroded English privileges and undermined their status. The logic of this is inescapable. Australia was a multicultural society with an immigration programme which officially paid no heed to race, colour or creed. Eligibility to settle permanently was determined by three basic factors: relationship to those already settled; skill and employability; and humanitarian rescue from persecution. The special status of British subjects had never been fully accepted by Australia because of the limitations on Indians or Africans imposed by the White Australia policy. The United Kingdom, which had accepted all British Commonwealth subjects, ceased to do so by restrictive laws of 1962 and 1968, and slowly moved towards a common European Union citizenship. There was no longer any moral obligation on either Britain or Australia to maintain special privileges for each other's citizens.

The invisible English

Charlotte Erickson described the English who went in large numbers to the United States as the 'invisible immigrants'.[5] English-language dominance and the original English settlement allowed them to disappear, despite being foreigners in a country which had fought two wars against Britain in the fairly recent past. Australia never saw itself as foreign and sent large numbers of its men to fight in any war which involved Britain (at least until Vietnam). Consequently, many of the English in Australia were even more invisible. This was not the case in the nineteenth century. Sir Henry Parkes was far from invisible. But once the native-born became the majority and public figures were increasingly drawn from them, the English faded into the background, numerous though they were.

Australian nationalists from the 1890s to the 1950s were anxious to assert that they were not English. The Australian labour movement took on a distinctively Irish character from 1918. It also was not very friendly towards the English, who were seen as conservative because of their domination of the upper levels of society and the stake of British capitalism in the Australian economy. Working-class English immigrants in the 1920s were visible if only for their cloth caps and malnutrition. But they were much less visible than the 'reffos' of the 1940s or the 'dagos' of the 1950s. Becoming invisible was thus made easier by the growing multiculturalism, and eventually multiracialism, of post-war Australia. That there are still almost one million English-born in Australia would surprise almost everyone, including them. This is more than anywhere else in the world outside the United Kingdom.

Immigrants in general have not reached the top of the national political pinnacle, and those of predominantly English origin are outnumbered from the 'Celtic fringe'. Even recently, the 'Anglo' John Howard has confronted three Labor leaders of Irish origin in a row – Keating, Beazley and Crean. Even his likely successor, Peter Costello, is of Irish origin on his father's side. A factor in English 'invisibility' has been this modest role at the pinnacle of political power. Ethnic origin may tell us little about the behaviour and views of prominent individuals. But an impression has been created that there is a smaller English-descended population than is actually the case. Perhaps immigrants who were not English had to try harder. Many successful and prominent English immigrants have come from prosperous and educated backgrounds. They have not needed politics or entrepreneurial business to rise in the social scale.

An ambivalent relationship

As part of the British Empire, Australia shared in the excitement and rhetoric which accompanied its expansion until 1914. But at least from the 1880s there was growing questioning of this role. As the English were the largest element in Australia from overseas, and as they also dominated British politics, this questioning was normally directed against them by critics of the imperial relationship. One influential critic was the Australian Natives' Association (ANA), formed in Victoria in 1871. Membership was confined to those born in Australia, thus excluding the large number of English immigrants arriving during the 1880s when the ANA was expanding. While this rule was later modified, the ANA was at the core of Australian nationalism in Victoria, including support for Federation and for White Australia.

The ANA stated quite clearly that only those born in Australia could really feel for the country. Obviously this excluded English and other immigrants. The ANA was non-sectarian, avoiding the strained relations between Protestants and Catholics which characterised the period of its greatest influence. But its attitude towards immigrants was uncompromising:

> Each man in its ranks first drew breath on Australian soil: his every fibre has been built up from her substance, and he is 'bone of her bone and flesh of her flesh'. To him she is all-sufficient ... However the immigrant ... 'he does not – he cannot – feel the harpstrings of his being trembling in sympathy with her every mood'.[6]

As the English were the largest immigrant element in Australia, this message was less than welcoming.

Another critic of the English was the large Irish Catholic population. Irish-born numbers reached their maximum level in 1891 at 250 000 and then went into decline. But Catholic influence continued, as did support for Irish nationalism. Catholics were highly sensitive to Protestant sectarianism, which was well organised and vocal, especially in New South Wales. Although many of the most rabid sectarians were of Scottish or Irish Protestant origin, the English as the dominant group and the traditional enemy of Ireland were often blamed for the widespread discrimination and denigration from which Australian Catholics suffered. The hanging of

Ned Kelly in 1880 continues to inspire anti-English sentiment, yet Kelly was condemned by an Irish Protestant judge for killing three Irish Catholic policemen. The only Englishman with any responsibility for Kelly's death was the Victorian premier Graham Berry, a Londoner who came to Melbourne during the gold rush.

The labour and socialist movement, despite the large English element in its leadership, attacked 'England' from a different viewpoint, as the centre of imperial capitalism. During the Boer War this often slid into anti-Semitism, with the figure of 'Cohen' allied with 'John Bull' seizing South African gold and diamonds. The split over conscription for overseas service in 1916 saw Catholics and socialists in alliance, if for different reasons. While there is no compelling evidence of ethnic allegiances during this controversy, it effectively marked the end of English and Scottish Protestant domination of the Australian Labor Party and the rise of a Catholic leadership of Irish origin which dominated the party nationally and in most States through to the 1950s. While often at variance, the Catholic, populist and socialist elements in the party coalesced around New South Wales premier Jack Lang between 1925 and 1932, when he was removed by the undoubtedly 'English' governor Philip Game. Game had a classical English background, coming from a respectable South London suburb, educated at public school and military academy and serving in the British Army in India and France. He was knighted on retiring from New South Wales in 1935 to command the Metropolitan Police in London. Anti-English feeling was exacerbated by the 'body line bowling' controversy of the same year, which saw English cricketers behaving in a distinctly unsportsmanlike way by aiming at the batsman rather than the wicket.

Hostility towards the English establishment and imperialism should not have rebounded on the English immigrants in Australia. But there had been a degree of hostility towards English immigration since the 1880s, especially in the trade unions. The miners' union had complained to a New South Wales parliamentary select committee of 1880 that English miners had been assisted to emigrate after wrongly claiming to be agricultural labourers. Numbers recruited from mining counties dropped afterwards, but the Hunter coalfield continued to recruit from the English Northeast. Union opposition to immigration was, of course, far more hostile towards Asians and other non-British arrivals. But the basic objection was that immigration increased the labour force and therefore lowered wages, and the English were the largest number arriving in the 1880s, between 1909 and 1914 and in the 1920s. It was one of the achievements of the Chifley Labor government to win the unions round to mass post-war immigration by promising that all arbitrated conditions and union membership requirements would be met. By then, many English arrivals were also unionised and unlikely to undercut local conditions.

Objections to English immigrants also reflected the failures of the 1920s and unrest among some during the mass migration of the 1960s. In the 1920s even conservative enthusiasts for mass English migration were often critical of the 'poor types' who were actually arriving – a reaction which goes back to the earliest days of assisted immigration nearly a century before. The 1920s experience was an unhappy one, with failure of the group settlement schemes, poor industrial relations and the eventual catastrophe of world depression. The feeling that England was, once again, unloading its unwanted was strengthened by the emphasis on solving British unemployment and the significant recruitment of orphans and deserted children. This was a less important criticism in the 1960s. But there was a strong public reaction against the 'whingeing Poms' who did not appreciate the benefits of living in Nissen hut encampments. A hangover from the 1920s, and even from earlier decades, was the belief that the English were much poorer than Australians and should be grateful to be allowed into the country.

This critical attitude was normally expressed in terms of the 'English' or the 'Poms'. The Scots, as in the past, escaped censure and the Irish had ceased to come. Patriotic and imperialist admiration of 'England' persisted within the parties which ruled Australia and most of the States during the 1920s and 1930s and from the 1950s to the 1970s, and in the still powerful Returned Services League. They were officially committed to the Empire, the Monarchy and the Union flag. 'God Save the Queen' continued as the national anthem into the 1970s and the new dollar almost ended up being called the 'royal'. Anglophile sentiment was strong in the middle classes and survived, presumably, among many English immigrants, if in a less fulsome form. There was, then, an ambivalent attitude towards England and the English which lasted until the early 1970s. Then the Whitlam government asserted Australian distinctiveness and began the processes which led to the dismantling of special privileges for the British and even challenges to the monarchical system.

The republic referendum of 1999

Debates about the importance, relevance or desirability of English influence have erupted in Australia from time to time since the 1890s. The constitutional referendum of 1999 was the latest, though not necessarily the last, of these debates. A clear majority of Australians, by compulsory vote, showed that they wished to retain the anomalous role of the Queen of England, as she was erroneously described. Had the populists and nationalists who opposed a 'politicians' republic' not sided with the monarchists, the result might have been different. But throughout rural Australia, where recent immigration has had least impact, large majorities rejected change.

Had a referendum been held on retaining the flag with its Union Jack quartering, the opposition to change would have been even greater. Opinion polling found that 'hostility to Britain was an important source of republican support; conversely, people who have warm, positive feelings about Britain were less keen on a republic'.[7] It further found a wide discrepancy between those born in the United Kingdom (mainly English), of whom only 40 per cent wanted a republic, and those born in Australia, of whom 48.5 per cent would vote 'Yes'. This difference held across party identification and was much greater for New Zealand-born and 'others' (mainly non-English-speaking-background immigrants). Anglicans and Uniting Church – the two largest English-derived denominations – had large 'No' majorities, but the Scottish-descended Presbyterians were even more opposed to the republic.[8]

The monarchist victory suggests that the English inheritance is not as weak or as irrelevant as many suppose. Despite the important role of English immigrants in radical and reforming politics, English symbols and loyalties have been associated with conservatism and resistance to novelty at least since the 1920s. The Liberal and National parties, the Returned Services League and the Country Women's Association all retained loyalty to the Crown in their constitutions well into recent years. While this is an ageing constituency, it still wields considerable influence. Ambivalence clearly remains. Prime Minister John Winston Howard publicly identified with English symbolism in the first few years of his tenure in a way unthinkable for his Labor predecessor, Paul Keating. That he was of English descent and Keating of Irish may not be coincidental. It was certainly commented on at the time.

Because English immigrants have become so invisible it is often assumed that they are fully integrated and assimilated. By one measure of assimilation, often used in the United States, this is not so. UK citizens have been notoriously reluctant to become naturalised. Before 1984, when they enjoyed all the benefits of citizenship including the vote, there was little reason for them to do so. As becoming Australian makes no difference to remaining British, it is hard to understand this reluctance. All British-born Australians could hold dual citizenship if they chose to swear allegiance to 'the Queen of Australia' – to whom they already owed allegiance as the Queen of the United Kingdom. They can now 'pledge their loyalty to Australia and its people', which also makes no difference to their retaining British citizenship. All those who had the vote before 1984 still have it – the largest anomaly in the otherwise rigorously administered compulsory voting system. As most British immigrants arrived before 1984 this is not a small number. This was a matter of great concern to republicans in 1999, who rightly believed that the English would support the monarchy, as 60 per cent did. It led Harold Scruby of Ausflag to call for their disenfranchisement. This did not happen. His complaint probably did not help the republican cause in Western and South Australia, where only one (out of 14) and 3 (out of 12) electorates had republican majorities. English voting behaviour is rarely studied or even important. But on an issue like the republic, it could be very significant. Only 15 per cent of South and Western Australian electorates voted 'Yes', compared with 28 per cent nationally.

Support for the monarchy was strongest in rural and provincial areas which normally support the National Party. These have few immigrants but their populations are overwhelmingly derived from the British Isles some generations back.[9] Voters in blue ribbon metropolitan Liberal and Labor electorates tended equally towards republicanism. Of more interest are those electorates with high English immigrant populations, which are almost confined to South and Western Australia. The republican votes in Western Australian electorates were Brand 33.7 per cent, Canning 32.7 per cent, Moore 42.6 per cent, Pearce 37.2 per cent and Tangney 46.5 per cent; and in South Australia, Makin 41.7 per cent, Bonython 33.3 per cent and Kingston 41.4 per cent. In the only other electorate with more than 10 per cent British-born (Dunkley, Victoria) the vote was only 45.3 per cent. The majority of these electorates were held, or had just been lost, by the officially republican ALP. They represent the core of concentrated English settlement. Of thirteen electorates with more than 12 per cent British-born in 1996, only Curtin (WA) voted 'Yes'. This does not conclusively prove strong British support for the monarchy but it is reasonably indicative. The repeated, incorrect and usually hostile republican references to 'the Queen of England' probably mobilised many English-born voters in her defence. Smart attacks on 'Betty Windsor' did not help the republican cause.

'British', 'English or 'just Anglo'?

The decline of English immigration to Australia, and thus of the English-born component of the population, does not necessarily mean that Australia will rapidly cease to be the 'most British' (and 'most English') society outside the United Kingdom. Englishness is clearly attractive at least to the more conservative elements who voted for the monarchy in 1999. It is typified to some extent by the thrice elected prime minister, John Winston Howard. With ancestors from Hertfordshire, a practising Anglican and former Methodist, and a self-proclaimed monarchist, he is arguably not only the most conservative prime minister since Federation (his own self-description) but also the most English. His belief that Don Bradman (ancestors from the Suffolk/Cambridgeshire border) was the 'greatest living Australian' was as much Anglophile as nationalist.

But this kind of Englishness, which is like Caledonian Society Scottishness, is not necessarily shared by most English migrants to Australia. The outstanding characteristic of the mass, mainly working-class, immigration of the 1950s and 1960s is that it has not produced a viable English community except in some areas of heavy concentration such as Elizabeth (SA), Frankston (Vic) or Perth. English organisations are few and far between. The Victoria League and the Royal Commonwealth Society are dominated by socially distinguished Australians seeking to assert their distant (preferably non-convict) origins. More overtly 'English' groups may border on the absurd, like the Royal Society of St George with its worship of thatched cottages, fox hunting, Winston Churchill and Margaret Thatcher.[10] The Society, which traces its origins back to colonial America, secured the patronage of Queen Victoria in 1896. Its presidents have included the Duke of Cambridge, the Duke of Windsor, Viscount Montgomery, the Duke of Devonshire and Rudyard Kipling. Their 'England' is even more of a fantasy society than the Scotland of Burns Nights. It harks back to the 'Old England' from which so many were seeking to escape over a century ago. The society has only 8 of its 72 branches in Australia, of which 3 are in Queensland. The English in Australia (TEA) is a recent and less conservative expatriate association.

'English' culture is every bit as varied, Americanised, class differentiated and media determined as Australian – and in some respects, such as regional accents, even more diverse. Most English immigrants have been in Australia for over thirty years and have lived wholly within the local English language culture, much of which has rubbed off on them. Unlike many other immigrants they cannot insulate themselves within ethnic subcultures, nor would most of them wish to. Outside Perth and Adelaide there are few social advantages in seeking out compatriots, as they are widely scattered and may have few common interests unless they come from the same English region. Unlike the Irish, Scots, Welsh and Cornish, the English do not have any strong sense of being a minority. There are more distinctively ethnic organisations for these groups than for the numerically larger English. Many of the 'Celtic' groups are, of course, based on those of distant immigrant origins. While there are organisations catering to recent Irish immigrants, historically most of their social needs were served within the Catholic Church.[11]

The 'Celts' increasingly became a minority within British society as emigration and economic decline reduced their numbers. England absorbed many right into the 1930s by internal migration, before being faced with new influxes from the Commonwealth from the late 1940s. The dominance of London and the Southeast, always of central importance in English emigration to Australia, became more marked. Middle-class migrants became more important from the 1980s as assisted passages were discontinued and highly educated migration given preference. There is now very little English working-class migration to Australia. The middle classes disperse more and fit more easily than did the assisted industrial immigrants of the 1950s and 1960s. They do not have regional accents or subcultures and many have no particular loyalty to or interest in their original British localities. They face no barriers to total assimilation, even if many still think of themselves as English and decline to become naturalised.

With steadily declining intake and an ageing immigrant population, the direct influence of the English on Australia will increasingly be marginalised. A stage will soon be reached when the post-war English immigrants die off without being replaced, as happened to the Irish a century ago. This does not overlook the fact that immigrants of British origin from outside the British Isles are steadily increasing. New Zealanders have outnumbered British immigrants since 1996 and now form the second largest 'migrant minority' after the English. While about 15 per cent are Maoris or Pacific Islanders, the rest are mostly of English, Scottish or Irish origins. The same is true of most Canadian and American immigrants. The growing numbers from South Africa are also largely of English descent. Altogether, these diasporic Britishers numbered about 500 000 in the 2001 census. Many may be more patriotically 'British' than those from the Old Dart, and their Britishness is likely to be conservative and middle-class. Nor is it likely to be obviously 'English' except in a nostalgic sense. 'Traditional Australian culture' has been only lightly modified by the one million British-born. Both this traditional culture and the English-born are slowly fading away!

Will they ever come back?

The decline of the English-born as a major component of the Australian people has been almost inexorable (see Tables 2 and 3). There are many reasons for supposing that the English will never again have the direct impact they exerted as late as the 1960s. Those days are definitely over. There are less measurable reasons for supposing that English cultural influence is also declining and will never recover either.

The English came because they regarded Australia as an English – or at least British – society; because it offered a better standard of living; because they were paid and actively encouraged to come; because it had a sunny and spacious lifestyle; and because they had relatives and friends there. Except for a handful of activists they did not come to enjoy political freedom and democracy; they did not expect a developed welfare state; they did not believe (except perhaps in the 1850s) that the streets were paved with gold; and they knew very little about the 'Australian way of life'. They did hope that their children would advance more rapidly than in class-divided England. But from the early convicts to the assisted immigrants interviewed by Appleyard in the 1960s, many had almost no idea of what Australia was like or what would become of them.[12] From at least the 1920s there was a suspicion that Australians were prejudiced against them. Apart from homesickness and general disappointment, this was an important factor in so many post-war immigrants going home, an option closed to most of their predecessors by distance and cost.

The economic pressures which drew the English working classes towards Australia also required that they be assisted to come. This is no longer the case. The cultural attractions of moving within the British Empire have also disappeared. It is now easier to move within the European Union. The employment prospects for unskilled manual workers are no longer there, are unattractive or are excluded under the points system for skill introduced and refined since 1979. Family reunion, especially for elderly parents, has become increasingly difficult. The English are treated as foreigners for immigration purposes and the only exceptions to the system of universal visas are the New Zealanders. Policy decisions made in Australia have progressively ended all the benefits the English once enjoyed.

Many do come, but as temporary visitors. The British entering as tourists are usually outnumbered only by the Japanese and New Zealanders – and young English backpackers dominate the working holiday visa system. Conversely, London still contains the largest Australian expatriate community of the one million Australian citizens who live abroad.

England is still socially divided. The economic reasons for emigration have not disappeared, but the English are no longer responding to them. The affluent Home Counties, from which many emigrated in the past, are now so rich that Australia has little to offer in the way of financial improvement. The industrial and former mining areas of the North and Midlands are still disadvantaged. But the skills of their redundant workers are no longer sought by a post-industrial Australia. Rural England is completely transformed. Villages within driving distance of large towns become commuter suburbs and retirement homes for those wanting to live in the remnants of 'Old England' but with all modern conveniences.

The great classes who were drawn to Australia by assisted passages in the past – farm labourers, domestic servants, coal miners, textile workers, soldiers, sailors and general labourers – have shrivelled away or almost vanished. Some low-paid occupations – clothing, transport and catering workers – are now dominated by those who emigrated to England from much poorer countries. This is most marked in London, from which Australia has drawn a disproportionate number of immigrants.

England is still 'two nations', but not on the lines originally drawn by Disraeli. One of these 'nations' – the South – has little incentive to emigrate except in remaining pockets of disadvantage in London. The other – the North – is losing its industrial skills and there is no demand for them in Australia. But in neither part of England is there the desperate poverty which encouraged labourers to cross the world. Moreover, while unemployment is higher than during the mass emigration of the 1960s, it is still normally below the Australian level.

Many Australians believe that emigration is driven by poverty and disadvantage, as was often the case. On that basis, three areas of England stand out as potential sources – inner-London, south Lancashire and the Northeast. In London, Tower Hamlets, Hackney and Southwark are still measurably deprived, as they were in the convict days. The old 'depressed' areas of the 1930s are the new 'deprived' areas of today, just as the old East End of London is today's new, multiracial East End. In 1992 the poorest households were in Northern and Midlands industrial or former mining areas, including parts of Manchester, Liverpool, Sheffield, Newcastle, Hull, Birmingham and the Black Country, Leicester, Sunderland, Bolton and Leeds. This is almost a roll call of industrial England of the Victorian era. Between 1979 and 1987 these areas lost 1.5 million industrial jobs, without any compensating gains in other employment.

If emigration to Australia was open to all the English and generously subsidised, as it was for 150 years, this is where they should come from. Conversely, almost all the richest districts of England are in the Home Counties. There is no financial incentive to come from this area. Current immigration policy encourages those with higher education and professional skills, who are concentrated in this very privileged belt around London.

Since the ending of special privileges and benefits for the English, emigration no longer has much to do with social or economic need. The stereotyping of the past is irrelevant for the present and future. English migrants living in hostels in the 1960s complained that Australians 'think we all come from Coronation Street'. That epic can still be viewed in Australia but has lost much of its impact. Even in Manchester, slum clearance has been so devastating that the programme's producers have had to build an artificial set as no intact 'Coronation Streets' still exist. Future understanding between the hosts and the newcomers depends on getting rid of the notion that Australia is much richer than England and is doing immigrants a favour by letting them in. By one imperfect measure – Gross National Product per capita – Australia was richer than the United Kingdom in 1988 but has been marginally poorer ever since.

The English 'contribution'

For two hundred years Australia was colonised by the English. Its language, institutions, many of its religious denominations and some of its collective wisdom and attitudes can all be easily traced to England. Its universities, churches, commercial and banking houses were often deliberately staffed from England. English workers developed the coal and steel industries, cleared and farmed land, joined the armed forces, the police and the prison systems, and bought or built new homes in the constantly expanding suburbs. They have good claims on the founding of the trade unions and their political wing, the Australian Labor Party, and of the Anglican and Uniting churches.

One lasting English inheritance has been suburban living. From the 1880s onwards English immigrants have preferred life in the major cities. Attempts to resettle them in the bush, especially in the 1920s, were a failure. By then the great majority of the English no longer had rural origins. In London and the Northwest, the two major sources of immigrants for many years, the English descended from three or four generations of townspeople. As in England their consistent aspiration was to establish a home in the suburbs where they could avoid the congestion and pollution of the city centre and have access to the country for brief trips. As in England preference is for an individual and well-serviced home, close to schools and transport and not too isolated.

Settlement patterns for a century have reflected this. The English in Newcastle and Sydney in the 1880s, and the English in Perth, Adelaide, Melbourne and Sydney in the 1960s, were strongly rep- resented in the outer suburban fringe. With almost mathematical precision the English-born proportion rises with distance from the city centre until it reaches the rural outskirts, when it almost disappears, to be replaced by the locally born. The English are no longer pioneers. They come from the suburbs to live in the suburbs. But they are coming in diminishing numbers and their impact on Australian society is less than ever before.

NOTES

1 Who Were the English?

1 G. D. H. Cole and R. Postgate, *The Common People 1746–1946*, London, Macmillan, 1963; Pelling, *A History of British Trade Unionism*.
2 Cole and Postgate, *The Common People*, p. 226.
3 A. Briggs, *A Social History of England*, London, Penguin, 1983, ch. 7.
4 E. Hobsbawm and G. Rudé, *Captain Swing*, London, Penguin, 1973; D. Kent and N. Townsend, *The Convicts of the* Eleanor, Sydney, Pluto, 2002.
5 D. Charlwood, *The Long Farewell*, Melbourne, Penguin, 1983, p. 107.
6 M. Goff, *Victorian and Edwardian Surrey from Old Photographs*, London, Batsford, 1972, p. 79.
7 W. Cobbett, *Rural Rides*, London, Penguin, 1967 (1830), p. 180.
8 *Report*, London, 1847, para. 4175.
9 Staffordshire Record Office, item D 3610/17/2.
10 Select Committee on Colonisation from Ireland, *Report*, para. 3026.

2 Convicts, Labourers and Servants

1 P. Quennell (ed.), *Mayhew's Characters* (from *London Labour and the London Poor*, 1851), London, Spring Books, n.d. See also Quennell (ed.), *London's Underworld*.
2 Quennell (ed.), *Mayhew's Characters*, p. 338.
3 P. Bean and J. Melville, *Lost Children of the Empire*, London, Unwin Hyman, 1990, p. 29.
4 Hammond, *The Village Labourer*.
5 Staffordshire Record Society, *Staffordshire Assize Calendars 1842–1843*, Stafford (UK), 1992.
6 N. Irvine, *Mary Reibey: Molly Incognito*, Sydney, Library of Australian History, 1982.

7 Irene Wyatt, *Transportees from Gloucestershire to Australia 1783–1842*, Gloucester (UK), Bristol and Gloucestershire Archaeological Society, 1988.

8 United Kingdom, *Census*, 1841.

9 Based on information supplied by East Sussex Record Office, Lewes.

10 E. Hobsbawm and G. Rudé, *Captain Swing*, London, Penguin, 1973; D. Kent and N. Townsend, *The Convicts of the Eleanor*, Sydney, Pluto, 2002.

11 J. Marlow, *The Tolpuddle Martyrs*, London, History Book Club, 1971.

12 Quoted in Kent and Townsend, *The Convicts of the Eleanor*, p. 250.

13 Hitchins, *The Colonial Land and Emigration Commission*, Philadelphia, University of Pennsylvania Press, 1931.

14 'Returns from those British Colonies where the Land Revenue is applied to Emigration' (1848), *British Parliamentary Papers, Emigration 1836–1847*, vol. 22, Dublin, Irish Universities Press, 1971, p. 314.

15 M. Crowther, *The Workhouse System 1834–1929*, London, Batsford, 1981.

16 'Emigration', leaflet issued at Bury St Edmunds (Suffolk) for the Queensland Agent General, 1883.

17 A. Lemon and M. Morgan, *Poor Souls They Perished*, 2nd edn, Melbourne, Australian Scholarly Publishing, 1986. The official report of 1846 is in *British Parliamentary Papers, Emigration*, vol. 22, Dublin, Irish University Press, pp. 277–96.

18 S. Surtees, *Emigrants' Letters from Settlers*, London, Jarrold, 1852, p. 4.

19 *Northampton Herald*, 22 June 1850.

20 NALU, *Annual Report*, Leamington, 1876.

21 B. Higman, *Domestic Service in Australia*, Melbourne University Press, 2002.

22 Letter from R. W. Hay, 1 January 1833, Colonial Office.

23 *Times*, 17 February 1916.

24 W. Cobbett, *The Emigrant's Guide in Ten Letters*, London, self-published, 1819, p. 40.

3 Farmers, Miners, Artisans and Unionists

1 M. Bassett, *The Hentys*, London, Oxford University Press, 1954.

2 A. Hasluck, *Thomas Peel of Swan River*, Melbourne, Oxford University Press, 1965.

3 M. Schumer, *Henry Dendy and his Emigrants*, Sallas Books, Melbourne, 1975.

4 *Hull Advertiser*, 11 September 1829.

5 *Report of the Poor Law Commissioners*, 1834, Recommendation xxii, pp. 199–219.

6 Colonial Land and Emigration Commission, *Report*, 1850; South Australia, Parliamentary Papers, 1864.

7 Victoria, *Hansard*, 4 April 1862, pp. 929–37.
8 *British Parliamentary Papers, Colonies, Australia*, vol. 5, 1837–40, Irish University Press, 1970, p. 98.
9 M. Kiddle, *Caroline Chisholm*, Melbourne University Press, 1996 (1950).
10 Kiddle, *Caroline Chisholm*, Appendix F.
11 Staffordshire Record Office, item 3708/4-13.
12 Robson, *The Convict Settlers of Australia*.
13 Victoria, *Censuses*, 1851, 1861.
14 J. Docherty, 'English Settlement in Newcastle and the Hunter' in Jupp (ed.), *The Australian People*, pp. 305–11.
15 G. Bebbington, *Pit Boy to Prime Minister*, Keele (UK), n.d.
16 Letter from R. W. Hay, Colonial Office, 1 January 1833.
17 Marriage records, Mortlock Library, Adelaide.
18 G. D. H. Cole and R. Postgate, *The Common People 1746–1946*, London, Macmillan, 1963; Pelling, *A History of British Trade Unionism*.
19 J. Rae, *Contemporary Socialism*, London, Swan Sonnenschein, 1891, p. 90.
20 Rae, *Contemporary Socialism*, p. 92.
21 D. Torr, *Tom Mann*, London, Lawrence and Wishart, 1956.

4 Class and Equality

1 J. Arch, *From Ploughtail to Parliament*, London, Cresset Library, 1986 (1898).
2 Quoted in Pelling, *A History of British Trade Unionism*, p. 80.
3 Staffordshire Record Office, item 3586.
4 See, e.g., N. Bleszynski, *Shoot Straight You Bastards*, Sydney, Random House, 2002.
5 Quoted in Jupp, *Arrivals and Departures*, p. 103.
6 Quoted in Richardson, *British Immigrants and Australia*, p. 92.
7 R. S. Neale, *Class and Ideology in the Nineteenth Century*, London, Routledge & Kegan Paul, 1972, p. 106.
8 J. Higley et al., *Elites in Australia*, London, Routledge & Kegan Paul, 1979, p. 88.
9 S. Judd and K. Cable, *Sydney Anglicans*, Sydney, Anglican Information Office, 2000.
10 G. Souter, *Heralds and Angels*, Melbourne University Press, 1991.
11 Martin, *Henry Parkes*, Melbourne University Press, 1969.

5 From Colonies to Commonwealth

1 F. Hitchins, *The Colonial Land and Emigration Commission*, Philadelphia, University of Pennsylvania Press, 1931.
2 *Chronicle and Industrial Review*, 15 January 1876.
3 M. Stammers, *The Passage Makers*, Teredo Books, Brighton (UK), 1978.
4 Quoted in Stammers, *The Passage Makers*, p. 175.

5 'Report of the Immigration Agent', Queensland Legislative Assembly, *Votes and Proceedings*, 1885, p. 791.
6 Queensland, *Census*, 1891.
7 New South Wales, *Parliamentary Papers*, 1877.
8 Roe, *Australia, Britain and Migration 1915–1940*.
9 Bolton, *A Fine Country to Starve In*, p. 29.
10 Church Emigration Society, *Annual Reports*, 1908–13.
11 Details in J. Menadue, *Things you Learn Along the Way*, Melbourne, David Lovell, 1999.
12 New Settlers' League (NSW Division), Fifth Annual Report, Sydney, 1927.
13 G. Sherington and C. Jeffery, *Fairbridge: Empire and Child Migration*, Perth, University of Western Australia Press, 1998.
14 Derived from Jupp and York, *Birthplaces of the Australian People*, Canberra, 1995.

6 Bringing Out Britons

1 *Daily Telegraph*, 8 July 1947.
2 Department of Immigration, *Assisted Passages to Australia*, no. 36, November 1968.
3 Ibid.
4 *Canberra Times*, 14 April 1967.
5 Jupp (ed.), *The Australian People*, pp. 316–21.
6 *Citizenship Convention Report*, 1958.
7 *Sydney Morning Herald*, 20 February, 1 October 1957.
8 *Citizenship Convention Report*, 1956.
9 J. Joynson, 'British Assisted Migrants and Hostels in the 1950s' in E. Richards and J. Templeton (eds), *Visible Immigrants Five*, Canberra, History Division, ANU Research School of Social Sciences, 1998, pp. 106–26.
10 *Australian*, 23 May 1967.
11 *Age*, 2 November 1952.
12 Melbourne *Herald*, 16 November 1965.
13 *Citizenship Convention Report*, 1953.
14 *Canberra Times*, 14 April 1967; *Age*, 24, 25 January 1967.
15 *Age*, 26 January 1967.
16 *Citizenship Convention Report*, 1965.
17 *Daily Telegraph*, 6 July 1965.
18 Dovey, *The Departure of Settlers from Australia*.
19 *Daily Telegraph*, 9 July 1965.
20 Appleyard, *British Emigration to Australia*; Appleyard et al., *The Ten Pound Immigrants*; Zamoyska, *The Ten Pound Fare*.
21 *Age*, 8 February 1958.
22 *Courier Mail*, 31 January 1967.
23 Mark Peel, *Good Times, Hard Times*, Melbourne University Press, 1995.

24 *West Australian*, 5 November 1964.
25 *West Australian*, 9 November 1964.
26 Peel, *Good Times, Hard Times*, p. 10.
27 Peel, *Good Times, Hard Times*, p. 1.
28 *Australian*, 8 January 1971.
29 P. Barry, *The Rise and Fall of Alan Bond*, Sydney, Bantam, 1990.
30 *Australian*, 2 May 1974.
31 *Canberra Times*, 18 April 1967.
32 *Adelaide Advertiser*, 6 August 1977.
33 *Adelaide Advertiser*, 9 August 1977.
34 *Canberra Times*, 22 January 1965.
35 J. Menadue, *Things You Learn Along the Way*, Melbourne, David Lovell Publishing, 1999.

7 The English Inheritance

1 Hartz, *The Founding of New Societies*, p. 275.
 2 Hartz, *The Founding of New Societies*, p. 282.
 3 G. D. H. Cole, *Chartist Portraits*, London, Macmillan, 1941.
 4 R. Knight, *Illiberal Liberal: Robert Lowe in New South Wales 1842–1850*, Melbourne University Press, 1966.
 5 Martin, *Henry Parkes*.
 6 J. Jupp: 'Ethnicity, Race and Sectarianism' in M. Simms (ed.), *1901: The Forgotten Election*, Brisbane, University of Queensland Press, 2001, pp. 135–50.
 7 H. V. Evatt, *Australian Labour Leader: the Story of W. A. Holman*, Sydney, Angus and Robertson, 1979 (1942).
 8 M. Sawer (ed.), *Elections Full, Free and Fair*, Sydney, Federation Press, 2001.
 9 G. Souter, *A Peculiar People*, Sydney University Press, 1981.
10 D. Torr, *Tom Mann*, London, Lawrence and Wishart, 1956.
11 V. Coleman, *Adela Pankhurst: the Wayward Suffragette 1885–1961*, Melbourne University Press, 1996.
12 P. Wilson, *Immigrants and Politics*, Canberra, Australian National University Press, 1973.
13 T. Brabazon, *Tracking the Jack*, Sydney, University of New South Wales Press, 2000.
14 W. Cobbett, *Rural Rides*, London, Penguin, 1967 (1830).
15 S. Surtees, *Letters from Emigrants*, London, Jarrold, 1852, p. 6.
16 K. Kumar, *The Making of English National Identity*, Cambridge University Press, 2003; Colls, *Identity of England*.

8 The English as 'Foreigners'

1 J. Jupp, 'Twilight of the Empire: Britain as a Foreign Power', *Reform*, Spring 1999, pp. 89–112.
 2 Alomes and Jones, *Australian Nationalism*, p. 20.

3 C. A. Price in Jupp (ed.), *The Australian People*, p. 82.
4 The Index volume (vol. 13), details English birthplaces for 1788–1939 at pp. 118–43.
5 C. Erickson, *Leaving England*, Ithaca (US), Cornell University Press, 1994.
6 'Advance Australia', 7 October 1898, quoted in Birrell, *A Nation of Our Own*, p. 9.
7 Warhurst and Mackerras (eds), *Constitutional Politics*, p. 119.
8 Warhurst and Mackerras (eds), *Constitutional Politics*, p. 110.
9 *See* Dixson, *The Imaginary Australian*; Partington, *The Australian Nation*.
10 See the Royal Society of St George website: <http://www.royalsocietyofstgeorge.com>
11 See P. O'Farrell, *The Irish in Australia*, Sydney, University of New South Wales Press, 1987.
12 Appleyard, *British Emigration to Australia*.

Abbreviations

ALP	Australian Labor Party
MLA	Member of the Legislative Assembly
MLC	Member of the Legislative Council
MP	Member of Parliament

FURTHER READING

Primary material

Berryman, I., *A Colony Detailed: the First Census of Western Australia 1832*, Perth, Creative Research, 1979.

Colonial Censuses, 1828–1901.

Commonwealth of Australia, *Censuses of Population and Housing*, 1911–2001.

Dovey, W. R., *The Departure of Settlers from Australia*, Canberra, Department of Immigration, 1967.

Forrest, R. and D. Gordon, *People and Places: a 1991 Census Atlas of England*, Bristol, School for Advanced Urban Studies, University of Bristol, 1993.

Jupp, J. and B. York, *Birthplaces of the Australian People*, Canberra, Centre for Immigration and Multicultural Studies, 1995.

'Report from His Majesty's Commissioners for Inquiring into the Administration and Practical Operation of the Poor Laws' (1834) in *British Parliamentary Papers, Poor Law*, Dublin, Irish University Press, 1971.

Books

Alomes, S. and C. Jones (eds), *Australian Nationalism: a Documentary History*, Sydney, Angus and Robertson 1991.

Appleyard, R., *British Emigration to Australia*, Canberra, Australian National University Press, 1964.

Appleyard, R. and A. Ray, *The Ten Pound Immigrants*, London, Boxtree, 1988.

Atkinson, A., *The Europeans in Australia: the Beginning*, Melbourne, Oxford University Press, 1997.

Birrell, R., *A Nation of Our Own*, Melbourne, Longman, 1995.

Bolton, G., *A Fine Country to Starve In*, Perth, University of Western Australia Press, 1972.

Broome, R., *Arriving*, Sydney, Fairfax Syme and Weldon, 1984.

Burgmann, V., *'In Our Time': Socialism and the Rise of Labor 1885–1905*, Sydney, George Allen & Unwin, 1985.

Coldrey, B., *Good British Stock: Child and Youth Migration to Australia*, Canberra, National Archives of Australia, 1999.

Colls, R., *Identity of England*, Oxford University Press, 2002.

Davies, N., *The Isles: a History*, London, Macmillan, 2000.

Dixson, M., *The Imaginary Australian*, Sydney, University of New South Wales Press, 1999.

Dunbabin, J., *Rural Discontent in Nineteenth Century Britain*, London, Faber & Faber, 1974.

Gill, A., *Orphans of the Empire*, Sydney, Millennium Books, 1997.

Goldsworthy, D., *Losing the Blanket: Australia and the End of Britain's Empire*, Melbourne University Press, 2002.

Haines, R., *Emigration and the Labouring Poor*, London, Macmillan, 1997.

—— *Life and Death in the Age of Sail*, Sydney, University of New South Wales Press, 2003.

Hammond, J. and B., *The Skilled Labourer 1760–1832*, Stroud (UK), Alan Sutton, 1995 (1919).

—— *The Town Labourer 1760–1832*, Stroud (UK), Alan Sutton, 1995 (1917).

—— *The Village Labourer 1760–1832*, Stroud (UK), Alan Sutton 1995 (1911).

Hartz, L., *The Founding of New Societies*, New York, Harcourt Brace and World, 1964.

Hassam, A., *Sailing to Australia*, Manchester University Press / Melbourne University Press, 1994.

Horn, P., *Labouring Life in the Victorian Countryside*, Stroud (UK), Alan Sutton, 1987.

Hughes, R., *The Fatal Shore*, London, Collins Harvill, 1987.

Jupp, J., *Arrivals and Departures*, Melbourne, Cheshire-Lansdowne, 1966.

—— *Immigration*, Melbourne, Oxford University Press, 1998, chs 2, 6.

Jupp, J. (ed.), *The Australian People: An Encyclopedia of the Nation, its People and their Origins*, 2nd edn, Melbourne, Cambridge University Press, 2001.

Kumar, K., *The Making of English National Identity*, Cambridge University Press, 2003.

Martin, A., *Henry Parkes*, Melbourne University Press, 1969.

Nicholas, S. (ed.), *Convict Workers: Reinterpreting Australia's Past*, Melbourne, Cambridge University Press, 1988.

Partington, G., *The Australian Nation: its British and Irish Roots*, Melbourne, Australian Scholarly Publishing, 1994.

Pelling, H., *A History of British Trade Unionism*, Harmondsworth, Penguin Books, 1963.

Quennell, P. (ed.), *London's Underworld* (Henry Mayhew's *London Labour and the London Poor*), London, Spring Books, n.d.

Richardson, A., *British Immigrants and Australia*, Canberra, Australian National University Press, 1974.

Robinson, P., *The Women of Botany Bay*, Melbourne, Penguin, 1993.

Robson, L. L., *The Convict Settlers of Australia*, Melbourne University Press, 1965.

Roe, M., *Australia, Britain and Migration 1915–1940*, Melbourne, Cambridge University Press, 1995.

Shaw, A. G. L., *Convicts and the Colonies*, Melbourne University Press, 1977.

Souter, G., *Lion and Kangaroo*, Sydney, Collins Fontana, 1976.

Thompson, E., *The Making of the English Working Class*, Melbourne, Penguin Books, 1968.

Ward, S., *Australia and the British Embrace: the Demise of the Imperialist Ideal*, Melbourne University Press, 2001.

Warhurst, J. and M. Mackerras (eds), *Constitutional Politics: the Republic Referendum and the Future*, Brisbane, University of Queensland Press, 2002.

Zamoyska, B., *The Ten Pound Fare*, London, Viking, 1988.

Theses

Crowley, F. K., British Migration to Australia 1860–1914, DPhil, University of Oxford, 1951.

Fedorowich, K., Foredoomed to Failure: the Resettlement of British Ex-Servicemen in the Dominions 1914–1929, PhD, University of London, 1990.

Hornsby, P., Factors Affecting the Realisation of Prior Expectations amongst British Migrants Coming to Australia, PhD, University of Adelaide, 1979.

McLennan, N., 'From Home and Kindred': English Emigration to Australia 1860–1900, PhD, Australian National University, 1998.

Pope, D., The Peopling of Australia: United Kingdom Immigration from Federation to the Great Depression', PhD, Australian National University, 1976.

R. J. Shultz, The Assisted Immigrants 1837–1850, PhD, Australian National University, 1971.

INDEX